Politics and Change
in East Germany

Map of the German Democratic Republic

Politics and Change in East Germany: An Evaluation of Socialist Democracy

C. Bradley Scharf

Westview Press • Boulder, Colorado

Frances Pinter (Publishers) • London

Copyright © 1984 by Westview Press, Inc.

Published in 1984 in the United States of America by Westview Press, Inc., 5500 Central Avenue, Boulder, Colorado 80301; Frederick A. Praeger, Publisher

Published in 1984 in Great Britain by Frances Pinter (Publishers) Limited, 5 Dryden Street, London WC2E 9NW

Library of Congress Catalog Card Number: 84-5183
ISBN (U.S.): 0-89158-945-7
ISBN (U.S.): 0-86531-451-9 (pbk.)
ISBN (U.K.): 0-86187-375-0
ISBN (U.K.): 0-86187-376-9 (pbk.)

Printed and bound in the United States of America

10   9   8   7   6   5   4   3   2   1

Contents

Tables and Figures

Preface

In writing this introduction to East German politics and society, I have in mind three purposes.

First, I want to provide a study that is readily comprehensible to English-speaking audiences. West Germans still provide much of the best scholarship on their neighbor to the east; yet translated texts reflect an inevitable preoccupation with "the German problem"—the (implicitly unnatural) division of Germany. Perhaps reflecting some sense of uncertainty over the past and future of their own Federal Republic, West German authors typically devote much effort to portraying the German Democratic Republic's (GDR) inferior record of material accomplishment and political liberty. In contrast, my intent here is to regard the GDR primarily in its own terms and to view its existence as yet another chapter in the discontinuous political history of the German people. The GDR is in many respects an anomaly, but no more so than is the Federal Republic.

Second, I believe that a comparative frame of reference enhances understanding. The German Democratic Republic is unique, as are all other states, yet many of its problems and processes are shared with other systems. For some purposes, the most useful comparisons are with allied nations of the "socialist-state community"; for other purposes, comparisons are more meaningful with Western Europe, Scandinavia, and even North America. In addition to specific illustrations, this approach involves a consistent application of the time-tested concepts of comparative political science. I reject the notion that the study of communist systems requires an entirely separate language of analysis; in my view, politics in the GDR is best understood as a specific manifestation of more or less universal political phenomena.

Finally, this book is joined together by a recurrent theme: the search for the national identity of the German Democratic Republic. Pursuit of this end requires that we cast off the academic residue of cold-war encounters with communist Europe. For more than three decades, memories of human tragedy and Western disillusionment have perpetuated the image of totalitarian rule in that region. Today most scholars recognize the shortcomings of the totalitarian model, especially its overwhelmingly propagandistic usages, its proclivity to exaggerate and reify discrete events, and its inability to distinguish one system from another or to account for change within a single system. But outside the community of specialists, this earlier image dies hard. Particularly in the case of East Germany, Westerners have been most reluctant to abandon a superficial, "totalitarian" interpretation.

A broader, more realistic interpretation recognizes that the present German Democratic Republic is a compound of at least four sets of influences. First of all, the people of the GDR are Germans, and their culture and politics are both a continuation of and a departure from historical German precedent. Second, the GDR lies very much within the Soviet sphere of influence. As a consequence, East Germany faces severe restraints in both its foreign and domestic policies, and it is frequently an object and a victim of East-West confrontations. Third, the GDR has a socialist economy, oriented toward skilled labor and technology. It is also deficient in raw materials and energy and, therefore, highly dependent upon foreign trade. Planning for sustained economic growth is thus a forbidding and treacherous task. Last, the GDR has created what is in many ways an advanced urban-industrial society. This social transformation has spawned problems quite familiar in many Western nations, including environmental pollution, urban crime, weaker family structures, and a lower tolerance for social inequalities.

German culture, Soviet hegemony, economic restraints, social change— all of these elements flow together to form a distinctive and increasingly significant political entity. To gauge the importance of each element, and the ways in which the people and political leaders of the GDR seek to make these elements compatible, is the imposing task of this rather short book.

Much of this work had its origins during my studies in Berlin in 1969. I am indebted to a great many colleagues who have shared their insights over the years. In particular, I wish to thank Arthur M. Hanhardt, Jr., Hartmut Zimmermann, and Gero Neugebauer for their encouragement and remembered kindnesses. I wish to express my gratitude to Seattle University for facilitating completion of the manuscript. Special thanks go to Ruth Tressel for heroic typing efforts and, most importantly, to Ann Scharf, my kind and constant critic.

C. Bradley Scharf

1
Past and Future in the GDR

The German Democratic Republic (GDR or East Germany) is largely a product of the collapse of the Third Reich and the subsequent division of Europe into hostile spheres of influence. Long viewed in the West as merely "the Soviet occupation zone," the GDR has experienced diplomatic isolation, economic discrimination, and political penetration. It accommodates a mighty Soviet military presence and exhibits a continuing fear of Western challenges. It also severely restricts civil rights on the grounds of fragile national security.

East Germans buy consumer goods from the Federal Republic of Germany (West Germany), watch West German television, denounce capitalism, and envy the prestige and material success of the Federal Republic. East Germans also buy raw materials from the Soviet Union, belittle Russian culture, struggle to make socialism work, and regard Soviet power with a mixture of fear and admiration.

East Germany's leaders, whether in the dominant Socialist Unity party (SED) or in one of its associated political or social organizations, share a commitment to "socialist democracy," an unfolding form of participatory rule based upon emerging standards of economic and social equality. They also share a refined sense of the policy restraints imposed by limited economic and fiscal resources, military dependence upon the Soviet Union, and deficient popular acceptance of official goals as worthy and the state as legitimate. Like the educated public, but perhaps more acutely, the GDR's leaders feel the pull of both East and West, the burden of a tragic past, and the fading inspiration of an ever-receding future.

The record of communist rule is not without its bright spots. Despite many unfavorable conditions, the GDR today boasts a high level of industrial and agricultural modernization, a steadily improving standard of living, a wide complement of progressive social policies, and an active role in world affairs. But the present is nevertheless a difficult time. These achievements are now perceived as modest and routine, and they have not supplanted the need to grapple with conflicting concepts of public purpose and national identity.

Ambiguous Roots

The problem of uncertain national identity is epidemic, affecting large nations and small, rich and poor. It occurs wherever history has brought together diverse cultures, as in North America, the Soviet Union, and many less developed nations. The problem arises also where former unity has yielded to division, as in Ireland, Korea, and Germany. In each example, the search for national identity has its own contours. Cases differ in the extent of public violence and in the scope of personal suffering. But in no case are the circumstances more intense and the implications for world affairs more profound than in the German Democratic Republic.

In both domestic and foreign sources, East German history is conventionally dated either from the Allied conferences at Yalta and Potsdam (February and August 1945), when the boundaries of postwar occupation were set down, or from the formal creation of the GDR on October 7, 1949. For their part, East German historians emphasize departures from a past of feudal and capitalist repression and from the tyranny of national socialism. Western historians, employing similar conventions, depict the present GDR as essentially having no past and, often by implication, as being unnatural or illegitimate. Both interpretations miss the mark.

The land and the people who today constitute the German Democratic Republic do indeed have a past, which cannot be selectively affirmed or denied. Like most nations in the world today, Germany has experienced social upheavals, wars, and changing political boundaries; but Germany has persisted through turmoil as an identifiable entity for a rather long time. In different periods, some German lands experienced degrees of detachment from the whole of Germany. But the sweep of German history has always encompassed the region long known as Central Germany and now identified as the GDR.

Sovereign states have existed here in various forms for over a thousand years. They include much of the Holy Roman Empire; the old Hanseatic city of Rostock; the early duchies of Brandenburg, Mecklenberg, and Saxony; and most of the Kingdom of Prussia. The present GDR was also once the integral central region of the Hohenzollern Empire, the Weimar Republic, and the Third Reich. In a most tangible way, cities, castles, churches, and war memorials stand as monuments to past governments, however ephemeral they may appear in modern history books.

German culture is even more pervasive and continuous. Culture traveled easily across the internal boundaries of old Germany, so it cannot be so readily identified with a specific locale. In a sense, an indivisible German culture—including the arts of Bavarian aristocrats, the commercialism of Hamburg entrepreneurs, and the radical philosophy of Trier's most famous native, Karl Marx—is not the exclusive legacy of the contemporary Federal Republic, but is also the inheritance of the people of East Germany.

Today, a tourist to the GDR can visit the University of Leipzig (Karl Marx) founded some two hundred years before the first Pilgrims landed in New England. Several such old and distinguished institutions mark the generations of prominent people who were shaped by, and in turn helped to shape, the culture of Germany and of much of the Western world. For this is the land of Johann Sebastian Bach and Richard Wagner, of Martin Luther and Otto von Bismarck, of Alexander von Humboldt and Max Weber. East Germany's cultural history includes enduring contributions to the arts and physical sciences, not to mention momentous scholarship in the realms of theology, philosophy, sociology, and government. The manner in which elites and ordinary citizens perceive this history plays an important part in identifying present purposes.

All modern governments have a central task of nurturing patriotism. Because nearly universal concepts of citizenship involve an assumed mutual obligation between the state and citizens, individuals are expected to comply with law in the expectation that the actions of the state will produce public benefit. However, public benefit may not always be evident, especially in individual cases. Governments therefore must seek citizen compliance through reliance on police forces and through a reserve of popular good will, whereby citizens voluntarily give their government the "benefit of the doubt" and generally uphold the legal order even in difficult times. When invested with highly emotional content, this reserve of good will is called patriotism.

In nations with extended territorial and political stability, such as the United States and Great Britain, governments devote little concentrated effort to developing patriotism—except perhaps in wartime. For the most part, patriotic themes emerge simply as a by-product of normal political processes and are transmitted by nongovernmental social institutions. However, in East and West Germany and in many Third World nations, governments cannot afford such a passive approach. Internal diversity, external threats, and a more restricted capacity to deliver promised public benefits create an urgent need for popular good will. Consequently, fostering patriotism becomes a major preoccupation of public officials. In the German Democratic Republic, official efforts to instill patriotism are authored by the SED Department for Culture and Science. Implementation of these efforts is at least the nominal responsibility of all public and private institutions in society.

Presented as part of a broader "socialist consciousness," this version of East German patriotism incorporates the past in two ways: one relates to cultural history, the other to political history. First, the great achievements of German culture receive strong emphasis in school curricula and in organized recreational activities for youth and adults. This emphasis encompasses mandatory instruction in music and art history, state encouragement of participation in groups of all ages for graphic and performing arts, and extensive public subsidies for repertory theaters and other cultural events. Such government support for cultural activity continues an older German tradition (present today also in West Germany), but it acquires added meaning in the search for national identity.

In the earlier years of more overt Soviet penetration, the SED undertook elaborate screening to insure that the performing arts were limited to the works of "progressive" authors and composers. On occasion, elegant exercises in sophistry were required to determine whether specific composers, regardless of the particular age in which they had lived, had demonstrated a revolutionary or sympathetic attitude toward "the working people." By the late 1950s, however, such arcane censorship had given way to the greater need to revitalize awareness of the breadth of German cultural history. Bach and Beethoven, for example, have been officially restored to a dimension of German culture that is essentially apolitical. Similarly, recent years have seen a new government emphasis on refurbishing old buildings, including castles, churches, and monasteries. Although relics of aristocratic privilege and reactionary values, these structures also testify to historic German achievement.

Other dimensions of German culture are somewhat more difficult to separate from the connotations of recent political history. Both foreign scholars and introspective Germans have observed that the prominent romanticism of German arts has been counterbalanced by a preference for reason and order in public life. This combination results in an almost legendary German industriousness in work habits and a noteworthy efficiency in administrative and military organization. Although certainly overdrawn, the widely recognized caricature of Prussian "iron discipline" is more than faintly reflected in East Germany's self-image. Even today, citizens of the GDR contrast their own putative efficiency and self-control with the assumed indolence and licentiousness of their Slavic neighbors. In return, these neighboring Slavic peoples recall the intimate linkage between Prussian discipline and the ruthless brutality of Hitler's National Socialist regime.

More than its cultural history, East Germany's political history is an awkward second component of patriotism. Official histories repudiate both Prussian aristocratic rule and the fascism of the Third Reich. Instead, the present state lays claim to a revolutionary legacy dating back at least to the mid-eighteenth century. In addition to Karl Marx and Friedrich Engels, whose *Communist Manifesto* appeared in early 1848, socialist revolutionaries such as Wilhelm Weitling and Moses Hess contributed to the events leading up to the German revolution of 1848–1849. That upheaval, which featured the first popularly elected parliament in German history, was scarcely a workers' revolution; rather, it was an early effort by the commercial middle class to wrest power from the aristocracy. As an experiment in democracy, this episode was soon repudiated, and it accomplished little more than an extension of Prussian authoritarian rule.

The spotlight shifted briefly to the laboring class, as Ferdinand Lasalle founded the General Association of German Workers in 1863. This more overtly socialist thrust soon waned under the weight of Bismarck's "enlightened" social policies (state-mandated disability insurance and social security), designed to undermine the appeal of the radical opposition. This tactic was followed by the antisocialist laws, which from 1878 to 1890 prohibited socialist or communist political activity.

After the fall of Bismarck, the Social Democrats reemerged as spokespersons for the working class. As their electoral strength increased, however, they turned sharply away from revolutionary goals. This excessively moderate orientation, coupled with Social Democratic defense of the empire, spawned the more radical Spartacus Union under Rosa Luxemburg and Karl Liebknecht, the organization that in 1918 formally became the Communist Party of Germany (KPD). This group promoted scattered workers' councils during the last weeks of World War I, stirred uprisings in several major cities, and introduced a four-week Communist Republic in Munich and Augsburg in the spring of 1919. The KPD also secured participation in the governments of Saxony and Thuringia until ousted by intervention of the Social Democrat–supported central government in the fall of 1921.

As a badly fragmented parliament struggled vainly to resist rightist pressures in the wake of military defeat and economic hardship, the KPD entered its own period of internal division. After receiving 6.3 percent of the vote in the 1925 presidential election, Ernst Thälmann steered the KPD toward closer cooperation with the Communist Party of the Soviet Union. The result was expanded recruitment among the workers and increased representation in the parliament, combined with tactics designed to hasten the downfall of the Weimar Republic. Ironically, these tactics paralleled those of the National Socialists and facilitated Adolf Hitler's accession to the chancellorship in January 1930.

When the parliament building was destroyed by fire one month later, Hitler blamed the KPD, ordered the arrest of some four thousand communists, and outlawed their party. Communists were thus among the first categorical victims of fascism. Many of the more active KPD members fled the country, going chiefly to Moscow, where they later formed the ten-man Ulbricht Group. Among the survivors in Germany itself, some communists attempted to resurrect secret party cells in the summer of 1941. However, little was achieved until the Ulbricht Group returned to Berlin nine days before the German Army capitulated. On June 11, 1945, the KPD was formally reconstituted, thus launching the four-year transition to communist rule in Germany.

As this brief history suggests, revolutionary politics in Germany has a checkered past. Radical initiatives, whether under Hess, Lasalle, or Luxemburg, invariably have been short-lived, often violent, and usually followed by a prolonged period of political repression. In this perspective, German revolutionaries may be perceived by the working class as harbingers of grief. On the other hand, more moderate approaches to expanding workers' rights in the process of parliamentary democracy have generated stalemate and disorder. In addition to sharpening antagonisms between Social Democrats and communists, these episodes did little to cultivate German faith in democracy or political parties. One might go so far as to argue that effective social change in Germany had occurred primarily under authoritarian regimes and that other experiments in political rule brought only disorder.

Efforts to cull patriotic themes from this mixed history are bound to be awkward—perhaps more so for East Germany than for West Germany. Beyond the obvious discontinuity, there is no clear thread tying together what the SED would identify as "progressive forces." Nevertheless, there is ample evidence of a heritage of radical socialism and even communism. Although communist political leaders have rarely been successful, some of communism's most articulate advocates have been German. From time to time, their ideas evoked significant popular support. It must be emphasized that German communism is not merely the creature of the Soviet occupation. Although communism is but one of many historical German themes, it is nonetheless an authentic German impulse.

This observation in no way diminishes the profound Soviet impact. Just as the proximity of Soviet forces and the corresponding U.S. and British policies undoubtedly impeded communist organization in the Western zones, so did the Soviet presence determine the shape of communist power in the Eastern zone. In fact, it is precisely this overwhelming Soviet participation that so severely handicaps the German Democratic Republic's search for a distinct identity.

Soviet Penetration

As a contemporary manifestation of German culture and political history, the German Democratic Republic is certainly a German state and a German nation. But it is German with a decided Russian accent, one that first began to appear when the Communist International, under Soviet direction, acquired influence in the KPD during the 1920s. During the Nazi period, the Ulbricht Group in Moscow was selected to insure that Soviet interests were properly represented in any postwar German government. Upon the surrender of the German armed forces, these men worked closely with the Soviet Military Administration to set up the beginnings of civil administration.

At this point, Soviet plans for Germany were only partially developed. It does not appear that Moscow's policy for Germany was initially formulated as part of a scheme to create an East European bloc of Soviet-controlled states. Rather, Germany was seen as a separate, if paramount, issue. Above all, the Russians were determined to exact reparations for war damages and to insure the end of the German military threat.

On August 2, 1945, U.S., British, and Soviet leaders signed the Potsdam Agreement. Among other provisions, it (1) affirmed Polish and Soviet annexation of German lands east of the Oder-Neisse line; (2) affirmed the creation of a fourth (French) zone of occupation; (3) created a Four-Power Control Council for Germany and a Four-Power Commission for Berlin; (4) granted supreme authority to the commander-in-chief of each occupying force in its own zone, while stipulating "uniformity of treatment of the German population . . . so far as is practicable"; and (5) provided that each nation should satisfy reparations claims from its own zone, except that substantial industrial equipment from the Western zones would be sent to the USSR (the value of the equipment to be partially offset by an exchange for specified food and raw materials). This agreement further included measures to eradicate what were judged to be the political and economic foundations of German fascism and militarism.

In retrospect, it is easy to see why these arrangements were unworkable. The most visible central issue of the dispute among the Allies was the exchange of goods between the Western and Soviet zones. Additional major obstacles were French short-run opposition to any central German authority and the British-U.S. plan to facilitate economic reconstruction by merging their respective zones. Citing this merger as a violation of the Potsdam Agreement, the Soviet Union abandoned the Allied Control Commission and in June 1948 blockaded land and water access to the Western sectors of Berlin. A U.S.-directed airlift provided residents nearly 1.5 billion tons of essential goods over the next eleven months and firmly charted West Berlin's future, as well as Germany's enduring division.

Underlying these increasingly hostile actions and the mutual charges of agreement violations was a fundamental political difference between the Soviet Union on one side and the United States, Great Britain, and France on the other. In the Soviet view, the Potsdam obligation to prevent the revival of fascism and "to prepare for the eventual reconstruction of German political life on a democratic basis" meant nothing less than the destruction of capitalism and the gradual introduction of socialist democracy adapted from Soviet experience. The Western powers, on the other hand, were eager to revive a private economy, a decentralized government, and a competitive electoral system.

Although neither the Soviet nor the Western concepts corresponded to past German practice, each had some popular roots in German history. While claiming to respect the will of the German people, each occupation regime undertook steps giving preference to indigenous groups who shared the victor's goals. In the Soviet zone, this overt preference frequently became indistinguishable from outright control. Citizen resistance grew not only out of the thoroughness of the de-Nazification program, which included confiscation of the property of Nazi officials and supporters, but also out of a pervasive anti-Russian sentiment, a sentiment that found only the weakest anti-American counterpart in the Western zones. The Russians, it must be recalled, were not only Germany's historic military adversaries; they were also perceived in German minds as culturally inferior. These sentiments were reinforced by the stringency of the military occupation and by the heavy burden of war reparations, which Western sources estimate at U.S. $15.8 billion in the years 1945–1953; in some years reparations payments equaled fully one-fourth of the GDR's national income.[1] Stories of Russian greed, vandalism, slovenliness, and stupidity still circulate privately among East Germans, illustrating the depth of popular feeling.

The emerging East German authority fought a nearly fruitless battle to distinguish itself from the Soviet military rule. Partly out of conviction and partly out of a reasoned desire to please its Soviet sponsors, the East German Communist party tirelessly pointed out that the German people were responsible for Hitler. The people had rejected the call for revolutionary socialism and instead had supported fascism, which was finally destroyed, not by a popular uprising, but at the hands of the Soviet Red Army. Special gratitude was therefore due the Soviet Union for providing the German people a chance to embark on a revolutionary path, to atone for a history of missed opportunities. But such gratitude would not mean an uncritical acceptance of Soviet methods, according to an official Communist proclamation of June 1945: "We are of the opinion that it would be wrong to force the Soviet system on Germany, as that would not correspond to the present stage of development in Germany. Rather, we are of the opinion that the important interests of the German nation in the present situation call for a different road for Germany, the road of establishing an anti-fascist, democratic regime, a parliamentary democratic republic."[2]

Despite the constraints of the occupation government, East German developments in the first three postwar years were consistent with the claim of a distinctive, parliamentary democratic road toward socialism. Agricultural land reform and nationalization of much industry produced short-range public benefit and received broad popular support. The creation of four political parties laid the groundwork for a parliamentary system, departing sharply from Soviet practice. In April 1946, the East German Communist party merged with the increasingly popular Social Democratic party to become the Socialist Unity party, the present-day SED. Evidence of overt Soviet pressure in this process supports the charge that the merger was designed to enhance Soviet control, thereby compromising the putative "German road."

Local elections in the fall of 1946 brought the SED a plurality in all five states. In a separate election for Berlin (all four sectors), where the two working-class parties had not been merged, the Social Democrats received 48.7 percent of the vote and the communists only 19.8 percent.[3] The Berlin vote probably confirms the wisdom of the forced creation of the SED, which deprived socialist voters of an anti-Russian alternative.

During the tense period of the Berlin blockade, the issue of Soviet hegemony assumed paramount significance. This period coincided with Stalin's efforts to undermine Tito's leadership in Yugoslavia because of Tito's refusal to accept Soviet authority on a wide range of problems. Communist parties throughout Eastern Europe were directed to sever political and economic ties to Yugoslavia and to purge "Titoists" from their own ranks. In the climate of the times, a Titoist could have been anyone who did not unreservedly endorse Soviet wishes. A wave of purges and prosecutions ensued, eventually reaching East Germany and the SED.

Although the SED purge did not exhibit the grotesque show trials and executions evident elsewhere, the effect was substantial. In the second half of 1948, SED membership fell by about 200,000, or 10 percent,[4] and most former Social Democrats were ousted from all leadership bodies. By January 1949, the SED had been fully restructured according to the pattern of the Communist Party of the Soviet Union. At the same time, all non-SED elements in the "antifascist bloc" of parties and social organizations were relegated to decidedly peripheral roles. Acting as the German People's Congress, and later as the National Front, this SED-directed bloc spoke against the formation of a separate West German state and drafted a constitution for the imminent German Democratic Republic.

The result of this turbulent year was to transform the East German political system according to the Soviet model, contrary to earlier stated intentions. Whether this change simply unveiled deliberate deceit, or whether a new policy was adopted in response to changed conditions, is not especially important. In any event, both SED members and ordinary citizens felt betrayed. The very visible hand of the Soviet authorities throughout this process must have extinguished the last remaining spark of legitimacy for the East German authorities.

It is not surprising, in view of these inauspicious beginnings, that East German emigrants and other Western observers came to regard the German Democratic Republic as nothing more than a disguised appendage of Soviet power. U.S. Secretary of State Acheson considered the "so-called" GDR as "without any legal validity or foundation in the popular will . . . , created by Soviet and Communist fiat."[5]

While such characterizations correctly highlight Soviet penetration of the East German system, they oversimplify and misrepresent the nature of the GDR's political leaders and their relationship to Soviet power. In coming to terms with the hostility of the West and the distrustful harshness of Soviet demands, such East German leaders as Wilhelm Pieck, Walter Ulbricht, and Erich Honecker did not thereby become mindless puppets or self-serving traitors. Nor did they abandon either their German heritage or their aspirations for future German peace and prosperity. Rather, like their "realistic" counterparts in the Western occupation zones, these leaders perceived that superpower support was the sine qua non for all East German goals, including the achievement of sovereignty and the implementation of socialism. Because of circumstances peculiar to the Soviet state, the price of support was high—unquestionably more severe than that experienced in the Federal Republic. Although Soviet penetration has meant radical political and economic changes, it is not at all clear that the GDR today more closely resembles the USSR than the Federal Republic resembles the United States.

Nevertheless, the visibility of Soviet influence and the deep anti-Russian feelings have left East German leaders a huge problem in their search for national identity. As will be shown in subsequent chapters, this search has combined accommodation to Soviet wishes with overt and covert efforts to distinguish East German interests and achievements.

Socialist Planned Economy

Perhaps the outstanding East German achievement has been the comprehensive introduction of socialism. In its simplest form, socialism is the ownership and management of the economy by public authorities. Modern societies typically feature public ownership of certain services, such as transportation, communication, electricity, and education. In addition, public authorities often manage the extraction of natural resources and the manufacture of products. Even in predominantly private economies, such as Great Britain and the United States, government-owned facilities produce steel, automobiles, fertilizer, and numerous other commodities.

What distinguishes a socialist economy, such as that in the GDR, is the scope of public ownership, the restrictions of private economic activity, and overall planning and management of the economy by government agencies. In the early postwar period a socialist economy was created by retaining the prior public ownership of transportation and communications, nationalizing the property of emigrants, and expropriating the land and business holdings of people who had used their wealth to support the Nazi regime. The legal processes involved were subject to abuse, of course, and the criteria applied to Nazi "collaborators" overlooked the coercion such people had experienced under the previous regime. Nevertheless, these measures elicited substantial popular endorsement.

By 1950 the GDR public sector accounted for more than half of the national income, including 68 percent of manufacturing, 41 percent of construction, and 61 percent of trade.[6] During the 1950s, socialist ownership was extended to agriculture in the form of state-directed collectives.[7] Remaining small-scale private enterprise was increasingly restricted through taxation and mandatory purchasing and marketing contracts. Reduced profits led to undercapitalization and opened the way for state investment in these private firms, thus creating a special category of semipublic enterprises. This category accounted for nearly 10 percent of the national income, until most of these firms were fully absorbed into the public sector in 1972.[8]

Today, East German private enterprise accounts for about 3.2 percent of the national income, while employing only .07 percent of the work force, primarily in construction, services, and agriculture.[9] Although the efficiency and absolute size of the private economy are significant, its relative contribution to national wealth is among the lowest in the world. Since the GDR apparently has a low tolerance for illegal and semilegal private economic activity, the relative importance of its private sector is probably smaller than is the private sector in other East European states. In this sense, East German socialism might be considered more "developed" than that of its allies.

Of course, as practiced in the German Democratic Republic, socialism involves far more than governmental ownership of the economy. It also encompasses government responsibility for development and distribution of the material and human resources to insure stable growth, the increase of standards of living, and a just distribution of the fruits of economic activity. According to the SED's Marxist-Leninist outlook, the ultimate aim of direct economic planning and management is the elimination of the economic foundation of social conflict and the economically based barriers to the full development of individual human personalities.

The sociological rationale for this perspective is quite familiar to most citizens in Western liberal democracies. It revolves around the claim that accidents of birth—being born to parents who are impoverished, uneducated, or belong to an ethnic minority—often render individuals the victims of lifelong discrimination. Such disadvantages, encountered early in life, are said to produce psychological, social, and economic handicaps. A young person acquires a low self-esteem and a feeling of inferiority toward those with higher, but unearned, social status. He or she finds that educational and career choices are closed and later discovers that the only available jobs are those permitting no individual initiative. Apart from work, the disadvantaged individual may have fewer leisure hours and less money to pursue the intellectual and recreational activities reserved for others. Such a syndrome of socioeconomic disadvantages may spawn a distinctive life-style and set of values that, when passed from generation to generation, result in a self-reinforcing cycle.

In Britain, the United States, and other liberal democracies, the last two decades have seen legislation based partly on an acceptance of this rationale. As a result, educational opportunities have been expanded, discrimination in housing and employment has been reduced, and social-work activity has become more aggressive in tackling the less tangible manifestations of the "poverty cycle."

The socialist impulse of Marxism-Leninism proceeds from similar assumptions, but there are also very important differences both in principle and in practice. The most critical theoretical difference is the SED willingness to ascribe virtually all basic social conflict to economic differences, primarily to differences between those who own economic enterprises and those who are merely employees. In theory, all social discrimination, even ethnic and sex discrimination, is perceived to derive from this fundamental economic distinction. The other main theoretical difference centers on the role of private property. In liberal democracies individual claims to private property generally are accorded legal standing equal or superior to claims of socioeconomic discrimination. In specific cases, conflicts between the two types of claims are resolved by legislative compromise or by uncertain and even arbitrary judicial standards.

In contrast, the East German approach regards the claims of inferior socioeconomic standing as decidedly superior. Consequently, the right to private property, though not abolished, is severely circumscribed. Above all, private property (the means of production) may not be used for economic activity that has the effect of perpetuating another persons' economic dependency and social subordination. Thus, all the means of production are owned and operated by the government; private property is limited to such things as personal possessions, savings, and residences.

The practical application of this rather intense search for social harmony in the GDR has created three major problems or distortions. First, the nominal "public" ownership of the means of production indicates that agencies of the central government, clustered in the Council of Ministers, are directly responsible for all significant economic decisions, regardless of where they are actually implemented. In reality, of course, many decisions are made by regional or local governments or in the factories and farms, but central agencies retain and exercise the right to overturn lower decisions. In addition, the Socialist Unity party, acting presumptively on behalf of the public interest, ultimately holds these central agencies accountable for the nation's economic performance. The result is a very large discrepancy in authority between those individuals who make basic decisions and those who must implement them. The ability of central decision makers to gather timely and accurate information is often overtaxed by the size and complexity of the national economy. Furthermore, all participants are plagued by the knowledge that the definitive level of decision will change from time to time. To protect themselves from adverse upper-level decisions, lower economic agencies may conceal certain kinds of information, thus aggravating the central problem of making effective and rational economic decisions.

A second major problem is the enhanced potential for arbitrariness, which results from the marriage of economic and political authority under East German socialism. There is irony in this outcome, because socialism initially prescribes public economic ownership as a remedy for the tendency of concentrated private economic power to resist or even dominate political authority. Whereas liberal democracies experience the countervailing forces of political and economic power—producing moderation or stagnation, depending on one's point of view—East German socialism has no such mutually offsetting forces. In the GDR, therefore, the governing elite enjoys the duality of political and economic power, fewer restraints on its behavior, and a greater separation between the governors and the governed than is common in the West. To be sure, the precommunist capitalist elites have been deprived of their power, but this condition of powerlessness extends also to the working class, the very people for whose benefit socialism was presumably introduced. In fact, everyone who is dependent for his or her livelihood on the political and economic authority of the state and party elite will find it extraordinarily difficult to exert individual sovereignty in the face of remote and concentrated power.

The third major shortcoming of East German socialism arises from the noncompetitive nature of its electoral process. As a general principle, other forms of socialism can avert many of the abuses of concentrated power by periodically exchanging public officials through competitive multiparty elections. But in the GDR all elected officials, whatever their organizational affiliation, are selected by the SED to appear on an uncontested electoral list. Consequently, citizens cannot apply direct sanctions against officials perceived as unresponsive to public wishes. Occasionally, the converse relationship is invoked, when a citizen is subject to sanctions for excessive criticism of a public official. Since such sanctions most commonly affect one's employment, East Germans must contend with potential economic disadvantages based upon political discrimination—virtually the reverse of the charge that Marxist-Leninists level at capitalist societies.

For those able to adjust to these problems (apparently a sizable majority), GDR socialism offers ample educational and employment opportunities, secure retirement and other social benefits, a relatively high standard of living, and a general socioeconomic status more oriented to individual achievement than to accidents of birth.

Both the benefits and the costs of the East German system are products of more than thirty-five years of experimentation and growth. German cultural and political history, Soviet penetration, and the GDR's leadership commitment to the Marxist-Leninist version of socialism have all played a part in shaping the nation's identity. But other forces are also at work, transforming the nation and posing new problems.

Ecological Issues of Social Change

A distinguishing feature of Marxism has always been its ecological, or systemic, view of human development. Work and leisure, family and group, physical and intellectual, cultural and political—these dimensions of life are not discrete segments; how an individual performs in one dimension is assumed to affect all others.

East German leaders, because they are politicians and not social philosophers, have often neglected this ecological perspective. They have preferred to concentrate their resources on resolving narrow political and economic problems in the short run, while ignoring or repressing long-term social consequences. However, in the late 1960s a more comprehensive view of social change began to surface in authoritative writings. This broader approach was both a logical outgrowth of economic reform and a sign of the more or less satisfactory resolution of basic political conflicts. It also reflected the fact that certain ecological issues had begun to assume sharper contours.

Governmental attempts to deal with these issues are summarized in subsequent chapters. For the moment, a brief review is necessary to complete the picture of the GDR's national identity. To some extent, the social ecology of East Germany reflects recent German history as well as peculiarities of SED-style socialism. At the same time, the nation reflects many characteristics found in any modern industrial society.

East Germany's 16.8 million citizens live in an area about the size of Ohio, or about four-fifths the size of England. With 402 people per square mile (156 per square kilometer), the GDR has the highest population density of the socialist states. It is seven times higher than that of the United States, but significantly lower than West Germany's and Great Britain's.[10] The total population has declined from approximately 19.1 million in 1947 (including a great many refugees from eastern and central Europe) and has approached stability over the last two decades.[11]

Three reasons account for this unusual decline. First, very high rates of emigration far exceeded the rates of immigration. From 1949 to the closure of the Berlin border in August 1961, West German and West Berlin authorities registered nearly 2.7 million refugees.[12] An additional 192,000 refugees have been received through 1982. Legal emigration from the GDR to the West—primarily pensioners—averages around 13,000 per year.[13] In contrast, immigrants to the GDR, mainly from West Germany, average fewer than 5,000 per year.[14] Second, the East German birthrate has declined steadily. In 1979, 11.6 live births per 1,000 population were recorded, compared to 14.7 in the United States, 12.1 in the United Kingdom, and 9.8 in the Federal Republic.[15] In part this decline reflects the personal choices made in modern societies—choices involving increasing affluence, more open employment for women, and a weakening of pronatalist religious values. In addition, the GDR has experienced a decline in the number of women in their child-bearing years. Third, the GDR has an unusually high proportion of elderly citizens. Some of these are men who were barely too old for military combat in World War II and are now in their eighties. But this disproportion is better explained by the fact that the middle age groups were reduced by both war and emigration. The demographic result is an annual death rate of 14 per 1,000 population, an excess of deaths over births.[16]

From an economic standpoint, the population structure is unusually unfavorable. For every 100 people employed, there are 65 who are not of working age (32 elderly and 33 children).[17] This means a very heavy burden on the working population in providing services for the others. By the late 1970s this imbalance began to shift slightly, but the effects will be quite evident for another fifteen to thirty years. In addition, there is a substantial excess of women aged forty and above. This situation complicates the problem of support for the elderly and conflicts with the desire of young couples for weaker extended family ties. It has also contributed to an annual divorce rate of 2.7 per 1,000 people and a marriage rate of 8.6, both among the highest in the world.[18] Another related problem may be the GDR's high suicide rate. Although not officially published as a separate statistic, the suicide rate may be as high as 30 per 1,000 people, compared to 12.7 in the United States, 7.9 in the United Kingdom, and 22.7 in West Germany.[19]

High rates of divorce and suicide are manifestations of social instability. Causes are difficult to delineate clearly, but they are especially associated with modern urban-industrial societies. Social psychologists have observed that such societies are characterized by high rates of social and physical mobility, a decline of extended families and religion-based norms, a strong emphasis upon individual achievement, and the concentration of people in impersonal urban environments. Public values and status criteria shift away from personal relations toward the accumulation of material possessions. Scholars hypothesize that such social changes place a very heavy emphasis on individual "success" in occupational and material terms. In the absence of strong personal support networks, the penalties for failure are especially severe. Loneliness, marital infidelity, suicide, and divorce are the price of frustrated aspirations and low self-esteem.

Despite occasional Marxist-Leninist discourse on spiritual development and the virtues of collectivism, East Germany has not escaped these symptoms of economic and social modernization. The fact that these problems are more severe in the GDR than in other East European socialist states is consistent with the GDR's more advanced stage of modernization.

It is also true that the magnitude of East Germany's social problems sometimes exceeds that of even the more developed states of Western Europe. The complicating factor of an unusual population structure has already been noted. Other explanations are rather speculative, but three points can be suggested. First, the path to success in the GDR seems to be narrowly prescribed. It is true that the equality of opportunity that initially awaits young people is broad, but deviation from the expectations of those in authority, especially teachers and work supervisors, can lead to the permanent loss of opportunity. An individual who exhibits an excessive religious orientation, public political dissent, or even ordinary social misbehavior may be forever deprived of the opportunity for significant personal advancement. Positions of responsibility are normally reserved for those with unblemished personal histories. This low tolerance for deviance and the unwillingness to permit "second chances" probably mean that many people experience severe frustration and deprivation from early in life. What distinguishes Western capitalist societies is not the absence of frustration and deprivation, but the hope that setbacks may be eventually overcome by hard work and good fortune.

Second, compared to their West European counterparts, East Germans have fewer opportunities to release their frustrations by indulging in relatively harmless deviant or escapist activities. Shared housing arrangements and a strong group emphasis in leisure and recreational facilities mean that individuals are seldom far from others who, out of commitment to an older morality or out of fear of appearing negligent, are willing to lodge a public reprimand for deviant behavior. Such social pressure is not unique to the GDR, but it is more intense and cannot be easily escaped by moving to a different community or changing one's circle of acquaintances.

Third, for those East Germans whose personal circumstances engender feelings of frustration and depression, the constant image of West Germany as holding a bright and unattainable future may further exacerbate a condition of despair and marginally increase the frequency of social problems.

One must be careful not to exaggerate the scope of these social problems. It is evident that a vast segment of East German society is able to find satisfaction within the prevailing system of values and rewards, and there is no way to measure the extent to which the "frustration" scenario has validity. But ample evidence of individual experiences suggests that, in addition to the problems generally associated with modern societies, some GDR citizens suffer from distinctive patterns of stress. Such patterns, even though they affect a small minority, are a significant element in East Germany's social ecology.

Ecological issues arise also from the impact of social change on the GDR's physical environment. Although the total population has declined, industrial and technological development has produced greater concentrations of people. Apart from the 1.1 million people of East Berlin, most of the population is found in a triangle reaching from Magdeburg in the west, to Erfurt in the southwest, to Dresden in the southeast. The GDR is more urbanized than other East European states, but it has only three cities of more than .5 million people. Instead of the giant metropolitan developments of Western industrial states, East Germany features extended clusters of moderate-sized towns. Nevertheless, the problems of mass transit, air and water pollution, housing shortages, and land-use planning pose complex ecological dilemmas in the GDR as in other industrialized nations.

In one other respect East Germany shares a critical developmental problem with other industrialized nations. Present standards of consumption and methods of production place a very severe strain on East Germany's natural resources. The amount of useful agricultural land (.67 acres per capita) is more favorable than in some West European countries, but the worst in East Europe. The shortage requires high applications of artificial fertilizers and a significant reliance upon imported chemicals and food. Manufacturing technology requires a large, steady volume of imported raw materials and energy. When all uses are included, the GDR's per capita energy consumption is by far the highest of the socialist countries and is, in fact, among the highest in the world. Although soft-coal production is significant, the GDR is heavily dependent upon increasingly expensive foreign sources of energy. Consequently, East Germany, too, faces the need for difficult choices and a restructuring of established patterns of consumption.

Dimensions of National Identity

When outsiders first endeavor to comprehend a nation such as the German Democratic Republic, it is tempting to isolate a single attribute as the most essential defining element. English-speaking peoples, much affected by their government's involvement in East-West confrontations, have long tended to see the GDR as simply a Soviet "satellite," an unredeemable renegade from its Western past. But reality is far more complex. The GDR is a nation at a crossroads in a very profound sense. It is pulled in four directions simultaneously. It is intensely aware of its German past, while aspiring vigorously to a socialist future. It is a West European nation because of its shared popular culture, its shared problems of advanced urban-industrial ecology, and the highly visible presence of the Federal Republic as a point of interest and comparison. It is also an East European nation because of its military dependence on the Soviet Union and its more or less compulsory adoption of Soviet forms of political organization and public values.

It is no exaggeration to say that the GDR is in the midst of an identity crisis. Contrary to expectations, the passage of time has not brought much relief. As old riddles remain, new forms of change have only added new dimensions to the problem.

The following chapters describe the major East German institutions and the public policies devised to accommodate these diverse influences and to forge a distinctive and widely shared sense of national identity.

Notes

1. Jochen Bethkenhagen et al., *DDR und Osteuropa: Wirtschaftssystem, Wirtschaftspolitik, Lebensstandard* [GDR and East Europe: Economic System, Economic Policy, Standard of Living] (Opladen: Leske, 1981), pp. 16–17. See also Doris Cornelsen et al., *Handbook of the Economy of the German Democratic Republic* (Westmead, England: Saxon House, 1979), pp. 1–3.

2. Cited in Carola Stern, "History and Politics of the Socialist Unity Party of Germany (SED), 1945–1965," in William E. Griffiths (ed.), *Communism in Europe*, vol. 2 (Cambridge: MIT Press, 1966), p. 64.

3. Peter C. Ludz et al., *DDR Handbuch*, 2d ed. [GDR Handbook] (Cologne: Wissenschaft und Politik, 1979), p. 148 [hereafter, *DDR Handbuch*].

4. Ibid., p. 950.

5. Cited in Ferenc Vali, *The Quest for a United Germany* (Baltimore: Johns Hopkins, 1967), p. 23.

6. Cornelsen et al., *Handbook of the Economy of the German Democratic Republic*, pp. 5–6.

7. *DDR Handbuch*, pp. 1175–1177. See also Rolf Badstübner et al., *DDR: Werden and Wachsen* [GDR: Becoming and Growing] (Frankfurt am Main: Marxistische Blätter, 1975), pp. 196–216.

8. *DDR Handbuch*, pp. 1180–1182.

9. Cornelsen et al., *Handbook of the Economy of the German Democratic Republic*, pp. 28–29.

10. Calculated from Statistisches Bundesamt, *Statistisches Jahrbuch 1981 für die Bundesrepublik Deutschland* (Stuttgart: W. Kohlhammer, 1981), pp. 630–631 [hereafter, *Statistisches Jahrbuch 1981-BRD*].

11. Zentralverwaltung für Statistik, *Statistisches Jahrbuch 1980 der Deutschen Demokratischen Republik* (Berlin: Staatsverlag, 1980), p. 1 [hereafter, *Statistisches Jahrbuch 1980-DDR*].

12. *DDR Handbuch*, p. 401.

13. *Statistisches Jahrbuch 1981-BRD*, p. 77.

14. Ibid.

15. Ibid., pp. 636–637.

16. Ibid., p. 637.

17. Calculated from *Statistisches Jahrbuch 1980-DDR*, pp. 84, 364.

18. *Statistisches Jahrbuch 1981-BRD*, p. 637.

19. *Statistisches Jahrbuch 1980-DDR*, p. 1.

2
Directed Democracy:
The People and Government

Every nation has a political culture, a set of widely shared beliefs about the appropriate functions of government and the proper relationship of citizens to their state. Any such set of beliefs has three related layers: (1) an official culture, or public myth, which depicts government purposes and citizen aspirations in the most noble, idealistic light; (2) an elite subculture, which explains the privileges of power and adjusts idealistic principles to accord with realistic limitations; and (3) a mass subculture, which accounts for differences between the governors and the governed and promotes uncritical acceptance of the less tangible ideals.

Political cultures vary greatly from one nation to another. In stable liberal democracies the official culture tends to be a loose agglomeration of values and precepts accumulated over generations. For example, virtually all Americans can recall phrases from the noted speeches of Lincoln, Wilson, Roosevelt, and other political leaders. Famous documents, such as the Declaration of Independence, the Pledge of Allegiance, and even the inscription on the Statue of Liberty, all contribute to the public myth, so often invoked in history lessons, political debates, and holiday speeches. The durability of this official culture is not diminished by its lack of philosophic coherence or its frequent failure to account for real political behavior. At the same time, the long evolution of U.S. political culture, its decided emphasis on pragmatism, and the nation's rather open systems of communication have gradually brought the three layers of political culture closer together. Thus, value discontinuities between the official, the elite, and the mass versions of political values are considerably less troublesome than in newer and less democratic systems.

The political culture of the German Democratic Republic is distinguished by a number of characteristics. Most important are the profound discontinuities in German political history, which have precluded the gradual evolution of political values, and the adoption of Marxism-

Leninism as the foundation for an officially propagated myth considerably divergent from the preceding myths of Imperial Germany, the Weimar Republic, and the Third Reich. An inevitable consequence has been a very wide discrepancy between the official myth and the elite and mass subcultures.

Marxism-Leninism

The official culture, or ideology, is an amalgam of ideas adopted from the German philosopher Karl Marx and the Russian political leader Vladimir Lenin. Like other communist parties throughout the world, the GDR's Socialist Unity party designates this ideological heritage by the term Marxism-Leninism. It is a complex heritage derived from the volumes of writings and subject to different interpretations according to the specific context.

Among his numerous works, the ideas of Karl Marx are best expressed in his *Economic-Philosophic Manuscripts* (1844), *The Communist Manifesto* (with Friedrich Engels, 1848), and *Das Kapital* (three volumes with Engels, 1867, 1885, 1894). Reflecting his German upbringing and later observation of life in England, Marx's early work is primarily a philosophy of social justice, in which he contrasts the natural dignity and creativity of human beings with the depraved conditions of life under industrial capitalism: poverty, long and hard labor, the constant threat of unemployment, ubiquitous inequality, and, above all, restrictive economic and political structures that deprived people of the opportunity to govern their own lives. *The Communist Manifesto* couples a much simplified distillation of Marx's social philosophy with a political polemic, an incitement to rise and seize control over the enslaving mechanisms of capitalism. *Das Kapital* is a lengthy and turgid exposition of the origins and evils of capitalism and the "scientific laws" by which capitalism will breed its own destruction.

Of course, subsequent economists and economic history itself have seriously discredited much of Marx's scientific claim. His earlier social philosophy, however, with its emphatic humanist morality, has many respected adherents in communist and noncommunist nations. Party agencies in East Germany speak of "creatively adapting" Marx's ideas, but they admit no basic shortcomings in any of his writings.

When Lenin emerged among the radical opponents to the Russian czar, he brought much inspiration from Marx but no practical guidance on how to remedy the injustice of a society still in the last throes of feudalism. Marx's polemic had been directed to the working class, or proletariat, in societies where feudalism had been long superseded by dynamic capitalism. Consequently, Lenin found it necessary to create numerous corollaries to Marx's "scientific laws" in order to justify a proletarian revolution in this backward Russian land of few proletarians.

By adroitly exploiting military and economic calamities, Lenin led the Bolsheviks to power in 1917. He then was forced to confront the greatest deficiency of Marxism, the absence of a strategy for creating a just socialist society. Whereas Marx had hoped that a mature workers' revolution would spontaneously chart a progressive path, Lenin perceived that Russia's unsophisticated masses required firm leadership. Consequently, he fashioned an elitist Communist party and instituted a severe "dictatorship of the proletariat" for effecting radical social and political change. This recorded experience, acquired in the course of improvised adjustments to Marxism and supplemented by some practices of Russia's subsequent regime under Josef Stalin, constitutes the body of Leninism.

For the purpose of understanding East Germany's official political ideology, it is important to emphasize that Marxism and Leninism are two separate, if related, components. Moreover, Marxism scarcely possesses the coherence or explanatory power that SED authorities would like to ascribe to it. East Germans have reason to find Leninism even less satisfactory, because it was created for the conditions of backward Russia—conditions sharply different from those of postwar Germany. Nevertheless, Marxism-Leninism is today the strongest, most sharply delineated influence in East German political culture.

Perspective on Democracy

The influence of Marxism-Leninism is most apparent in the official SED view of political democracy. Because this view differs significantly from views regarded as self-evident in Western liberal democracies, a note of caution is in order. Although in the early transitional phase SED pronouncements deliberately invoked vague expressions of democratic principles in order to attract the widest possible support, it is misleading to ascribe subsequent endorsements of democratic ideals solely to deceit or cynical political tactics. Reflecting the inspiration of Marx, the SED view of democracy springs from an ultimate concern for individual sovereignty. Consequently, despite frequent and obvious violations of individual rights in everyday life, the official culture is not fundamentally antidemocratic. If pure democracy means complete sovereignty for all citizens, an antidemocratic system means that all power is invested in an absolute monarch or fascist dictator. In the German Democratic Republic, the official myth aspires to democracy—not to its opposite.

In its East German expression, Marxism-Leninism has a distinctive concept of political democracy, according to which political institutions can never be simply neutral mechanisms for integrating the diverse wills of nominally equal groups. It would be naive to expect such "neutral" institutions to produce policies serving the public good. In a capitalist, or bourgeois, democracy—this critique continues—contesting groups cannot be equal, since the unequal distribution of wealth and economic ownership inevitably distorts political processes to the benefit of privileged social segments.

Electoral contests, legislative squabbles, and interest-group pressures are seen as the special province of influential elites. Such activities do indeed constitute political democracy, but only for the capitalists; for workers and for all others whose livelihood depends on service to a large, privately owned enterprise, "democratic" government assumes a dictatorial character. In the SED interpretation, the main function of such a government is to uphold the unequal division of economic and political power. To the extent that the dependent majority derives social benefit from such a system, it does so only because the majority provides the human resources upon which capitalism is built. For the ruling elite, therefore, wages and social expenditures are not a matter of justice and equity, but simply a prudent investment in a productive resource. Even beneficent policies are possible, but only so long as the foundation of privilege remains unaffected.

Interest-group pluralism, recognized in the United States and Europe as a modern form of democracy, is condemned by Marxist-Leninists as a sort of "bread-and-circuses" distraction. It provides the dependent classes with a vicarious sense of participation, while inhibiting the formation of a class consciousness necessary to grapple with the more basic question of power. Consequently, East German leaders put forward a cynical, if not wholly negative, view of political democracy. In principle, political democracy is a potentially decisive instrument for eliciting individual and collective sovereignty. In the SED public myth, however, this potential can be tapped only under carefully circumscribed conditions.

East Germany's official political culture stipulates two prerequisites for the attainment of "authentic" democracy. First, basic economic inequalities, derived from differences in individual relationships to the means of production (i.e., owner or employee), must be eliminated, along with the attendant inequalities in social institutions and privilege. This requirement is not to be misunderstood as a denial of differences in individual abilities, interests, and personalities; on the contrary, the purpose is to abolish artificial barriers and to create a broad equality of opportunity, through which individual uniqueness can be fully expressed. Second, from the lack of economically focused conflict there must emerge a universal acceptance of the common good, which is compatible with the good of every individual. As even the most idealistic East German political philosopher would acknowledge, this is an awesome challenge.

Following Lenin's example, the SED emphasizes the voluntaristic side of Marx's social philosophy: "Men make their own history. But they do not make it just as they please, out of whole cloth, but out of conditions directly encountered and transmitted from the past."[1] Thus, the prerequisites for this special form of democracy are not expected to arise spontaneously: They must be consciously created. East German efforts to create these prerequisites and to lend substance to the official political culture center around the need to shape a common political will and corresponding governmental forms.

Corporatism and Political Representation

During the first fifteen years of communist rule in East Germany, the regime struggled to eliminate hostile elements in the population—first Nazi supporters, then small entrepreneurs and Social Democrats. The nationwide uprising in June 1953, sharp clashes with the labor unions in 1957–1958, the high-level SED purge in 1958, and the repeated waves of emigrants across the open border to West Berlin—all of these events illustrated the profound lack of unity in the nation.

By the early 1960s, however, the GDR appeared to have reached a turning point. The construction of the Berlin Wall in August 1961 dramatically reduced emigration and stabilized the work force. Economic growth became more predictable, and political opposition was more thoroughly repressed.

In 1963 the SED issued its first Party Program, a comprehensive recital of national achievements and goals. This document exuded great confidence, claiming that economic transformation and a new unity of all the people had laid the foundation for the "comprehensive building of socialism." Although the society still contained many different segments, with diverse needs and abilities, an unprecedented unity of will had emerged. The task of the SED, then, was to insure a continuing and constructive role for each of these segments.

This portrayal of East German society was premature, to say the least. Nevertheless, it illustrates the principle of corporatism around which the political system is organized. Because political theorists have employed this principle in connection with fascism, as well as with contemporary Scandinavian democracies, the term *corporatism* is not mentioned in SED treatments. But the corporatist principle fits well the Socialist Unity party and its attempt to weld all citizens into a single social organism, with each part—like the parts of the body—performing an essential task.

In the GDR today, corporatism is far more a goal than a reality. The reality is a set of political organizations that, with their numerous pyramidal and cross-cutting linkages, encompass virtually the entire population. Thus the form of a corporate society has been created; however, its substance is a rather different matter.

The formalism of this scheme is best expressed in the National Front, the loosely structured umbrella association for all political organizations. This includes the five political parties: SED, Christian Democratic Union (CDU), Liberal Democratic Party of Germany (LDPD), National Democratic Party of Germany, (NDPD), and Democratic Farmers' party (DBD). It also includes the four main mass organizations: Free German Labor Union Federation (FDGB), Free German Youth (FDJ), Democratic Women's Federation (DFD), and Culture Federation (KB). Each of these nine constituent organizations has its own interests and conducts most of its activities independent of the National Front.

The National Front itself has threefold significance. First, the National Front symbolizes the goal of extending some form of political responsibility to all citizens and of enlisting all responsible citizens in a single organizational expression. Nominally distinct from both the government and the dominant party, it promotes community and national pride through its publications and media campaigns. Second, community branches draw together members of the constituent organizations, and other citizens as well, for community-action projects such as fairs, holiday celebrations, and beautification campaigns, much in the fashion of civic clubs in Western democracies.

In its third function the National Front assumes a more overtly political character; it is responsible for promoting elections, coordinating the nomination of candidates for elected assemblies, and helping citizens to monitor the activities of their elected representatives.[2] In each electoral district, delegates from the political parties, mass organizations, and even residential associations gather at open National Front meetings to propose candidates. After an initial screening, a list of qualified, exemplary citizens is presented to additional public meetings. Candidates are listed in preferred order, usually a few more than the number of seats available; on rare occasions, these public meetings alter the order of candidates.

On election day voters may strike the names of unwanted candidates or simply place the unmarked list in the ballot box. The top names on the ballot will be elected, unless stricken by a majority of the voters, in which case the seat will go to the next-lower name of the list. Informal East German sources intimate that, in past elections, urban voters sometimes voted down many approved candidates. Embarrassed by its low support from working-class districts, the East German "workers" government felt compelled to publish artificially affirmative election results. This problem has apparently diminished over time, either because of the voters' sense of futility or because of improved nominating processes.

According to the official political culture, the National Front's political role insures that the process of selecting public officials belongs to the whole people rather than to some narrow socioeconomic elite. The pivotal role of the SED, as the creator and most authoritative segment of the National Front, ostensibly guarantees an equitable process and the selection of high-quality candidates. Of course, there is no assurance that the SED officials involved will not introduce both institutional and personal prejudice into the process. On the contrary, a degree of systematic intervention is evident in the consistent application of SED-originated, nonpublic rules of proportional representation, according to which the distribution of seats on assemblies at all governmental levels conforms to preestablished quotas. As a result, the percentage of seats distributed by sex, age, occupation, and organizational affiliation remains about the same from district to district and election to election. Obviously, such an outcome requires considerable behind-the-scenes coordination of the nominating process. The ultimate effect is a more inclusive, more proportional representative system than could be achieved through a more spontaneous process; it also reinforces the SED's image of a corporatist polity.

Unitary, Parliamentary Government

The corporatist principle is also reflected in the formal structure of government. The German Democratic Republic has the most common governmental structure in the world today: a unitary, parliamentary system. Unlike federal systems, East Germany has no provinces or states exercising independent authority; territorial divisions of government possess only that authority specifically delegated by the national government. This system corresponds to the unitary system of France, for example, and to the relationship of counties and cities to U.S. states. Unlike presidential systems, East Germany employs no separation of powers or checks and balances at the national level; all authority is vested in the National Assembly (Volkskammer). This arrangement is one of parliamentary supremacy, like that of Great Britain, and is similarly justified by the claim that no authority can be higher than the will of the people, of which the National Assembly is the best institutional expression. Thus, the absence of either vertical or horizontal divisions of authority expresses a determination to create a corporate society.

Because the National Front policy eliminates competitive elections, a formal agreement assigns a fixed number of the 500 National Assembly seats to each National Front organization: SED—127; CDU, LDPD, NDPD, and DBD—52 each; FDGB—68; FDJ—40; DFD—35; and KB—22. Because many deputies from the four mass organizations are also members of a political party, the SED share actually exceeds 50 percent.[3] In actual practice, since virtually all National Assembly votes are unanimous endorsements of prior decisions, the partisan distribution of seats is relatively inconsequential.

The formal operation of the National Assembly resembles that of the many modern parliaments. Because of the brevity of its sessions and the absence of significant public discussion, however, its role is more like that of parliaments in less developed nations than that of parliaments in industrial democracies. GDR deputies are elected for five-year terms and meet in three or four annual plenary sessions, some lasting only one day. They formally elect the State Council, the Council of Ministers, the chairman of the National Defense Council, the attorney general, and the Supreme Court justices. In practice, however, all of these positions are filled by processes outside the assembly's control.

The unicameral National Assembly creates its own twelve-member Presidium, a sort of collective presiding officer. This body includes the assembly president (Horst Sindermann was reelected in 1981 for a second five-year term), three additional SED deputies, and a senior deputy from each of the eight remaining National Front organizations. The Presidium is simply a coordinating agent for assembly business. Its relatively modest function is indicated by the fact that the chairmen of parties and mass organizations do not occupy Presidium posts. Thus, the National Assembly Presidium has less stature than the Presidium of the USSR's Supreme Soviet.

The National Assembly also forms fourteen standing committees with jurisdictions corresponding to major areas of public policy, such as foreign affairs, health, and labor and social policy. The activities of these committees are poorly reported in the public media, so relevant evidence is only fragmentary. The size of each committee is not always fixed. National Assembly deputies, who usually include state and SED officials employed in the area of committee concern, constitute the majority of each committee's membership. Additional members may be drawn from outside the assembly; these individuals are chosen because of their professional expertise or because they belong to affected groups, regardless of their partisan affiliation. For example, a "representative" elderly widow may be added for a review of social-security law, or a psychologist may be added for a review of laws defining juvenile crime.

Each committee meets at least once every year to receive reports from responsible government and SED officials, nominally satisfying the constitutional requirement that the government be accountable to the people. For sensitive policy areas, such as foreign affairs or national defense, the National Assembly committees do not go beyond this level of formalistic legitimation. But in some areas of social policy—less ideologically sensitive and having more immediate impact on individual citizens—assembly committees sometimes receive proposed legislation at any early stage and utilize working sessions to review and modify the proposals. This practice is justified both as an expansion of democracy and as a means to devise better laws. During the 1970s this consultative-deliberative role of assembly committees became more visible, as large segments of the GDR legal code (e.g., family law and labor law) were thoroughly publicized and revised. It is not known whether this comprehensive activity is part of a general upgrading of the National Assembly or merely a temporary phenomenon.

The State Council

Between sessions of the National Assembly, many of its functions are entrusted to the State Council. Following the death in 1960 of Wilhelm Pieck, the first and only president of the republic, the State Council was formed to fill the role of a collective head of state. Some of its functions resemble those carried by elected presidents in Western parliamentary systems: It designates ambassadors, receives foreign emissaries, grants state honors, calls elections, and formally promulgates laws of the National Assembly.[4] From 1960 to 1973, the chairman of the State Council was Walter Ulbricht, simultaneously first secretary of the SED until 1971. During Ulbricht's joint tenure, the State Council gradually expanded its competence. Disruptive reorganizations of the Council of Ministers in the early 1960s permitted much executive authority to flow to the State Council, which even began to issue orders affecting relatively routine matters in specific ministries. In addition to these intrusions against the executive, the State Council occasionally adopted major legislation, bypassing the formal requirement of National Assembly action. Curbing of State Council authority began in 1971 and was formalized by constitutional amendment in 1974. The former authority of the Council of Ministers has been restored, and the National Assembly has acquired a more active role in formal legislation.[5]

In retrospect, it appears that Ulbricht's enlargement of his State Council role may be construed as an abuse of personal power. Because the authority of the large SED underlies the entire government structure,

Ulbricht's effort to become not only head of the party and head of state, but de facto of the government as well, may have been both unnecessary and unwise. On the other hand, Ulbricht may have perceived the Council of Ministers as an obstacle to major economic reforms. Thus, a transfer of authority to the State Council may have been the most effective way to circumvent administrative resistance. Both interpretations may be correct.

Walter Ulbricht was removed from his post of SED first secretary in June 1971, but he retained the chairmanship of the State Council until his death in January 1973. The main legislation restoring authority to the Council of Ministers was enacted in October 1972. Willi Stoph, chairman of the Council of Ministers since 1964, abandoned this office to become Ulbricht's replacement as State Council chairman. In view of the legislative reallocation of authority between the two bodies, Stoph's transfer may be seen as a demotion and a way to emphasize that the new SED leader, Erich Honecker, was unquestionably in charge. Stoph may have been well suited also to assure the appropriate dismantling of the swollen State Council staff.

Accurate appraisal of the State Council's function is further complicated by the fact that in October 1976 Willi Stoph returned to his former office as chairman of the Council of Ministers. Erich Honecker, whose SED leadership title was changed to general secretary, acquired the additional role of State Council chairman. Because the State Council chairman is titular head of state, Honecker's acquisition of this post now permits him to enjoy the diplomatic visibility befitting the leader of the governing party. (The following year a similar change was effected for Soviet leader Leonid Brezhnev.) Although the State Council staff was expanded slightly, there has been no evidence of a renewed effort to strengthen the State Council at the expense of the Council of Ministers.

Following the national election in June 1981, the State Council consisted of Erich Honecker as chairman, three vice-chairmen (Willi Stoph, also chairman of the Council of Ministers; Horst Sindermann, president of the National Assembly; and Paul Verner, SED secretary for security questions), and seventeen others. Four of the remainder represent the remaining National Front parties; the others are all from the SED, including eight who also sit in the Politburo. Although this closer overlapping of membership may suggest enhanced prestige for the State Council, in practice the council continues to exercise mainly ceremonial functions, functions that in other communist states are served by a National Assembly Presidium. Thus, the State Council is something of an anomaly, a surviving expression of the corporatist National Front image.

The Council of Ministers

In parliamentary language, the GDR's real executive power—the "government"—is the Council of Ministers. The Council of Ministers encompasses forty-five ministers and heads of other government agencies. It is smaller than analogous bodies in France and the Soviet Union, but larger than the British or U.S. cabinets. The functional areas of the council correspond roughly to ministerial divisions in Western democracies, except that several additional ministries and coordinating committees have been created to administer the national economy. Thus, alongside such ministries as Defense, Finance, Health, and Justice, one finds ministries for Chemicals, Electronics, Machinery, and Construction. Because those ministries most directly connected with production are legally and operationally different from the more conventional ministries, their inclusion in the council is not as peculiar or confusing as it might appear at first glance.

It is difficult to formulate generalizations about the membership of the Council of Ministers. Some ministries have experienced several major reorganizations, amalgamations, and divisions in thirty years. The authority role of the council itself has changed from its origin as completely subservient to the Soviet military governor to its present exercise of considerable functional autonomy. Turnover in ministerial posts has been variable, with average tenure of ministers ranging from more than ten years (Interior, Justice, Finance) to less than four years (Agriculture). Personalities and political conditions sometimes change quickly in young states, so that general principles are seldom valid for long.

With a few rather special exceptions, the selection of members to the GDR Council of Ministers is not designed to elevate individuals on the basis of their political leadership skills. For purposes of contrast, it is useful to recall that the British cabinet, for example, is made up of more or less distinguished politicians, who are placed on the "government team" because of their personal prestige and because of their contribution to electoral victory. Over time, some British politicians will serve in several cabinets, moving to more prestigious ministries, until they emerge as contenders for the role of prime minister. In the British cabinet, administrative skills and technical expertise are decidedly less important than more overtly political talents. For most positions in the GDR Council of Ministers, on the other hand, this order of relevant criteria is reversed.

Most GDR ministers are not part of a political stratum superimposed on an administrative hierarchy; rather, they are themselves products of that administrative hierarchy, professionals promoted through the ranks. This does not mean that ministers are merely the aged survivors of a lethargic seniority system. In high-technology areas, the emphasis is on technical expertise, and age may even be a handicap. Wolfgang Junker, for example, became minister for construction at the age of thirty-four, following extensive technical training, six years of management, and three years as deputy minister.[6] Junker's first acknowledged political position, candidate member of the SED Central Committee, was acquired only after he had been minister for more than four years.

The Council of Ministers as a group is closely linked to other organs of political authority. Twenty-seven council members are also deputies to the National Assembly, and forty-one belong to the SED. Most of the SED ministers have been (or will be) elected to the SED Central Committee, mainly because they have risen to important government posts. The significance of these linkages is explored more fully in the later discussion of the SED structure.

At this point, an exceptional subset of the Council of Ministers deserves closer attention. As with any large body, the council has its own smaller executive committee, again known as its Presidium. Since 1972 the Presidium has been authorized to act on behalf of the entire Council of Ministers, and consequently it constitutes the highest executive authority of the government. With respect to the remainder of the council, however, the Presidium's role is not strictly a directive one. Full meetings of the council are held almost weekly, permitting an element of collective consultation. The precise relationship of the Presidium to individual ministries depends upon the subject of ministerial competence and, to a lesser extent, upon the prestige of the ministers themselves.

A key to evaluating the Presidium is found in its composition (here described as of mid-1983). The Presidium is headed by its chairman (roughly, the prime minister) and two first-deputy chairmen, all with distinguished service in SED offices. Chairman Willi Stoph began his career in SED agencies concerned with construction, raw materials, and—later—general economic planning. From 1952 to 1955, he served as minister of the interior, where he was responsible for creating the present structure of internal security. From 1956 to 1960, he was minister of defense. In 1960 he assumed a special role for coordinating SED–Council of Ministers relations. Except for his brief service as head of the State Council, Stoph has been in the Council of Ministers Presidium since 1962. He has been a member of the SED Central Committee since 1950 and a member of the Politburo since 1953. In addition to his long record of service in the highest SED offices, Stoph is distinguished by his practical administrative experience both in economic affairs and in the areas of security and defense.[7]

Alfred Neumann, a first-deputy chairman and oldest member of the Presidium, spent twelve years working his way through the SED organization in East Berlin. In 1958 he became a member of both the

SED Secretariat and its Politburo. During the Council of Ministers reorganization (1961–1965), he headed the National Economic Council (since abolished). Since 1962 he has been on the council Presidium, usually without a designated functional responsibility. Neumann has been a member of the SED Central Committee since 1954 and a member of the Politburo since 1958.[8] Werner Krolikowski, the other first-deputy chairman, held several SED offices in Rostock County before moving to the critical industrial region of Dresden, where he headed the SED organization from 1960 to 1973. He then spent three years as leader of the national SED Department for the Economy, until assuming his present post in 1976. Krolikowski has been a member of the SED Central Committee since 1963 and a member of the Politburo since 1971. His older brother, Herbert, is deputy minister for foreign affairs.[9]

Despite radically different personal backgrounds, Neumann and Krolikowski have two major experiences in common: extended service as a high SED official in a major industrial region, with ample opportunity to display talents in leadership, decision making, and personnel recruitment, and intensive service in a high position of economic responsibility. Both men can be considered professional politicians, in some respects resembling politicians in Western parliamentary systems. They have moved upward, because they supported successful people above them. But equally important, they have earned their own bases of support through personality, proficiency, and their disposal of resources with which to reward loyalty.

Similar generalizations apply to the remaining nine members of the Presidium, known simply as deputy chairmen. In their case, however, less emphasis is placed upon party functions and more on technical expertise. Five deputy chairmen are SED members; four belong to the other National Front parties. All have held party offices, and all have had experience in economic planning and management. Unlike Stoph, Neumann, and Krolikowski, each remaining Presidium member holds a specific council post: State Contracts Court, Justice, Vehicles and Farm Machinery, Material Supply, Environment and Hydroeconomy, State Plan Commission, Communication, Science and Technology, and Council for Mutual Economic Assistance. Except for the minister of justice (a former specialist in private enterprise), all deputy chairmen are directly responsible for a dimension of economic policy.

Given the legislative definition of the Presidium as the leading group for the entire government, this one-sided selection of economic officials to the council Presidium is both surprising and revealing. It appears that the Presidium is not, in fact, the coordinating and directing body for the entire Council of Ministers. Instead, the Presidium functions more narrowly as the most authoritative government organ for the administration and planning of the national economy. As will be discussed in the next chapter, this concentration of expertise has implications for the exercise of SED authority in economic questions. For council agencies outside the economic area, executive oversight falls primarily to Chairman Stoph, his first-deputies, and their staff in the Bureau of the Council of Ministers.

Individual ministries function according to specific statutes. During the 1970s, many of these statutes were rewritten to reflect the expanded authority of the council and to provide ministries with greater resources for policy initiation. The hierarchic principle of authority, common to most European administrative systems, was reaffirmed, and provisions have been included for larger personal staffs for each minister, staffs that comprise small groups outside the normal chain of command. It is not known whether these changes have notably altered any minister's authority; much would depend upon the extent of a minister's discretion in selecting the personal staff.

Another change in ministry structure is the revival of the collegium, which had fallen into disuse in the early 1960s. Each minister is supposed to call regular meetings of the ministry's collegium, which includes deputy ministers, state secretaries, department heads, and, as needed, consultants from outside agencies and SED offices. Whereas the collegium had been created originally to promote scrutiny of the minister's performance, the present emphasis casts the collegium more in the role of a forum for explaining ministerial policy and exchanging information about the effect of proposed changes. If this image is accurate, the ministerial collegium in the GDR may begin to resemble consultative commissions attached to ministries in West European parliamentary systems.

Local Government

Below the national organs of government, the GDR has three territorial levels: 15 countries (*Bezirke*), 219 districts and urban boroughs (*Kreise*), and about 90,000 towns and communities (*Gemeinde*). Each features an elected assembly, the composition of which is controlled by local National Front committees under guidelines somewhat more flexible than those applied to the National Assembly elections. Each assembly is supported by a structure of committees, organized around policy areas of local concern and including both deputies and nondeputies. Nearly .5 million citizens (one out of every 28 adults) serve on an assembly committee at some level, and 200,000 are deputies.[10] Official sources proudly point out that this ratio represents a far higher level of citizen involvement than is found in Western democracies. The positive aspects of such participation should not be discounted; the consequent requirement of public accountability, if squarely addressed by local officials, may well produce better government, higher legitimacy, and broader citizen cooperation. It is worth noting that, in recent years, Western democracies have begun new experiments in citizen consultation committees, especially in urban settings, to help reduce the gap between the governors and the governed.

In the German Democratic Republic, to be sure, the effectiveness of citizen participation is rather severely circumscribed by the authority of local government executives—who in practice are selected by higher officials—and by the narrow limits of action set down by the central government. Local governments have no independent right of policy initiative; all local policy must be derived from explicit authorizing legislation or a ministerial order at the national level. Similarly, local government expenditures are all channeled through the unified central budget. In this respect, the GDR resembles the French unitary system and departs considerably from federal systems or even the looser British form of unitary government.

But East German local governments are not merely passive recipients of central allocations; they are participants in the budgetary process. The counties compete for larger shares of central allocations; the wealthier argue for proportions based upon revenue generated, while the poorer emphasize a need for compensatory or equalizing formulas. Individual districts and communities seek to finance special projects through supplemental grants from central ministries—for housing, for example. The outcome of such efforts hinges upon past performance, adroit leadership, and the cultivation of friends in higher offices.

Regardless of the source of funding, local expenditures generally must be distributed among competing needs. Which theater will be renovated, which streets will be repaired, where new housing or schools or restaurants will be located, how the burdens of household chores can be lightened, how juvenile crime can be reduced—such issues affect citizens in their daily lives. It is here that local mechanisms of citizen participation begin to bear fruit.

In recent years, higher political authorities have responded to complaints about the relative impotence of local government.[11] Central budget allocations have been inadequate and somewhat unpredictable, with the result that some community projects remain uncompleted for years. Expansion in the economic sector may place greater burdens on public services without a corresponding increase in local government funds. The Council of Ministers is working to project and guarantee local funding over longer periods, so that extensive projects can be planned over several years. New legislation has been enacted to compel production enterprises to bear part of the cost of public services. Although cooperative agreements between factories and local governments have existed for some time, local governments now have a strengthened legal right to sue factory management for failure to adhere to these agreements. It remains to be seen whether these changes will gradually transform East German local government into something more than a hollow exercise in frustration.

In addition to these profound financial and policy restraints, local governments are handicapped by their lack of authority over much of their administrative staff. Executive councils are nominally selected by local assemblies to exercise executive functions. These local officials are charged with administering the various policy areas related to local concerns. Although formally accountable to local assemblies, these officials are actually recruited, trained, and assigned by the central ministries in East Berlin. In effect, each central ministry operates its own civil-service system, which provides functionally trained personnel for the whole nation. Local governments have no separate source for administrative personnel. In legal terms, a local administrator is accountable both to local assemblies and to his or her central ministry. Because the central ministry disposes of career opportunities, however, any local administrator can easily calculate where the greater loyalty should be placed.

In the worst case, this imbalance may mean that most local government activity is simply the arbitrary application of policy handed down from a remote and unresponsive central bureaucracy. Efforts to utilize the local executive council as a collective, coordinating body may be futile. And executive accountability to the local assembly may amount to an endless series of explanations for why citizen expectations cannot be met.

Official public commentary suggests that citizen perception of local government has often corresponded to this worst case, and it is widely acknowledged that such futility in local government grievously undermines the goals of socialist democracy and the search for legitimacy. Improvement must be pursued along two avenues: Local government executives must be given more control over the diverse economic and administrative activity within their territorial jurisdictions, and they must be provided sufficient resources and incentives to respond more directly and effectively to representative citizens.

The Socialist State

The official political culture of the German Democratic Republic, nested in the legacies of Marx and Lenin, presents an ambivalent view of state power and popular sovereignty. In principle, the two concepts are perceived as mutually contradictory, since history reveals that the power of the state has always been used to exploit and repress the majority of the people. Furthermore, it is not possible to ignore the fact that even the new state of the GDR had been compelled to employ repressive methods against those elements in the majority who did not perceive the urgency of social and economic transformation.

But now, according to the public myth, those days are past. Reactionary elements have been eliminated or reconciled to the new order, and the great majority of the working people are joined shoulder to shoulder in creating a fully developed socialist society. State power is no longer repressive, since it now enjoys the full support of the citizenry. The executive organs of government are married to the assemblies of popular representation, forming the centerpiece of the new "socialist democracy." Thus, for the first time in German history, it becomes theoretically possible to strengthen both state power and popular sovereignty simultaneously. Or, to put the matter more strongly, only through an extension of popular sovereignty will the state be empowered to carry through the tasks of social transformation.

Viewed abstractly, this interpretation sounds like good Marxism. It is an attempt to move beyond Lenin's emphasis on the dictatorship of the proletariat to a more reciprocal image of the relationship between the state and society. Accordingly, the early stage records a highly concentrated state power effecting a dramatic economic and social transformation. Subsequently, the new society in turn transforms the character of state power, making it more responsive to the popular will. A symbiotic relationship ensues that, proceeding in cyclical fashion, gradually draws the two forces together until they become indistinguishable. Recalling the Marxist idiom, the end point of this process should be the full "withering away" of the state.

Although the public GDR myth occasionally invokes this nearly poetic imagery, more realistic and less sanguine appraisals are more common. The present organs of state power, it is conceded, are defective. Far too often government agencies are uncoordinated and inefficient. They define tasks from a narrow, self-serving viewpoint. And they seek to govern through arbitrary bureaucratic methods. At the same time, the assemblies of popular sovereignty fail to seriously exercise their function of expressing the public will, demanding accountability, proposing solutions, and sharing the burdens of governing. Deputies and other distinguished citizens are too easily satisfied with mere ritual and formalism. Again the mutually reinforcing interaction of state power and popular sovereignty is noted, but with emphasis on its negative consequences. The effect can only be to impede the quest for legitimacy.

The formal government structures described here represent the legal skeleton around which the East German political system is shaped. The official political culture depicts these structures as rational, efficient components of a single entity, expressing the will of a corporate, democratic society. However, reality is both less promising and more complex. It is less promising, because both the society and the government contain highly divisive, contesting elements; because abuses of power are many and richly rewarded; and because few people have reason to believe the democratic myth. The recent structural changes noted here implicitly recognize these shortcomings, for they are attempts to rationalize the distribution of authority and make it more accountable and more open to wider circles of participants. Reality is also more complex, because it must incorporate the many institutions and diverse functions of the omnipresent ruling party.

Notes

1. From Karl Marx, "The Eighteenth Brumaire of Louis Bonaparte," cited in T. B. Bottomore and Maximilien Rubel, *Karl Marx: Selected Writings in Sociology and Social Philosophy* (London: C. A. Watts, 1963), p. 54.

2. Günter Erbe, et al., *Politik, Wirtschaft, und Gesellschaft in der DDR* [Politics, Economy, and Society in the GDR] (Cologne: Westdeutscher, 1979), pp. 112–119.

3. Ibid., p. 118.

4. Peter C. Ludz et al., *DDR Handbuch*, 2d ed. [GDR Handbook] (Cologne: Wissenschaft und Politik, 1979), pp. 1038–1039.

5. Siegfried Mampel, "DDR-Verfassung fortgeschrieben [GDR Constitution Revised]," *Deutschland Archiv* 7, no. 11 (1974), pp. 1152–1157.

6. Günther Buch, *Namen und Daten: Wichtiger Personen der DDR* [Names and Dates: Important Persons of the GDR] (Berlin: J. H. W. Dietz, 1979), pp. 141–142.

7. Ibid., p. 313.

8. Ibid., p. 226.

9. Ibid., p. 174.

10. Zentralverwaltung für Statistik, *Statistisches Jahrbuch 1980 der Deutschen Demokratischen Republik* (Berlin: Staatsverlag, 1980), p. 395.

11. Klaus Sieveking, "Kommunalpolitik und Kommunalrecht in der DDR [Local Government Policies and Law in the GDR]," *Deutschland Archiv* 16, no. 11 (1983), pp. 1163–1174.

3
Directed Democracy:
The Party Role

The dominant role of the Socialist Unity party (SED) is an overwhelming fact of East German life, but its actual impact is exceedingly difficult for citizens of Western democracies to comprehend. Of course, foreigners quickly perceive that the SED differs radically from political parties in the U.S. or British senses. Yet it is misleading to conclude, therefore, that the SED is totally unlike more familiar parties. Reflecting a deep-seated fear of communist subversion in capitalist and underdeveloped nations, Westerners often try to apply a conspiratorial model to the SED. Unconsciously projecting a caricature of revolutionary Bolshevism, one expects SED members to gather in secret cells, there to plot ways to deceive the masses and to harness the force of government in order to impose their bizarre ideals on an unwilling population.

Although the means by which communist parties have come to power are somewhat diverse, it is true that the conspiratorial model has been validated by several historical incidents. However, this model never really corresponded to events in East Germany, even in the early postwar years. From the first days of the Soviet occupation, the activity of the German communists (initially known as the Communist Party of Germany) was highly visible. Rather than plotting in secret, the party stated its purposes openly and publicly recruited support among the general population. There was no design to "take over" the government, since the party and the government were built simultaneously and in tandem.

Today, the new political system has been completed. Standing at the center of the system, and involved in virtually every dimension of public life, is the Socialist Unity party. In organizational terms, the party is very large and internally diverse, reflecting much of the diversity of the society from which it springs. Because of its operational methods and its commitment to certain basic purposes, the SED has altered the shape of East German society. The pattern of influence is reciprocal, however, and the character of East German society has also helped to shape the SED.

38

Two Views of SED Precedence

The official political culture defines the SED as "the Marxist-Leninist party of the labor class and of all the working people of the socialist German Democratic Republic."[1] By this definition, the party seeks support from all segments of the population, since only outright capitalists would be excluded from the "working people" category. The overriding purpose of the SED is to strengthen the conditions "for the gradual transition to the building of communist society."[2] Thus, the party selects from all segments of society the most enlightened, skilled, dedicated, and patriotic individuals. Working together, these exemplary citizens chart the path of change, supply critical human resources for effecting basic policies, and encourage the contribution of ever-widening circles of the people toward the creation of a better life for all. Actively responsible party members are portrayed as public servants of the highest order, accepting personal sacrifice and giving extra effort for a noble cause. They are what Americans might designate as community leaders and "good citizens," except that they exhibit a greater certainty of purpose and a stronger reliance on the strength of their organization.

All individuals who occupy, or are preparing to occupy, positions of public responsibility—including government office, leadership in labor unions and other social organizations, or prominent leadership roles in the economy—are asked to consider making the commitment to SED membership. Party membership is more than a declaration of support for national goals and for the existing political system; it also provides each member regular access to the common resources of the organization, as well as opportunities to serve the nation beyond his or her normal employment. This commitment is not to be undertaken lightly; each party member, in public and private life, is a model for other citizens.

As depicted here, the character of SED members may appear too good to be true. It should be noted, however, that such people do exist in other societies. They may be found in public office, especially in local government, and they occupy critical roles in charitable and social service clubs, youth organizations, and religious institutions. In fact, without the contributions of such people, the societies of most liberal democracies would be far different. Although East Germany is governed according to quite different political principles, similar traits of altruism and orientation to public service are undoubtedly present. The extent to which these traits are embodied in the SED is, of course, a matter of serious dispute.

In the GDR today, there is a segment of public opinion, a sort of political "counter-culture," that stridently disputes the idealistic version of SED precedence.[3] According to this opposition viewpoint, the SED retains the basic attributes acquired under the occupation regime. At that time, the infamous Ulbricht Group arranged a tacit compact with Moscow in which the party elite received the personal trappings of power in exchange for totally subordinating East German sovereignty to the military and economic needs of the Soviet Union. As the party expanded, the presence of former Social Democrats and authentic communists complicated the tasks of the highest elite, until all were compelled to acknowledge the hard realities. To be sure, the SED leaders initiated policies to improve economic performance and to extend social benefits to the people. But these effects have always remained secondary to the twin goals of assuring Soviet hegemony and strengthening the central elite's monopoly of power. The goal of "building communism" is judged to be illusory, since it involves nothing more than a simplistic imitation of Soviet policies, without regard for their effect on the East German nation. The SED's claim to be "following" the Soviet Union on its "revolutionary path" is regarded as absurd, since the GDR is demonstrably more advanced than its Slavic sponsor.

The motivation of SED members is also directly challenged. Nowadays nearly everyone appreciates the naiveté of idealism. Since idealists are frustrated at every turn, critics claim, the SED is now populated chiefly by opportunists, who join in anticipation of material rewards. Party membership brings preferred access to housing, special shops, and recreational facilities. It also brings highly prized personal connections, through which one can arrange career advancements and privileged educational opportunities for one's children. In effect, the entire SED is a system of institutionalized nepotism and corruption. Career success depends not on merit, but on patronage. And the higher one rises, the larger one's share of the spoils. In this dissident interpretation, self-aggrandizement, not altruism, is the hallmark of the modern SED.

These two views of the SED, and the means by which it asserts precedence over the rest of society, are radically divergent. But they are not mutually exclusive. The party encompasses 2.2 million people,[4] and it is certain that they approach membership in many different ways and with varying mixtures of motivations.

Apart from the official political culture, there exists an elite subculture, which many SED members share. While asserting the continued role of long-range ideals, this set of values allows for a more realistic and pragmatic approach to everyday life. If the preservation of power and subordination to Soviet hegemony often seem to take precedence over some of the higher values of democracy and social equality, it is because the latter are distant and vague, whereas the former are tangible and ever present. Besides, politicians everywhere acknowledge that, in order to implement any kind of policy at all, it is first necessary to hold political power. This pragmatism also acknowledges the unequal distribution of material rewards. Because the GDR is an imperfect society, it is not governed by angels. Ordinary human beings require special recompense for assuming extraordinary responsibilities. And it is only prudent to try to build a better life for one's family. Political leaders do not surpass other citizens in greed, only in opportunity. At the same time, an ostentatious life-style must be avoided, since that would cause popular resentment.

The mass subculture provides yet another view of the SED. In principle, the general public does not seriously question the party's dominant role: It is simply a fact of life. But neither is there much positive attachment to the SED as an institutional expression of the nation. The public perceives little distinction between party and government elites, which together appear as a distant, generally unresponsive "establishment," a role East Germans attribute to ruling elites in most other nations of the world. If the East German people have recorded significant achievements, this has occurred more likely despite, rather than because of, their political leaders. Among the mostly widely held popular criticisms is the perceived failure of the SED to mitigate the more blatant consequences of Soviet influence.

The mass subculture includes no generalizations about the character of SED members. Party members are encountered every day, as public officials, employers, fellow workers, and neighbors. Some prove to be hardworking and helpful, others are self-indulgent and pompous. Taken together, they are much like any other people. To be sure, party members are known to enjoy special privileges, some of them undeserved. But inequality is an understood feature of every society. At least in the GDR, it is believed, most people are not systematically excluded; for those who can prove themselves and are willing to pay the price, there are open avenues into the party.

At this point, a basic definition of the dominant SED is still out of reach. It has been possible to summarize two opposing views and the efforts of the mass and elite subcultures to reconcile these views with reality. Such perceptions are a large part of the truth. But a better understanding of the party also requires a look at some more objective membership attributes, a review of organizational structure, and an account of its actual functions.

Party Membership Recruitment

The SED desires to affect and draw support from all segments of society. Consequently, its membership recruitment process seeks to be broadly representative.[5] On the other hand, the party also needs to incorporate the most skilled and educated citizens, since it is from this segment that future political, administrative, and management leaders will be drawn. By incorporating highly qualified members, the party not only performs more effectively, it also enhances the legitimacy of party precedence and the prestige of party membership. This, in turn, facilitates the subsequent recruitment of able young people. Consequently, membership criteria are also somewhat selective.

In addition to questions of representation and qualifications, party recruitment is also affected by self-selection on the part of potential members themselves. Not every eligible person actually chooses to join the SED. Despite the tangible rewards, some people conclude that membership obligations are too burdensome or that joining is incompatible with cherished personal beliefs. Young people seldom face a dramatic point of decision regarding party membership. Those who have done well in school and have avoided conflicts with the authorities know that they might one day be asked to join. They are also guided by personal orientations acquired primarily from their parents. Just as some U.S. parents assume that their children will eventually attend college, so many East German parents assume that their children will grow up and join the SED. Such children learn that "the way to get along is to go along." As more young people grow up in a stable GDR political system, this accommodative orientation becomes more widespread and party recruitment becomes more routine.

SED recruitment is actually a rather minor activity. The party grows very slowly, and each year only about twelve thousand members die or resign (disciplinary expulsion is very rare). Consequently, only around sixty-five thousand new members are added annually.[6] Selection is the function of the basic party organization (bpo), of which there are now more than seventy-nine thousand.[7] Since a bpo at a college or university may recruit two or three candidates in a year, it is evident that some bpo's may not recruit any members for several years.

More than 50 percent of SED recruits have just graduated from a university or technical college. To become an SED candidate at this point, a young person needs a combination of academic achievement, a record of at least nominal membership in the communist youth organization, a proven willingness to peform public-service tasks, and a past free of overt conflict with police and school authorities. Written recommendations from local SED officials are required, and the informal support of an influential parent can be very helpful. In a loose analogy, the ideal SED candidate looks something like the kind of person who might seek appointment to a U.S. military academy.

Additional avenues of recruitment are the upper echelons of the youth organization, labor unions, and the professional military service. In these cases, eligibility criteria are similar, except that academic achievement is less important and greater stress is placed upon proven leadership abilities.

During a one-year candidacy, the prospective member is expected to volunteer for extra assignments at his or her work place, undertake a part-time study course in political or technical training, and lead voluntary projects in communist education or public service. Most candidates pass the review at year's end and become full party members.

One out of every eight East Germans between the ages of eighteen and twenty-five, and one out of every six adults, is a party member or candidate. If membership is taken as a measure of political participation, these ratios represent a rather high level of political activity compared to the liberal democracies. They also demonstrate the extent to which the SED is rooted in, rather than segregated from, the general population.

Of course, the party is not scattered evenly throughout the society. Some effort is made to maintain the class background of SED members at the same proportion as the nation as a whole. If class background is defined in terms of father's occupation (a common Western usage), nearly 75 percent of the party originates from the working class. If class is figured according to one's occupation at the time of joining, the SED is about 56 percent working class, according to official claims.[8] That share is close to the percentage of workers in the entire labor force. In fact, except for the underrepresentation of farm workers and the overrepresentation of government and academic professionals, the shape of the SED rather closely resembles the shape of GDR society. In this statistical sense, the SED is far more representative than any major party in any liberal democracy. As in the West, women are underrepresented in the GDR: Women make up one-third of the party but more than half of the nation. Even this ratio compares favorably to most other systems.

Because of its Marxist-Leninist self-concept, the SED has worked hard to achieve this class balance, with a primary emphasis on workers. However, it is probable that ongoing social change will make this balance less meaningful in the future. For one thing, the working class will soon begin to decline as a percentage of the population. Second, a lower working-class proclivity to high educational achievement means that the recruitment emphasis on educational qualifications increasingly conflicts with the party emphasis on working-class representation. As a result, SED claims to be a working-class party (always an overstatement) must depend on a redefinition of the "working class" category. With the modernization and differentiation of the occupation structure, differences within the working class itself often are more profound than differences between the working class and other social segments. In real sociological terms, it might be said that the GDR is in the process of displacing the

Marxist notion of class with a more significant social hierarchy based upon educational achievement and technical expertise—what British social philosophers have termed a "meritocracy." Meritocratic criteria are far from having transformed the entire SED, but they have made an unambiguous imprint on the party's younger generation.

Basic Party Organization

The Socialist Unity party is organized according to two rather different perspectives, only loosely linked together: the perspective of the basic party organization and the perspective of the hierarchical structure of political leadership.[9]

For about 98 percent of the SED's 2.2 million members, party life consists almost exclusively of the bpo. A bpo is created wherever a sufficient number of SED members are employed; the average size is about twenty-seven. Bpo's exist in schools and universities, in factories and hospitals, in restaurants and retail stores, in government bureaucracies and military units. In rural areas, where small employment units have few SED members, a local party organization may be formed on a territorial, rather than an occupational, basis.

The density of party membership (i.e., the ratio of SED members to the total number of employees) varies from one setting to another. In general, those areas of employment that require more education and technical training will have a high ratio of party members. Thus, SED density is lowest among farm workers, retail clerks, letter carriers, barbers, and so on. It is highest among university faculty, higher government administrators, and military officers. In full-time SED agencies, of course, party density is 100 percent.

In offices and work places where the membership ratio is very high, monthly bpo meetings are scarcely distinguishable from ordinary staff meetings. In other cases, the bpo represents a subset of employees, who periodically gather to review the contribution of their work unit to the fulfillment of the party's political and economic goals. Most of their attention is concentrated on ways to better fulfill the unit's normal work plan. They may consider ways to reassign work loads, improve cooperation with other units, or improve working conditions. They may adopt plans to raise job qualifications or to raise the morale of their fellow workers.

SED guidelines also require that each bpo discuss its contribution to local community projects and National Front events. On exceptional occasions, the bpo may be asked to discuss public reaction (i.e., the reactions of coworkers and neighbors) to major events, such as the decision to restrict heating-fuel consumption or the outcome of workers' strikes in Poland.

The bpo also collects party dues and recommends potential new members. In principle, quarterly and annual reports of bpo activities are submitted to an office of the district party organization. The business of the bpo is managed by an unpaid elected secretary, who is never the same as the work supervisor or unit director. This poses the sometimes awkward situation in which a bpo secretary will conduct an evaluation of the performance of his or her own employer, also a member of the bpo. Available evidence suggests that a bpo secretary rarely indulges anything but the most circumspect criticism of a boss.

Every two and a half years, each bpo sends a delegate to a district party conference to hear speeches about party achievements and problems. These conferences formally elect the district party leaders, but it is clear that such officials are more or less self-selected or designated by a higher level in the party hierarchy.

For most SED members party activity begins and ends at the work place. Occasionally, an enterprising member may use wider party channels to resolve a work problem or to seek personal assistance in finding a new job or better housing. Only those with extraordinary abilities and determination, as well as those with influential friends and relatives, are able to move out beyond the bpo and enter the world of the SED hierarchy.

Party Hierarchy

Lower Party Hierarchy

The professional SED hierarchy, consisting of no more than twenty-five thousand full-time party officials at all levels, presents a sharply different perspective on the party's role in the GDR's directed democracy. The SED hierarchy is composed of leadership bodies at the district, county, and national levels. Except for differences in scale, district and county levels can be treated in the same descriptive terms.

At two-and-a-half-year intervals, each of the 219 districts holds a conference of delegates from the bpo's, and each of the 15 counties (*Bezirke*) holds a conference of delegates from the districts. The actual party authority, however, is exercised by a first secretary and additional secretaries (four to six), assisted by their full-time staffs (ten to twenty in districts, up to two hundred in counties). These small secretariats conduct regular enlarged meetings (ten to twelve participants in districts, fourteen to sixteen in counties), which include top local government and economic officials and the heads of the local labor unions and youth organizations. These larger bodies authorize permanent and ad hoc committees of party volunteers to organize special SED events and to study problems of continuing local concern. These committees are one avenue by which an activist member may broaden his or her personal contacts and cultivate the chance for recruitment into responsible party roles.

In principle, the district party leadership (Kreisparteileitung–KPL) and the county party leadership (Bezirksparteileitung–BPL) are the axis around which revolves all the political, economic, and social activity in their respective territories. In each case, the first secretary of the KPL/BPL is universally recognized as the dominant political authority. For KPL leaders, this authority may be narrowly circumscribed by a vigorous county organization; the strength of BPL control over the KPL depends on the personal style of the county first secretary, the physical distance of the district from the county seat, and the extent to which the district's main economic activity is integrated with the rest of the county. The fact that the BPL staff is more differentiated and many times larger than that of the KPL suggests that, for much party activity, the county is the effective level of operational direction. Even in those instances where district first secretaries direct the business of their own secretaries (e.g., the district secretary for the economy), these officials may be found to be actually more responsive to their counterparts in the BPL.

Having noted these marked disparities between the district and county levels, we turn to the five main functions of the lower party hierarchy— exercised in varying degrees, at both levels.

Five Lower Party Functions

It may be useful to group these functions into two categories. The first category includes the personnel and socialization functions. These functions express the SED's image as the creator of a new type of political-social system. In this image, the party selects and trains the most qualified citizens to assume leadership positions in all governmental and social institutions. It also provides the people with the education, values, and information necessary to make the system work in an integrated, harmonious, and progressive fashion. Were the party ever to fulfill these two functions perfectly, of course, it could theoretically dismantle its own hierarchy and go out of business, for it would have created the sort of utopian, self-regenerating society that Marx envisioned. Such a society would consist exclusively of enlightened, happy people, joined in a common will and administered by selfless, competent public servants.

Because present reality in the GDR falls far short of these millenarian conditions, the SED hierarchy must carry out another set of functions. Whereas the first image presents the party as the creator of a societal machine, the remaining functions depict the party as directly operating the machinery, noting design flaws, and making occasional emergency repairs. In this second image, the SED does not stand apart from society; rather it is an immediate participant. This participant role is exhibited in the three remaining functions: monitoring the performance of the system, coordinating the interaction of its various components, and intervening to assume direct control.

Personnel. No SED function is more critical than the selection and training of political administrative leaders. This is obviously a function of political parties in liberal democracies, as well. In the GDR this function, concentrated under a single umbrella, also extends beyond overt political roles to include economic management and virtually all social organizations.

The SED's personnel function (*Kaderpolitik*) consists of two parts. First, higher party agencies identify the key positions in public life that demand the most careful personnel selection. Separate lists (*Nomenklatur*) are constructed for the hierarchical offices in the SED, government, economy, and mass organizations. Each list is further divided according to the territorial level of the office.

Second, the party agencies at each level are charged with maintaining a personnel pool (*Kaderreserve*) from which the *Nomenklatur* offices may be filled. The greater part of this charge lies with the district (KPL), whose Secretariat attempts to maintain records on all local people who have advanced formal schooling, who have assumed extra political duties (such as voluntary work with a city council or National Front committee), or who have been cited for exceptional work performance. All new SED members will usually be included, as well as a few nonmembers. A great emphasis is placed on people in their early twenties. Those who fail to demonstrate a strong interest in personal advancement, including a majority of SED members, are eventually dropped from this personnel pool. Those who remain are recommended for further schooling and promotion. Following good performance, many are then passed on to the personnel pool at the county level, where this process is repeated.

Apart from its own hierarchy, where it exercises exclusive jurisdiction, the SED shares its personnel function with several nonparty agencies. Each government ministry, economic branch, and mass organization maintains its own personnel process, which is more inclusive and generally independent of direct SED concern. The party's personnel function is narrower and concentrates on the obvious leadership positions, which operate within the area for which a given party agency is responsible. Thus, the district SED secretary will be involved in selecting local labor-union officials and city-council members. The county SED secretary will be involved in selecting district party officials, mayors, and factory directors.

Most appointments are made as a result of normal promotion through these separate hierarchies, not because of overt intervention by SED officials. Most frequently, SED officials are simply called upon to ratify personnel changes proposed by the relevant nonparty officials and employers. It is true that SED members are generally promoted faster and farther than nonmembers; this occurs not because of party intervention, but because SED members are usually the most qualified.

On the other hand, it sometimes happens that certain SED members are promoted unfairly. This results from a patronage bias, which relies upon informal networks within the SED. Influential friends and relatives can sometimes use personal party connections to facilitate entry to special schools and prestigious jobs. Such distortions violate the principles of the SED's personnel function, but they are a real part of life in the GDR, as in any country where people know how to exploit personal "contacts." These biases also emphasize the sweeping politicization of the employment structure.

Socialization. Socialization describes the sum of the processes by which new generations of citizens and political leaders acquire the basic knowledge and values necessary to function harmoniously in the prevailing social system. In cases where a new governing regime is attempting concerted social change, the socialization function assumes special significance due to the disparity in values between the political leadership, on the one hand, and families and other social institutions, on the other. For the GDR, this disparity was initially far smaller than has been the case in traditional peasant societies. In important respects, the Marxist-Leninist value system was congruent with the antecedent values of industrial Germany. Nevertheless, considerable effort has been exerted to enable the people to accommodate themselves to the political expectations of SED rule and to the demands of continuing economic and social change.

In order to fulfill its socialization function, the SED employs full-time agencies at all levels to assure the consistent expression of appropriate values in most areas of public communication. School curricula and the public news media are both significant components of any socialization process and relatively easy to control. To a lesser extent, value lessons can be instilled through youth organizations, labor unions, and similar peer-group settings.

Among the five secretaries in the typical KPL, two are primarily responsible for socialization: the secretary for schools and culture and the secretary for agitation. These officials work very closely with nonparty agencies to insure that Marxist-Leninist values and patriotic themes characterize a significant part of public life. Apart from portraying a correct understanding of the capitalist-socialist struggle and a positive attachment to the SED, socializing efforts concentrate heavily on the values of public service, self-improvement, and individual achievement. Consequently, district party officials provide resources to promote voluntary community projects through the National Front, as well as career education and job training programs through the schools, youth groups, and labor unions. In this way, the socialization function becomes rather closely aligned to the personnel function.

Monitoring. In addition to the tasks of helping to provide human resources for building the new society, the SED endeavors to constantly monitor (*kontrollieren*) the performance of all institutions. For this purpose, much of the SED hierarchy serves as a large service for gathering information. District party officials compile written reports from the basic party organizations and supplement this information by frequent consultation with trusted people holding the key positions already noted.

Theoretically at least, this process should provide the KPL first secretary with multiple perspectives on each major area of activity in the district. From a local factory, for example, routine sources of information include management officials, union leaders, youth-organization leaders, and the bpo secretary. From a branch of city administration, information comes from the department head, the union official, and the bpo secretary. In extraordinary circumstances, additional information may be provided by local police or State Security officers. The mere fact that multiple sources of information are available does not necessarily insure that the KPL receives an accurate picture of performance. Since the various information sources depend on one another in their daily work, they share an incentive to portray themselves and each other in positive, harmonious terms.

In any event, the information arriving at the KPL should be sufficient to permit the relevant party officials to carry out their personnel function. Much information about the performance of economic units, the delivery of public services, and numerous other activities is distilled and forwarded to the county-level SED offices, where it becomes part of a broader effort to monitor governmental and societal performance. Finally, selected information is forwarded up to the national level to the departments of the Central Committee.

Despite the widespread German reputation for efficiency, this information system suffers from two main defects. First, as information is passed from lower to higher levels, it is handled by an increasingly differentiated SED bureaucracy. Although the KPL first secretary can call together a small staff to construct a composite appraisal of local affairs, the BPL first secretary has to deal with a much larger, fragmented set of officials. This differentiation is magnified at the national level. Second, SED offices at all levels are reluctant to report shortcomings to their own hierarchical superiors. Even when these shortcomings lie outside the party (for instance, in local government or a local factory), the lower SED office may be blamed for allowing the problem to develop.

Over the years, various measures have been devised to counteract this tendency toward concealment. Currently, the GDR relies upon the Workers-Farmers Inspection, a set of hierarchically organized committees intended to speak on behalf of the public interest in monitoring the behavior of public officials. Little is published about the actual work of the inspection. In many areas it probably exists only on paper, as a list of *ex officio* representatives from several party, government, and social institutions. Because the purposes of the inspection so clearly duplicate the monitoring function of SED agencies, local party officials can be expected to insure that the work of the inspection will not reflect badly on the SED hierarchy itself. In other words, if the Workers-Farmers Inspection is supposed to expose party inefficiency in its monitoring function, there is little reason to expect success.

Coordination. Despite the aim of creating an integrated, corporate society, the operational structure of most GDR institutions is heavily oriented toward a vertical chain of command. Thus, local factories usually operate as subsidiaries of regional enterprises, which in turn take direction from national ministries. Local labor unions are similarly guided by county and national boards. Local news media are managed by central authorities. Even government services, such as education and health care, are highly centralized.

As a result, local affairs in any district are made up of the end products of central directives sent downward along a host of unrelated chains of command. The potential for conflict and disintegration is very real. As an illustration, suppose a food canning plant is to be erected on the outskirts of a medium-sized town, significantly increasing the size of the local work force. In order to effect this change, separate actions will be required by Berlin ministries for food industry, transportation (for commuting workers), housing (for new residents), education (schools for workers' children), culture (recreation and leisure facilities), health (for a resident physician), police, and so on. Because all these actions must be implemented through separate authority structures, there is a high probability that implementation at the local level will be incomplete, inconsistent, and occasionally contradictory.

The district SED leadership (KPL)—above all, its first secretary—exists to coordinate all such local activities. In a limited way, the local government council and its mayor may try to coordinate some public services. But only the KPL has authority to guide the broad scope of interrelated activities. In addition to collecting information through routine channels, the first secretary may create a special coordinating committee of representatives from all affected groups. Where such a project is completed with a minimum of conflict, delay, and wasted resources, the first secretary expects credit from superior officials at the county level. By accumulating such credit, a first secretary can look forward to later assignment to a more important district.

Intervention. After the party's continuous effort to recruit and train public personnel, to monitor their performance, and to coordinate their activities, it sometimes happens that fundamental malfunctions occur. Economic activity may break down because of problems in one link in a chain of interdependent enterprises. Public services may be interrupted because of faulty maintenance or because funds have been improperly diverted. A work stoppage may take place, because workers have lost faith in incompetent union leaders. Or severe weather may threaten to exhaust the district's supply of heating fuel.

Such malfunctions are crucial, both because they require fast action and because they have ramifications that reach well beyond the competence of any single public agency. In such instances, the KPL first secretary assumes extraordinary authority to intervene directly into nonparty institutions, substituting his or her own directives for those of regular employers and officials. For example, the first secretary may order repair crews from a local factory to assist city employees in restoring public services or may arbitrarily announce his or her own plan for coal rationing.

Any such decision to disrupt normal authority structures entails risk for a first secretary. In the first place, the need to exercise the intervention function may be perceived as evidence of poor performance in carrying out the personnel, socialization, monitoring, and coordination functions. Second, repeated intervention into nonparty institutions can permanently undermine the authority of their officials. Employees are not likely to respect a factory director or chief administrator who is frequently overruled by SED officials. In such situations, the KPL first secretary could become the de facto head of a factory or administrative department, and this de facto role could reduce the time available to carry out his or her other party responsibilities. Finally, any time a first secretary intervenes into a nonparty institution, that action must later be justified to his or her own superiors and to the central authorities of the affected institution. If intervention has brought a swift resolution of the crisis, the first secretary will be praised and rewarded. On the other hand, if the intervention seems to have engendered greater problems than it solved, the first secretary may lose any hope of personal advancement. Rather clearly, the measure of an astute KPL official is his or her ability to correctly calculate these risks.

Upper Party Hierarchy

The five functions that occupy the district SED organizations also characterize the party's county-level work. Personnel policy becomes even more critical for the BPL. The socialization function is more narrowly defined, however; it is concentrated primarily on regional communication and on specialized educational institutions. The monitoring and coordination functions are also decisive at the county level. But the intervention function may be carried out somewhat more cautiously, especially in dealing with large-scale economic activity at the county level. On the other hand, BPL intervention downward, into the jurisdictions of local government and district party organizations, is quite common.

BPL influence reaches in the upward direction, as well. The first secretary and the full-time secretaries for the primary functional areas enjoy good access to national SED officials. In fact, many county party officials participate directly in the SED bodies that formulate national policy.

The national level of the SED assumes overall responsibility for the exercise of party functions, including the five functions. Because both party and government authority are somewhat more concentrated at the top, a more cooperative partnership arrangement is possible. The nature of the partnership varies from one policy area to another, and it can never be an equal partnership. For it is ultimately the SED—not the government—that establishes basic policy goals. The goal-setting function must therefore be added to the list of SED tasks.

The Central Committee

In traditional Western imagery, the Central Committee is probably the most misunderstood component in the SED structure. In the early postwar days, the Central Committee was composed of a distinguished, trusted cadre, who could be sent out to assume leadership functions in major administrative, economic, and social organizations. This early Central Committee was correctly portrayed as a small, Soviet-sponsored elite, superimposed on East German society in an effort to subordinate existing institutions to a new central authority.

Much has changed in the intervening years. Today's Central Committee is linked to society not by its reaching downward, but by society's reaching upward through the continuing recruitment of the nation's politically astute citizens. The Central Committee is no longer an "alien" element; instead, it is composed of people who are firmly rooted in society and who have been promoted through a variety of party and nonparty structures to become leaders in their respective fields.

Although its membership is affirmed by a large party congress every five years, the Central Committee is actually appointed (as a result of consensus among members of the Politburo and Secretariat) according to implicit criteria of functional, regional, and sectoral representation. Reflecting the corporatist conception of East German society, the Central Committee is essentially an *ex officio* body. It reaches far beyond the ranks of SED officials to encompass—by virtue of their holding specific offices—the top leaders of every political, governmental, economic, and social institution in the nation. It is a sort of designated "establishment," the "steering committee" of East German society. Because all of these individuals become party members long before rising to such prominent posts, it is natural that this gathering take place in the form of a principal SED institution. From a symbolic perspective, Central Committee meetings are certain proof that the SED—in the form of its most distinguished members—is the leading force of the nation.

The Tenth Central Committee (1981–1986)[10] has 213 members, of whom 57 are alternates. (Between party congresses, only alternates may be chosen to replace voting members.) These seats are distributed as follows: full-time party officials, 38 percent (about half are national, county, or city secretaries); government officials, 26 percent (more than half from the Council of Ministers); economic managers in industry and agriculture, 9 percent; leaders of the mass organizations, 10 percent; administrators in science and culture, 16 percent; others, 1 percent. Over time these percentages have changed very slowly, showing a gradual decline in the share for party officials and proportional increases for all other categories. At the Tenth SED Congress, roughly 90 percent of the preceding Central Committee members were reelected, a high rate of continuity. Allowing for deaths, retirements, and twelve new positions, the new Central Committee includes thirty new members. These additions reflect expanded representation for the professional staff of the "central apparatus," the armed forces, the foreign service, the news media, and creative artists.

The Central Committee meets two or three times annually for sessions of three to five days. Each session features lengthy presentations of a specific problem area (usually an economic issue) plus routine reports on other phases of party activity. Often proposals are outlined for subsequent discussion, but spontaneous debate during the session itself almost never occurs. Reports are submitted to the session for formal approval; there is no public record of a report having been rejected, but Central Committee members register dissatisfaction by withholding applause and informally voicing their concern outside the hall. In general, higher officials will not submit a formal policy declaration until it is assured of strong majority support through prior consultations. Inner party leaders have a strong incentive to avoid clashes with a Central Committee majority; after all, the Central Committee is composed of able and influential people, upon whom the highest leaders depend to implement party goals.

Departments of the Central Committee

The professional staff of the national SED organization, about two thousand select individuals, is employed by the forty departments of the Central Committee, informally known as the "central apparatus."[11] Many department heads are senior, second-echelon SED officials, occasionally entitled to present a report to the Central Committee. The departments concentrate on collecting data from the lower party offices, producing endless "guidelines" for the work of lower party officials and bpo's, monitoring the performance of national government ministries, and cultivating personnel pools for high-level party and nonparty positions. Junior staff in the departments often includes younger, upwardly mobile people. Having recently completed a course of study in a higher party institute, such individuals are exposed to work near the center of power, before resuming mid-level careers in party, government, or other hierarchies.

The functional divisions of the Central Committee departments roughly parallel those of the Council of Ministers, except that the departments are far fewer and smaller. They also suggest a different emphasis, with relatively more personnel devoted to matters of special SED concern: education, culture, communication, and foreign affairs. Ten party departments parallel more than thirty ministries and state committees for economic affairs. Only three or four departments are concerned with the general business of government, and four departments are apparently devoted only to internal SED affairs. All department heads are members of the Central Committee.

Secretariat of the Central Committee

The highest body of full-time SED officials is the ten-member Secretariat. Nominally elected by the Central Committee, this group manages the entire SED hierarchy. Its leader is General Secretary Erich Honecker. The remaining members are assigned specific areas of responsibility: international communist affairs, party organs, agriculture, culture and science, agitation, commerce, women and social policy, economy, propaganda, and security.

The Secretariat displays extraordinary continuity. The average tenure is more than sixteen years, and all but three officials have been members since at least 1963.[12] Career backgrounds reveal something about the secretaries' areas of expertise. Five current secretaries have held high office in the communist youth organization, including Honecker. Three have held party posts for security matters, and two have been promoted through work in agitation and propaganda. Three have had significant experience in district and county SED organizations, and two have had professional careers almost exclusively in the realm of economic planning.

There is no direct evidence concerning the relationship between the Secretariat and the Central Committee departments except that the departments are clearly subordinate. It is obvious that department workers come and go, but the Secretariat remains a very long time. Quite probably, the ten secretaries wield a great deal of authority over their professional staff. Thus, they dispose of a formidable instrument for gathering information and constructing policy recommendations.

Above all, the power of the Secretariat is expressed in the fact that all ten secretaries have acquired places in the Politburo.

The Politburo

If the Central Committee is really a microcosm of the leading social elements, then the Politburo is, in turn, a microcosm of the Central Committee. It consists of twenty-five members, of whom eight are alternates.[13] They represent the party hierarchy, the government, and the mass organizations.

Party officials make up a majority of the Politburo. All ten members of the Secretariat are included, following a practice observed more or less faithfully since 1963. As always, the Politburo includes the head of the party Control Commission, an appeals board for questions of SED membership rights. Also included are the first secretaries of two county party organizations (Berlin and Cottbus). The mass organizations are represented by the head of the labor unions and the head of the youth organization, both with considerable experience as party officials.

Government officials constitute another significant group. The Council of Ministers currently (mid 1983) supplies seven members, including its chairman and two first-deputy chairmen. Other council representatives are the head of the State Plan Commission, the minister for machinery and vehicles, the defense minister, and the minister for state security. The last two are among the most recent additions. Somewhat anomalous is the Politburo representation from the agricultural sector, the head of a giant agroindustrial complex in Neubrandenburg County. The Politburo is completed with the president of the National Assembly and—the most recent addition—the editor of *Neues Deutschland*, the party newspaper.

The rationale for selecting Politburo members is not self-evident. Although average tenure is a little less for the Politburo than for the

SED Secretariat, there has been a great deal of turnover in this highest political body. Consequently, it is difficult to identify recruitment patterns. In general, three considerations seem to be at work. First, the principle of corporate representation requires that many positions are filled *ex officio*. In this category belong the senior members of the Secretariat, the top three officials of the Council of Ministers, and the labor-union leader. This principle also insures the inclusion of at least one woman. Second, a new General Secretary needs to assert primacy over the system by including a number of individuals with personal loyalty in the Politburo. Actually, the extent of the changes implemented for this reason is far less in the GDR than in other systems. The accession of a new U.S. president or British prime minister, for example, is always followed by major personnel adjustments, even when there is no change in party. Finally, the Politburo retains a residue of its early revolutionary days, when it was primarily a group of disciplined generalists who could be periodically assigned to strategic positions in other agencies in an effort to assure SED dominance. This "sending-out" principle is the reverse of the corporate-representation principle. Today, the Politburo reflects a mixture of all three recruitment principles.

The Politburo and the Policy Process

The Politburo is the capstone of the East German political system. It symbolizes the indisputable fact of SED rule. All Politburo members are seasoned party veterans, accustomed to the privileges and burdens of power. All share a basic commitment to preserving the existing pattern of SED precedence, above all the prerogatives of the Politburo itself. They also agree on a broad set of goals for insuring national security, advancing the socialist economy, and extending progressive social benefits to the people.

In the present setting, this goal agreement is not as meaningful as it was thirty years ago. In the early days of the Republic, the official SED viewpoint set these leaders apart from the rest of the nation. But today most people have become accustomed to SED goals, and many people even endorse them. Consequently, shared values among the party leadership represent less of a bond. Given the complexity of governing a modern East German society, the existence of shared values may be less important than disagreements that arise concerning the relative priority to be assigned to each goal under specific conditions.

The Politburo claims collective responsibility for all public achievements. In reality, of course, the Politburo is mainly a symbol for the many political, governmental, economic, and social hierarchies—each working to achieve common goals, but each with a different institutional perspective and emphasis. The Politburo rarely participates directly in most of these institutions. Instead, it expects these institutions to be mostly self-starting and self-regulating.

The Politburo meets weekly to assess the performance of all public organizations. Some topics on its agenda, such as review of the annual economic plan, appear at prescribed intervals. But most topics arise as unanticipated problems, caused by external events or by unresolved shortcomings in a governmental or economic sector. Such topics may include the suddenly increased price for Soviet oil or the effect of East African turmoil on East German technical assistance advisers. Special attention may be given to such problems as coping with increased West German tourism, the increased visibility of GDR dissidents in foreign news media, or threatened work stoppages in Leipzig. More often the issues are less dramatic: how to overcome bottlenecks in the delivery of chemical fertilizers or how to resolve a conflict between the Ministry for Agriculture and the Ministry for Food Processing. Remedial action usually involves formulation of a public policy statement, a general recommendation on how the affected agency can improve its work, and the assignment of a Politburo member to follow up on resolution of the problem. As a rule, Politburo action tries to adhere to established chains of command; the Politburo collective is most reluctant to circumvent the authority of one of its own members.

Below the Politburo effective government takes place primarily in the interaction between the Council of Ministers, headed by its Presidium, and the Central Committee departments, headed by the Secretariat. It is commonly believed that this relationship is always dominated by the party agencies. But this belief can be fundamentally misleading. In the last analysis, SED dominance rests more on the fact that party members hold all public offices rather than on the power of specific party offices over officials in other sectors. There is no convincing evidence that a minister in government (e.g., for education, defense, or foreign trade) is always "outranked" by a corresponding official in the SED hierarchy. And it is probably not helpful to characterize authority relations in such terms. Similarly, it is fallacious to assume that policy is determined exclusively by party officials, with the top government officials merely "administering" party policy.

At the national level, the relationship between government ministries and party agents is much more cooperative than antagonistic. Although one side emphasizes its executive function and the other side its monitoring function, major policy decisions are likely to emerge in joint consultation. Partnerships arise between government and party officials concerned with the same policy area. Thus, the Ministry for Education and the Central Committee Department for Education will work together to secure priority funding for schools. Similarly, the Ministry of Justice and the Department of State and Law will seek priority for the training of judges. Since most political issues in the GDR involve such marginal adjustments in public priorities, political contests often pit one government-party linkage against another.

This process can be illuminated by an analogy from U.S. politics. For this purpose, a parallel can be drawn between East German ministries and U.S. cabinet departments. Another parallel exists between the SED departments and the standing committees of the U.S. Congress. In both systems, the latter bodies monitor the performance of the former. But it is also common, for example, to see the U.S. Department of Education working jointly with the House Education Committee to expand federal spending for schools.

Returning to the GDR, we see that policy conflicts among various government-party linkages are resolved in a distinctive fashion. Each policy partnership can seek support from interested members of the Central Committee. But it is very important that the issue move toward consensus rather than conflict and that the process not be revealed in public disagreement. When consensus is not possible, the issue must be referred to the Politburo for final decision. On such occasions, the Politburo acts as an arbitrator between opposing views, in which various government and party bodies are arrayed on either side of the issue.

Rounding out this skeletal view of policy formation in the GDR, it should be noted that major policies are usually transformed into formal law through a more extended process. After the Central Committee and the Politburo have worked to resolve the contest, a new law is drafted by the appropriate offices in the Council of Ministers. The draft law is then routed through the National Assembly committees and then to the entire assembly. Although very minor changes are possible in this last phase, the new law is always guided through the National Assembly by the same government and party officials who drafted it and who are ultimately responsible for its implementation.

The Integrative Network of Party and State

By this point it should be apparent that the presence of SED and the authority of its leadership stratum is pervasive. Its personnel and socialization functions are evident in virtually all dimensions of public life. The activities of party officials in monitoring, coordinating, and intervening in the leadership structure of governmental and social institutions is an ever-present reality. Although none of these functions are executed with mechanical precision, they do provide a predictability in political affairs, which surpasses even that of most other communist-governed systems.

At the heart of this stable system, conceived and executed by the SED elite, is a refined scheme of specialization and integration. This scheme is represented in Figure 3.1, a highly simplified diagram intended to suggest the main relationships among virtually all organized structures of political, economic, and social life.

The lowest level of the figure includes production enterprises, academic and research institutions, labor unions, and other social organizations (e.g., Free German Youth, Democratic Women's Federation, Democratic Farmers' Party). These organizations constitute the context in which the majority of the people conduct their public lives; they are also places where potential future leaders are discovered and nurtured. The multiplicity of such organizations (much more varied than depicted in Figure 3.1) reflects the diversity of the population and of the social roles they occupy. Each organization itself usually incorporates a great deal of internal diversity and structural complexity; for example, the Labor Union Federation, composed of both sectoral and territorial divisions, is far more complex than even the SED structure.

As shown in Figure 3.1, each of these economic, academic, and social organizations is linked to the state and party structures in four ways. First, all such organizations are created by government statute, and they operate within the framework of laws and policy directions received from the hierarchy of the government executive. For the smaller, lower-level organizations, policy directions are transmitted by city and district councils and by their administrative officials. Larger organizations and their national-level officials receive policy directions from regional government or from the national Council of Ministers; thus, the nationally organized industrial units and the national boards of industrial labor unions communicate directly with the highest government officials and employ their own considerable hierarchies to transmit policy downward, bypassing intermediate and local levels of government. Of course, such patterns are not mutually exclusive: Substantial duplication of information flow may be involved.

Second, all economic, academic, and social organizations are under the continuous, general supervision of the party executive. Since each organization is expected to contribute, in its own way, to the task of "building socialism," the activity of each is monitored by SED officials. Using the medium of SED members active in each organization, party executives at the local, regional, and national levels monitor periodic reports of performance and issue directives for the attainment of conscientious party work appropriate to the various organizational settings. General policy directions are received through different channels, de-

Figure 3.1: Principal Party, State, and Social Organizations in the German Democratic Republic

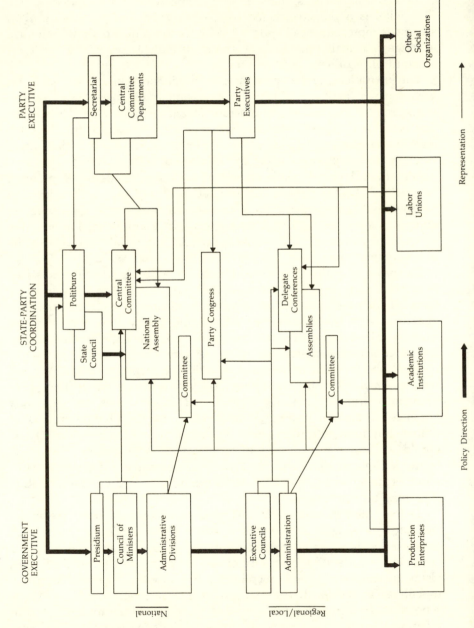

pending on the size and level of the organization, as is the case with government directions.

Because all public organizations are in some sense subject to policy directions emanating from both government and party executives, a word is appropriate concerning the relative importance of each hierarchy. As a general rule, the more specific an organization's function and the more it relies on expert knowledge to carry out that function, the more it will receive its primary policy direction from some segment of the government executive. Conversely, organizations with rather diffuse functions will rely primarily on leadership from the SED executive. This distinction is suggested in Figure 3.1: The more specialized economic and academic organizations are located to the left, nearer the structure of government; the labor unions—with functions nearly as comprehensive as those of the SED itself—and other social organizations are located to the right, nearer the party hierarchy.

The third linkage between public organizations and the ruling authorities occurs through the "organs of popular representation." These city, district, and county assemblies, along with the National Assembly, are represented in Figure 3.1 as part of the dual central core. As noted in the preceding chapter, the National Front mechanism is used to screen and coordinate lists of candidates to elected assemblies at all levels. Because all public organizations are direct or indirect elements in the National Front, they are assured representation in these assemblies. At the lower levels of government, such popular representatives constitute the majority of assembly deputies. For the National Assembly, such representatives are a substantial minority of deputies. The remainder of the deputies in each case come from the government and party executive structures.

The fourth linkage is found in the periodic conferences of SED delegates at each level. In a sense, these conferences are approximate counterparts to the elected assemblies, hence, they are depicted as the other part of the dual central core. But two distinctions in membership composition may be noted: First, while non-SED members are elected to popular assemblies (a majority of local assembly deputies are nonparty), only SED members may be elected to city, district, and county delegate conferences and to the Central Committee; second, at all levels the delegate conferences allocate a considerably larger share of the seats to officials of the government and party executives—and a smaller share to representatives of economic and social organizations—than do the popular assemblies.

Although the mix is varied, both popular assemblies and party conferences at all levels employ a tripartite mode of representation: Each includes representatives of the government executive, representatives of the SED executive, and representatives of the economic, academic, and social organizations. In some cases, an individual from one of these sectors may serve simultaneously as a deputy to an elected assembly and as a delegate to the corresponding party conference. Thus, several heads of Central Committee departments are both deputies to the National Assembly and members of the Central Committee. Similarly, a member of a local labor-union board may serve on the city assembly and attend the city party conference. The result is considerable overlapping of membership, ranging from one-fifth to one-third of the total.

Such an overlapping membership provides useful continuity in harmonizing the work of the two representative bodies. Neither body requires a great deal of time; plenary sessions are brief and infrequent. Consequently, participation in either elected assemblies or party conferences is always an adjunct to each members' major role as leader in some other institution. The primary significance of both governmental and party representative bodies lies not in the formation of policy, but in providing an institutional reference point for an elaborate network of informal consultation among its members and a forum for registering prior consensus.

In principle, this complex of interconnected and overlapping institutions is intended to provide integrated policy direction and comprehensive representation of all elements of public life. How well this works in practice, of course, depends upon the elimination of certain obstacles, the impact of which varies from time to time and from place to place. Examples of arrogant leadership and bureaucratic arbitrariness, information bottlenecks and passive noncooperation are routinely highlighted in party and government publications, as well as in the periodicals devoted to each of the major social institutions. But the persistence of such negative phenomena has not altered the nominal commitment to, and the ostensible belief in, the efficacy of comprehensive social integration.

Summary

This extended chapter is devoted to challenging common misconceptions about the dominant role of the Socialist Unity party. To be sure, the SED differs sharply from political parties in liberal democracies. Yet there remain enough similarities in function, and enough parallels in behavior, to reveal that the SED is not a wholly alien institution.

Western observers sometimes dismiss the study of East German politics with the simple assertion that "the party decides everything." Of course, this assertion is true, insofar as the occupant of every position of public leadership is an established member of the SED. Because party membership is so pervasive the SED is necessarily an element in virtually every activity of social significance.

On the other hand, to describe "the party" as if it were a single, undifferentiated entity obscures more truth than it reveals. At the very least, one must distinguish great differences between the SED as revealed in basic party organizations and the formal hierarchy. Distinctions are evident also between the district and county organizations and the several SED bodies at the national level. Yet another visage of the party is revealed by the thousands of SED members who hold leadership posts in the government and other nonparty institutions.

Once one recognizes these differences among the various levels of organization and categories of membership, it is possible to proceed further; for within each level and category there exists disagreement over which short-term steps will most likely bring about the long-range goals of the SED. It is at this point that the real study of East German politics begins.

Notes

1. "Das neue Programm der SED," *Deutschland Archiv* 9, no. 7 (1976), p. 744.

2. Ibid., p. 747.

3. For example, see "Das 'Spiegel Manifest' und die Reaktion der DDR," *Deutschland Archiv* 11, no. 2 (February 1978), pp. 199–219.

4. *Protokoll des X. Parteitages der Sozialistischen Einheitspartei Deutschlands* [Protocol of the Tenth Party Congress of the Socialist Unity Party of Germany] (Berlin: Dietz, 1981), p. 133.

5. The following discussion draws heavily from Gert-Joachim Glaessner and Irmhild Rudolph, *Macht durch Wissen: Zum Zusammenhang von Bildungspolitik, Bildungssystem, und Kaderqualifizierung in der DDR* [Power Through Knowledge: On the Relationship of Education Policy, Education System, and Cadre Training of the GDR] (Opladen: Westdeutscher, 1978), pp. 27–110.

6. Calculated from data supplied in *Protokoll des X. Parteitages*, p. 133.

7. Ibid.

8. Peter C. Ludz et al., *DDR Handbuch*, 2d ed. [GDR Handbook] (Cologne: Wissenschaft und Politik, 1979), pp. 950–951 [hereafter, *DDR Handbuch*]. See also *Protokoll des X. Parteitages*, p. 133.

9. Material on the SED structure for the following discussion is drawn chiefly from *Statut der Sozialistischen Einheitspartei Deutschlands* (Berlin: Dietz, 1976). See also *DDR Handbuch*, pp. 946–950.

10. Johannes Kuppe and Siegfried Kupper, "Parteitag der Kontinuität [Party Conference of Continuity]," *Deutschland Archiv* 14, no. 7 (1981), pp. 714–737.

11. *DDR Handbuch*, p. 1205.

12. Kuppe and Kupper, *Parteitag der Kontinuität*, pp. 716–717.

13. Ibid., pp. 715–716.

4
Economic Policy

The East German economy is socialist, which means simply that no significant economic activity may be privately owned. It should be recalled that, according to Marxist assumptions, private economic ownership produces alienation, deprives workers of benefits in proportion to their labor, and turns political power to the preservation of basic social inequality. Such reasoning concludes that public ownership of the economy is a prerequisite to achieving social justice.

In principle, public ownership may assume different forms. For example, a given economic unit—a factory or farm—may be owned by its own workers, or it may be owned by the local community, as in Yugoslavia. In Soviet-type systems, such as the GDR, public ownership means ownership by the central government. The fact that central-government ownership is nominally held "in trust" for the whole people is of no practical consequence.

An underlying rationale for central economic ownership in the GDR is the perception that the nation is engaged in a vital struggle against hostile capitalist forces; in order to avert defeat, the nation's scarce economic resources must be harnessed in a concerted effort. Particularly in the case of the GDR, this perception was early rooted in reality. Neighboring West Germany, along with its Anglo-American allies, unquestionably posed a threat to the socialist German Democratic Republic. The result for the GDR leadership (if not for the general population) has been a feeling of urgency akin to the crisis atmosphere that envelopes industrial democracies during wartime mobilization.

Nearly all sectors of the East German economy have been gradually absorbed by the central government. Only a very small private sector remains, mostly in food production, handicrafts, and professional and personal services. Some people legally engage in the private economy in addition to their regular public-sector jobs. There also exists a "second economy," consisting of bartered goods and labor beyond the reach of both the economic planners and the tax collectors. Occasionally this activity is outright illegal, involving theft of public property and black-market exchanges. But on the whole, the GDR's "second economy" is thought to be smaller than that in other socialist states. More than 98 percent of all economic activity is probably encompassed within the national plan.

When compared to the indirect U.S. system of fiscal and monetary controls or the French system of indicative planning, the East German government operates a centrally directed economy. This means that the basic allocations of economic resources, the usage of raw materials, the variety of commodity production, and consumer prices are not primarily the outcome of supply and demand interactions or of decisions by producers and consumers. Instead, the whole economy is shaped by priorities decided by the central government, including how much of the nation's wealth should be assigned to production and consumption, how much money should be spent developing specific types of goods, and how much each category of employees may be paid. Thus, East German consumers cannot encourage expanded production of tape recorders, for example, simply by being willing to pay higher prices; the volume of tape-recorder production depends on a central planning decision to allocate resources for this purpose. Similarly, an East German factory cannot recruit better workers simply by offering higher wages than other employers; wage rates are established by a central agency.

The Central Plan Process

The GDR economy falls under the direction of the State Plan Commission (SPK), a very large national agency with subordinate offices in the counties and districts. Working in close consultation with the highest political authorities, the State Plan Commission continuously charts the desired evolution of the economy, taking into account the availability of material and human resources, anticipated technological progress, foreign-trade potential, and the need for regular improvements in the standard of living. These changes are expressed in medium-range goals (Five-Year Plan) and in short-range tasks (Annual Plan).

For each economic sector, tentative plan targets are annually separated from the national plan and transmitted to the central economic ministries. From here the targets are further divided and sent to subordinate bodies.

Below the central ministries, several organizational forms exist. The first is combined industries (*Kombinate*), vertical monopolies that theoretically encompass all factories engaged in the production of interrelated commodity groups (e.g., automobiles, cameras, wire cables), including most factories making semifinished goods for components in the final products. *Kombinate* emerged as significant economic units during the transition from the New Economic System (1963–1967) to the Economic

System of Socialism (1968–1973). This shift was a first step toward correcting the macroeconomic imbalances arising in the uneven implementation of managerial discretion under the experiment with decentralized authority. For certain critical industries, *Kombinate* provided much closer coordination of production and investment among related enterprises, as primary authority was reallocated upward from enterprise managers to *Kombinate* general directors. At the end of the decade, the formation of combined industries was greatly accelerated; by 1981 some 130 *Kombinate* had become the predominant form of the centrally managed industrial sector.

A second form—smaller factories and service enterprises, especially those like bakeries that produce locally consumed items—functions separately from the central ministries and *Kombinate*. Instead, such enterprises are directed by a County Council for Local Industry, which is in turn subordinate to a corresponding national ministry. The third type, agricultural cooperatives and state-owned farms, is directed by county and district councils for agriculture and food, also under the guidance of a national ministry.

Plan targets make their way downward along these hierarchies to the basic production units. At each level, a proposed plan is developed, based upon estimates of the amount of resources needed to meet or exceed the initial targets. Workers are enjoined to participate in this process through their union representatives. In principle, worker contributions should challenge management to achieve higher output, more efficient use of resources, and increased income for all employees. Management and worker plans are aggregated upward through the Council of Ministers and again to the State Plan Commission.

Here the various elements of the plan must be integrated, differences between the initial targets and the aggregate plan reconciled, and the "material balance" insured. The material balance is the most troublesome element, since it involves a determination of the amount of material goods needed for all finished products and—reasoning backward—the amount needed at each intermediate stage of production, all the way back through the production cycles to the point where original raw materials are produced or imported.

Once this process is completed, the Council of Ministers and the State Plan Commission present summary reports to the Politburo, the Central Committee, and the National Assembly. After taking into account further recommendations from the high-level party bodies, the SPK fixes the plan in the form of balances and indicators for each economic sector. These figures include estimates for total production, investment in productive capacity, investment in research, average rates of profit, and expenditures for wages, technical improvements, bonuses, improved working and living conditions, profit taxes, and so on. Plan indicators are refined and sent down the hierarchies, just as in the earlier "target" phase. At the lowest levels, the actual annual plan is further subdivided into quarterly and monthly plans for each production unit.

The Enterprise and Its Director

All GDR enterprises actually engaged in production—whether they are individual factories, *Kombinate*, state farms, or agricultural cooperatives—are legal entities. They own equipment and hire their own employees; they enter into contracts to purchase supplies and services, as well as to sell their products; and they can sue and be sued. They collect their own income and disburse their own expenditures. They make a profit, borrow money, and pay taxes. In these respects, the GDR enterprises resemble corporations in capitalist economies.

However, important differences arise in the context of centrally directed socialism. East German enterprise directors are selected by central economic ministries. Salaries, wages, and prices are centrally determined. The allocation of profit to taxes, investment, and employee benefits is closely limited by legal guidelines. There are no stockholders and no stockholder dividends. There is no competition among enterprises for sales, and all product improvements must be centrally approved. All management decisions must conform to the national economic plan, and management authority can be superseded by high government and/or party officials, when necessary to meet urgent economic difficulties.

The obligation of enterprises to operate within the plan has led observers to characterize the GDR economy as a "command" system. This appellation was quite accurate in the postwar reconstruction period, when most nationally owned enterprises received very detailed instructions from central authorities regarding every aspect of their operations. Over time, however, central mechanisms have become more complex and less direct. The job of an enterprise director no longer consists of simply carrying out orders. Rather, it consists of interpreting a variety of SED goals as they apply to the life of the enterprise. Above all, these goals involve increasing the quantity and quality of production, while reducing the use of labor and materials. For these purposes, enterprise performance is measured in terms of fulfillment of the plan indicators. In principle, management and worker bonuses and prospects for career advancement are directly linked to plan performance. Failure to fulfill the plan is not a criminal offense; it simply leads to lower incomes, career stagnation, and declining worker morale.

Ideally, a successful director would be an efficient director, since rewards should go to the enterprise that achieves maximum output with minimum resources. But an enterprise director needs other skills as well. Plan fulfillment is easier (and bonuses larger) if the director can bargain for lower indicators. Enterprise income is higher if the director can secure a favorable price revision for products. Total product output is insured if the director can pressure suppliers for timely delivery of materials. And sales are improved if contracted purchasers can be persuaded to buy low-quality products along with those of higher quality. Thus, successful enterprise directors must cultivate friends in higher offices and make creative "deals" with managers in other institutions.

In addition, an enterprise director must be able to deal diplomatically with demands emanating from local government and from the labor union. The presence of a major enterprise has a profound impact upon both the need and the ability of local government to provide services. Enterprise funds are used to build housing and to supplement government expenditures. City councils constantly ask for more enterprise spending, while they seek to prevent enterprise needs from overwhelming those of the local community, such as the desire for rational transit planning and reduced air pollution. Great tact may be required to avert clashes with the local mayor.

Similarly, the enterprise labor union has legal claims against management. National legislation provides workers with rights to consult in certain management decisions, protection against arbitrary dismissal, free job training, safe working conditions, bonuses in proportion to effort, and cultural and recreational benefits in the work place. In light of an already complex set of tasks confronting him or her, an enterprise director may perceive labor-union claims as merely a further extraneous limitation on the freedom to manage effectively. Since it is primarily the union that aims to enforce these claims, the enterprise director seeks to comply only minimally, while persuading union representatives— through force of personality or complex technical argument—that further compliance would result in lower incomes for all workers.

It is true that union officials, local government, and even the basic party organization in the enterprise can lodge protests to the SED hierarchy. Experience shows, however, that an enterprise director with a good record of plan fulfillment has little to fear from such appeals to outside authority.

Structural Economic Problems

The task of managing a complex and sophisticated economy is enormous. For the SED, the task is crucial, because economic strength is the linchpin of all promised political and social change. In addition, economic performance provides the single and most visible standard by which people judge the SED's claim to rule.

Consequently, economic management is the all-pervasive preoccupation of GDR politics. Vast resources are devoted to economic education for the people and management training for the elite. Economic questions dominate nearly every newspaper and political speech. Some of the nation's best minds search for the correct forms of organization, the correct system of incentives, the correct application of investments. Yet fundamental problems remain. The following items, all quite familiar to the GDR's own economic experts, illustrate the difficulties of a centrally directed economy.[1]

Plan Inaccuracy. The national economic plan embraces more than eight thousand industrial, agricultural, and service enterprises, plus numerous government agencies. Reports on their past performance are the foundation of any plan, and the sheer complexity of record keeping poses severe problems. For each enterprise, the plan consists of at least thirty items, many of which are aggregated in the SPK documents. At the lower levels, very little of this information is computerized, so that a data base has a high potential for error—even assuming that reporting agencies are unbiased.

But bias does enter the system, because enterprises have an interest in understating their assets and otherwise reporting their operations in the most favorable light. Further inaccuracy occurs simply because of the time required to actually compile the plan. For example, the 1985 plan is initially formulated during 1984, based upon performance data from 1983, some of which are incomplete. As the end of the planning cycle approaches, it proves very difficult to revise data on the basis of estimates for current economic activity.

Lack of Scarcity Pricing. Internal GDR prices are not the result of market forces; that is, they do not necessarily reflect the scarcity of commodities or fluctuations in supply and demand. The practice of setting prices through a central state office—retained, in part, as a means to avoid inflation, "socially wasteful" consumption, and other capitalist ills—frequently inhibits calculations of economic efficiency. To the extent that prices are intended to reflect the cost of production, cost variables are generally out of date. Moreover, the ways of defining and calculating costs are subject to change according to competing political and economic criteria. Consequently, over time the relationship between the prices of goods and their costs of production may diverge markedly.

Even though there exists a strong nominal commitment to shift the emphasis of the national economy toward the more efficient (and more profitable) sectors, the rigidity and diversity of pricing formulas render the calculation of relative efficiency virtually impossible. As an illustration, the GDR national economy might benefit by shutting down its production of rolled steel and applying the saved resources to the production of higher-grade metals, which could then be sold to Poland in exchange for Polish rolled steel. A decision to make this shift depends, of course, on a calculation of the efficiency of steel production relative to the efficiency of high-grade metals production. But this relative efficiency cannot be calculated without a more accurate reckoning of the actual cost of the factors of production. From time to time, such structural shifts are indeed undertaken, but they are usually too late and too haphazard to bring about the potential gains in overall efficiency.

Pricing problems also interfere with efforts to induce optimal performance from enterprise managers and *Kombinat* general directors. Past reforms have often incorporated profit as a synthetic measure of enterprise performance and a primary yardstick for bonus income and managerial career advancement. But able managers necessarily calculated profitability on the basis of unrealistic state prices, so that profit maximization was frequently accompanied by the increased production of goods that the government did not want and the increased consumption of raw materials that the government wanted to conserve. Lacking the means to bring all prices up to date and being unwilling to surrender control of prices to market forces, the government combated production distortions by placing numerous additional restrictions on managerial decisions (more plan indicators) and relegating profit to a secondary role in measuring enterprise performance.

Waste of Raw Materials. The depletion of domestic natural resources, increasing costs for extracting coal and minerals, and rising world prices for raw materials mean that the GDR, like all other highly industrialized economies, faces a critical need to reduce waste in manufacturing. Despite repeated government injunctions to conserve resources, East German achievements lag far behind comparable Western nations.

Amid the numerous indicators added to the basic plan are nominal financial incentives for reduced consumption of raw materials. However, the rewards are far greater for increased production than for more efficient use of raw materials. Thus, the system virtually encourages waste. Moreover, the absence of scarcity pricing means that enterprise cost for certain raw materials may diverge sharply from world market prices. In some cases, producing enterprises find it more profitable to utilize scarce—but artificially underpriced—materials, even when abundant materials could be substituted. For this reason, East German manufacturers have been slow to follow the shift of Western capitalists toward the use of some synthetic materials, for example, in consumer goods.

Waste of Labor. GDR employers have two good reasons to retain excess workers. First, effective labor legislation protects workers from simple dismissal. In this area, at least, labor unions usually insist that grievance procedures be observed. Where a reduction in the work force can be justified, the employer still bears a responsibility for placement in a new job and, if necessary, for job retraining. Unlike workers in many capitalist nations, East German workers are spared much of the burden of structural unemployment. Capitalist Sweden also has comprehensive proemployment policies, but their cost is more widely shared through a system of insurance and government support. In contrast, the cost of GDR policies is borne by individual enterprises, so that it often makes sense to simply keep extra workers on the payroll.

Second, the cumbersome supply system in the GDR occasionally means delayed deliveries of materials and lost production time, with a consequent need for later accelerated production in order to fulfill the plan. Periodically accelerated production is best accomplished when the enterprise has workers in reserve. During normal or slack periods these reserve workers must be considered underemployed. From the standpoint of the whole economy (but not from the enterprise standpoint), this condition is a waste of labor resources.

This waste of labor is ironic in the face of East Germany's chronic labor shortage. (Custodial, repair, and other services routinely experience "temporary" labor shortages, lasting for months or even years.) Since 1966 the labor shortage has been partly covered by foreign workers (mostly Poles, Vietnamese, and Hungarians), a policy curiously similar to the *Gastarbeiter* in the Federal Republic. With the turn toward increasing automation, the importance of foreign workers has fallen off to about .6 percent of the GDR work force.[2]

Low Capital Productivity. The productivity of capital is expressed as the ratio between investment in fixed assets and the value of goods and services produced by those assets. Investment in new production capacity may be considered irrational when the cost of investment exceeds the value of new product output. This situation can arise in the GDR when the value of increased production is overestimated or when the cost of new production facilities is underestimated by failure to account for construction delays or increasing equipment costs. Delays occur when planned investment resources (e.g., major construction equipment and manpower) are "temporarily" diverted to rescue some other enterprise that has fallen behind in its plan. Although this problem is not nearly as severe as in the Soviet Union, uncompleted and underutilized capital equipment is a primary cause of East Germany's low capital productivity.

Awareness of these problems has recently led to much shorter plan targets for bringing new equipment into service, as well as an emphasis on investment to modernize existing enterprises, rather than to initiate new ones.

Growth Imbalances. During the middle and late 1960s, enterprise plans were arranged so that greater emphasis lay with maximizing profits. This emphasis coincided with experiments to extend the discretion of enterprise directors. For enterprises with more skilled leadership, more favorable commodity prices, and/or a history of generous investment, this experiment allowed them to attract scarce supplies and better workers away from less favored enterprises. Since these high-profit enterprises were concentrated in the high-technology branches of industry, they experienced accelerated growth while other branches lagged behind. Eventually, the interdependence of all branches became evident, and this imbalanced growth produced a slowdown in the entire economy.

In the last years of Ulbricht's leadership, profit maximization was deemphasized, and central ministries resumed more authority over investments. New investments were concentrated on what were termed "structure-defining industries," still mostly high technology. The result was another round of imbalanced growth with similar consequences.

Neglect of Infrastructure. A special example of these imbalances has been the continuing neglect of the economic infrastructure, broadly defined. This includes underdeveloped institutions for finance, marketing, and commercial law, all related to what are, by the standards of advanced industrial economies, retarded conditions in the field of communications and data processing.

Perhaps more significant is the relative neglect in the development of the transportation system, especially motor transport, and the systems of energy and water supply. These deficiencies alone account for much of the wasted investment already noted. There are, for example, numerous instances of new production facilities operating at partial capacity as a result of a lack of sufficient electrical power.

Slow Technological Change. Since 1963 the GDR economy has been ostensibly engaged in "mastering the scientific-technological revolution." This concept is sometimes broadly interpreted to include the "science" of management and other social sciences. Most frequently, however, it is applied to product innovation and improved production methods, especially in such areas as agronomy, chemistry, metallurgy, and the use of industrial lasers and other sophisticated technology.

Most research has been undertaken by centrally funded, specialized institutes, which have been criticized for their failure to develop production-related technology. Experiments with more dependence on funding through enterprise-institute contracts for specific projects have been only marginally successful. Most recently, the shift toward *Kombinate* as the major production organization has permitted the assignment of specific research units to individual *Kombinate*, subject to the general directors and financed as an integral part of the *Kombinat* operations.

Such a measure of decentralization may not be sufficient to overcome the calculated reluctance of production enterprises toward new production methods. Innovation involves risks: The introduction of new processes means lower output in the short run, as installations are modernized and new problems are uncovered and resolved. Because of the plan emphasis on short-term targets, such output reductions mean the loss of bonuses and other benefits. Once the new processes are successfully implemented, centrally determined prices are then established on the basis of current production costs. In some cases a modest price surcharge can be arranged for the first three years of new production, but it is still frequently more rewarding to expand production with old methods than to introduce new methods and new products.

In large measure, the protectionism afforded by a centralized trading system permits East German enterprises to resist technological change without the discipline of foreign competition. A further factor is, of course, the rigidity of central pricing.

The current catchword, *robotics*, applies to a form of technological innovation to save labor through automated production. This transformation has its own disincentive, since consequent labor-force reductions can mean a lower classification for management salaries and a reduction in certain enterprise funds that are also tied to the number of employees.

Uncertain Allocation of Authority. In their continuing effort to attain better economic performance, SED leaders have never achieved agreement on the proper allocation of policy authority. Questions persist concerning how best to allocate authority in three sets of relationships: (1) between the Council of Ministers and the economic departments of the SED Central Committee; (2) between economic planners in the State Plan Commission and economic administrators in the Council of Ministers; and (3) between the Council of Ministers, the intermediate levels (*Kombinate*, county councils), and the production enterprises.

The first relationship, the national level of government-party interaction, has seen a gradual diminution of direct involvement by Central Committee departments in economic-policy formation. This evolution has not been continuous, however. Specific intervention by national party agencies has occurred periodically, especially in such troubled areas as agriculture and retail trade. More general party intervention has coincided with significant economic reform; this was most notable during 1961–1965, when major economic ministries were more or less directly subordinated to the SED Secretariat. Beginning in 1965, however, the conventional form of economic ministries was restored. Their authority was strengthened in the general Council of Ministers reform of 1972 and further reinforced by personnel shifts in 1976.

As indicated in Chapter 2, the present Presidium of the Council of Ministers represents a prestigious collection of economic planners and administrators. With the exception of Günther Mittag, SED secretary for the economy, party agencies cannot match the Council of Ministers Presidium in terms of expertise and seniority. Although close government-party cooperation is assured through informal communication and through Politburo meetings, it appears that a division of responsibility has emerged in which the council Presidium holds the greater authority for making economic policy.

The second relationship, between planners and administrators, was a particularly sensitive issue during the first years of Honecker's leadership. One of the main criticisms of previous economic policy was that party leaders had grown excessively fond of their "systemic" view of society. According to this critique,[3] Ulbricht and his followers—in their zest for theoretical innovation—had persuaded themselves that the national economy had developed into a smoothly operating mechanism, a "cybernetic" system: In order to achieve desired performance from the economic system, it was necessary only to plug in the proper plan indicators. This concept had led to a rather sharp distinction between planning activity and actual economic administration, whereby planners were not allowed to interfere in ongoing economic activity.

In Honecker's view, Ulbricht's "cybernetic" imagery was hopelessly unrealistic. It failed to anticipate the inevitable growth imbalances, and it discouraged timely remedial intervention. The earlier emphasis on systemic concepts—the New Economic System (1963–1967) and the Economic System of Socialism (1968–1973)—has disappeared; today, the GDR has simply a "developed socialist economy." Earlier references to the tasks of economic "planning and management" have been switched to "management and planning," reflecting the integration and subordination of planning to hierarchic principles of central direction.[4]

The third relationship, involving authority allocations among the three levels of economic administration, is a perpetual riddle. Many of the nation's basic economic problems can be attributed to excessive centralization of authority. In fact, a main feature of the 1963 reforms was an effort to decentralize authority, to give wider latitude to management decisions in *Kombinate* and basic enterprises. But the appearance of growth distortions led to the reimposition of central restraints in 1968 and 1970.

Still, the problems of plan rigidity persist. The recent thrust to expand the *Kombinate* is the latest in a sequence of attempts to find an optimal subnational institution that can incorporate both policy authority and operational management.

Organizational Instability. After this review' of the key defects in the GDR's planned economy, it should not be surprising that the search for solutions has become a problem in itself. In the last twenty years, economic management has been subjected to three major structural reforms. Each reform has been imperfectly implemented, and each brought new uncertainties concerning development priorities and the allocation of policy authority. In addition, intervening periods have been characterized by almost endless alterations in the system of plan indicators and incentives. Enterprise directors could not be sure from one year to the next exactly how their performance would be evaluated and how bonuses would be calculated.

Institutes engaged in training new economic managers found that much of their curriculum had become obsolete by the time students completed a course of study. Labor-union institutes, supposedly training union representatives to become consulting partners with enterprise management, were simply overwhelmed by the complexity of the changes.

For the great majority of enterprises, all of this confusion was handled by a kind of formalism. Management, union representatives, and the basic party organization tried to observe the formal requirements as best they could. The enterprise director would prepare his annual plan, the union would prepare its "counter-plan," and the bpo would convene all the stipulated meetings. Since few of the people involved had a sure grasp of the consequences of this process, however, all this activity had little purpose, except to satisfy higher authorities. Beneath this veneer of formalism, then, all participants would strive to keep the actual operation of the enterprise unchanged. If preserving old routines was unlikely to bring progress and large bonuses, it at least avoided the risks of embarking on a poorly charted course of change.

Possibly the greatest contribution of Honecker's leadership has been an end to frantic, and somewhat visionary, economic reform. Since the mid-1970s, economic managers have enjoyed relative organizational stability. Central planning has become more cautious and more realistic. Although the present government seems to be addressing fairly directly many of the problems noted above, none has been clearly resolved.[5] National economic efficiency is still impaired by price rigidities, and the task of management is still burdened with a great many incompatible plan indicators. The economic system may be functioning more predictably, but there remains an obvious need for some variety of further reform.

Environmental Dilemmas

A great many of the GDR's present economic difficulties can be attributed to defects in the system of centralized management and planning, but another set of problems is independent of that system. External factors, including adaptation to the physical environment and adjustments to world trade, pose immediate concerns, which aggravate structural problems and—at the same time—make the resolution of structural problems more difficult.

Like other industrialized nations, the GDR has become acutely conscious of environmental deterioration.[6] The current constitution stipulates environmental protection as a national goal. In 1971 the Ministry for Environment and Hydroeconomy was created with broad coordinating authority and included in the "economic cabinet," the Presidium of the Council of Ministers. At first glance, the institutional prominence of environmental concerns in the GDR is impressive; yet the task is diffuse, and the resources meager.

Water pollution is an especially severe problem, mainly because the amount of available water per capita is 30 percent below the European average.[7] East German sources claim that their ratio of water resources to consumption is the worst of all industrial economies. Most water is consumed by industrial users. For a great many years, industrial wastes have been discharged into the nation's rivers, especially in the counties of Halle, Leipzig, and Magdeburg, where chemical plants are concentrated. This process has destroyed much inland fishing and endangered drinking-water supplies. At projected rates of expenditures, only about 17 percent of the water can be made potable. In addition, salt contaminants have flowed downstream to damage agriculture in the neighboring Federal Republic. The GDR is also a significant contributor to the persistent concentrations of sulfur wastes in the Baltic Ocean, with consequent damage to the fishing industry.[8]

Since the mid-1960s, government sources have linked air pollution to a substantial increase in deaths from lung cancer and respiratory diseases. Dust and sulfur dioxide emissions also damage buildings, crops, and forests, particularly around Cottbus and Leipzig. Manufacturing is the primary culprit, with the worst effects accompanying the processing of cement, coal, and minerals. The nation's heavy reliance upon domestic soft coal for household heating generates great amounts of smog in every urban center. Toxic auto emissions are a further cause of air pollution.[9]

Hearing impairment due to excessive noise is the most frequently reported job-related ailment in the GDR. Noise pollution is a frequent complaint of city dwellers, who endure the sounds of heavy traffic on poorly constructed streets. Medical studies have attempted to demonstrate the physical and psychological costs of excessively noisy machinery, poorly insulated apartments, and general urban crowding.

Open-cut mining is the cause of pronounced environmental damage, mainly in the coal-rich counties of the southeast. In addition to scenic and recreational costs, large areas of agricultural and forest lands have been destroyed through his process. Restoration is extremely slow and expensive.

Although the GDR preceded many of its neighbors in creating institutions and laws to deal with environmental pollution, severe problems persist. The Ministry for Environment and Hydroeconomy directs efforts to set ceilings on allowable pollution, provide guidelines for pollution prevention, and coordinate consultations among officials in the areas of health, worker safety, urban planning, and transportation, as well as in the economic ministries. But the Ministry for Environmental Protection must depend on others to implement innovations and to enforce the sanctions of the antipollution codes.

The 1971–1975 plan included large increases in investments for water storage and purification, coal-lands reclamation, clean refuse-disposal sites, and several long-term test and study projects. All of this was encompassed in a supplemental environmental plan. This special attention diminished considerably in the second half of the decade.[10] Rapidly increasing costs for raw materials, especially oil, produced severe increases in production costs. This intensified the reluctance of manufacturers to utilize systems of filters and waste recovery, which slowed production rates and consumed extra energy. Similarly, the rising costs of imported consumer goods placed an extra burden on the government treasury, with fewer resources available to subsidize and monitor antipollution measures.

After an initial rush of enthusiasm, ecological scientists again found themselves on the defensive. Unable to document the social costs of environmental deterioration, ecologists were characterized as engaged in "unproductive" activity. Environmental protection soon lost ground to other tasks, the fruits of which could be measured in terms of growth in national income.

Global Economic Change

Before World War II, the present East German lands delivered more than half of their production and received more than half of their consumption in commerce with other German regions or with foreign nations. The postwar division of Germany, coupled with compulsory deliveries to the Soviet Union, meant a profound disruption in trade patterns. Yet the nation's small size and shortage of raw materials, as well as its historic production emphasis on industrial specialization, require substantial involvement in foreign trade.

Today, the GDR's total trade volume ranks fifteenth in the world; its per capita trade is the highest in the East European community.[11] The internal significance of foreign trade can be measured in terms of the export ratio (i.e., commodity exports as a percentage of gross domestic product). In the late 1970s the East German export ratio was over 25 percent, about the same as for the Federal Republic.[12] This ratio was lower than those for Hungary and Poland, but it was about three times higher than those for the Soviet Union and the United States. This rather substantial foreign-trade involvement means that domestic economic development and planning is directly affected by the shape of the global economy.

From the mid-1950s to about 1970, the global price structure of raw materials and finished goods was especially favorable to any nation with a strong industrial base. The relative abundance of raw materials meant declining prices, while accelerating demand for industrial capital goods and consumer goods brought higher prices along with increased sales. Compared to the experience of its West European neighbors, East Germany's benefit from this favorable price structure was limited, but nevertheless significant.

Because of tautness and discontinuities in its domestic economy, the GDR had very little potential for surplus production with which to enter new foreign markets. For the most part, present and future surpluses were already earmarked for export to the Soviet Union and other East European states. The structure of world prices was advantageous to the GDR, even in this context, since this trade consisted mainly of exported finished goods and imported raw materials. Within the socialist bloc, less developed nations objected to their emerging dependency upon the processing centers of East Germany. The regional economic grouping, the Council for Mutual Economic Assistance, arranged a number of specialization agreements in which Hungary, Bulgaria, and Romania would emphasize primary-goods production to be exchanged for higher-stage industrial goods from the GDR and Czechoslovakia. Objecting that such arrangements would perpetuate an inferior economic status for some countries, Romania led the resistance to Soviet–East German efforts to further integrate the East European economies.

Despite this initial GDR price advantage in East European trade, long-term price agreements insulated much socialist-bloc trade from further world market price changes. In the early 1960s, shifts in world prices became even more favorable to the industrial economies. Thus, East Germany found guaranteed markets in expanding East European trade, but only at the cost of forgoing the potentially higher returns from trade in the world market.

This arrangement suited most GDR leaders rather well. After all, the potential for trade with underdeveloped nations was extremely limited, especially since it would require substantial credit financing from the limited state budget. Trade with the industrial West was hampered by the frequent inability of GDR goods to compete on the world market. Moreover, East German leaders feared that Western nations would resort to political manipulation of trade ties in an effort to weaken the SED regime, a temptation to which West Germans had yielded on a number of occasions in the past.

By 1963 the wide-ranging discussions surrounding the New Economic System had cast a different light on the function of foreign trade in the GDR's strategy for economic development. Expanded trade with the industrial West was proposed as a means to spur technical innovation through foreign-product competition, as well as a means to secure new technologies. A general increase of trade would be necessary in order to sustain longer production runs and increased revenues with which to finance new investments.

Generally more favorable economic and political conditions permitted limited application of this departure. From 1960 to 1975 East German foreign-trade turnover increased at an average annual rate of 9.7 percent, more than twice the growth rate for national income.[13] The greatest increases appeared in trade with the industrial West, which jumped from 19 percent of total GDR trade to more than 27 percent.[14]

On the whole, the expected benefits for domestic economic growth were somewhat less than expected. This is explained partly by the East German inability to adequately adapt internal production organization to the requirements of newly purchased capital goods. As a result, imported West German machinery, for example, had a much smaller effect on labor productivity in an East German factory than similar machinery did in a West German factory.

In addition, the GDR's increased reliance upon imported capital goods from the West indirectly exposed the East German economy to some of the worst effects of worldwide inflation. After about 1968, the favorable global price structure began to shift. Prices for many raw materials began to increase faster than prices for finished goods, thus reversing the trend of the preceding two decades. This shift accelerated, and in the period 1972–1974 prices for agricultural commodities, industrial raw materials, and petroleum skyrocketed.

To some extent, socialist-bloc trade arrangements had a cushioning effect. Most of East Germany's imported raw materials and energy sources come from the Soviet Union and East Europe under long-term price agreements, which reflect world prices only on a delayed basis. With respect to petroleum, this beneficial delay was sharply reduced in 1975, when the Soviet Union compelled other members of the bloc to accept a new price formula more closely reflecting current world prices.

But the GDR felt an even greater impact in an indirect fashion. The 1973 embargo by the Organization of Petroleum Exporting Countries (OPEC) against several Western nations, coupled with dramatic increases in the world market price of crude oil, generated higher production costs and overall inflation in the industrialized West. Expanded trade ties to the West now confronted the GDR with strong inflationary problems. In response, East German corporations reduced their purchase of Western capital goods. But in order to derive benefit from previous purchases of machinery, it was necessary to accelerate production of commodities heavily dependent on minerals and chemicals imported from the West. Inflated prices for these items, as well as for needed consumer-goods imports, sent an inflationary shock through the East German economy.

Although the GDR had usually experienced modest trade surpluses throughout the preceding decade, global inflation quickly produced a trade deficit in 1974. Like other East European states, the GDR was able to secure loans from Western banking consortia as a means to finance imports of Western technology and consumer goods and to make short-term oil purchases on the world market. East German efforts to translate imported technology into increased exports encountered very limited success as the global recession deepened. Additional credits were needed to finance raw-materials imports from Western markets, as well as increasingly substantial imports of U.S. grain. By the end of 1981, the East German foreign debt in Western currency (excluding debt to the USSR) exceeded U.S. $8.6 billion;[15] calculated on a per capita basis, this indebtedness was even higher than the deficit that so severely aggravated Poland's economic crisis. Only as a result of a strenuous and abrupt reduction of imports over the following year was a major payments crisis averted. With the encouragement of the Bonn government, West German bankers took the lead in arranging large new loans to the GDR in the spring of 1983.

Economic Performance

The complexities of centralized economic management, environmental deterioration, and resource depletion, along with the shifting conditions of foreign trade, all present severe obstacles to East Germany's goal of stable economic growth. In important respects, some of these problems are the same as those now increasingly encountered by the urban-industrial liberal democracies, which are themselves struggling to find politically acceptable modes of expressing government responsibility for effective economic performance.

Although a nation's economic activity can be measured by an almost infinite variety of quantitative data, any attempt to evaluate the result is necessarily arbitrary. Arbitrariness enters because one must select only a few indicators and reference points. For example, an economy may be judged according to per capita income, sustained rate of growth, increases in labor productivity, or return on capital investments. If economic activity is perceived as more than an end in itself, the national economy might be judged by the ability to maintain a "proper" balance between investment and consumption, to provide a "satisfactory" standard of living for its citizens, or to promote social equality—all highly subjective criteria.

After one has selected from a wide choice of indicators, it is still necessary to compare a national economy to some point of reference. "Good" performance is relative. Relative to what? Depending on the chosen reference point, quite different evaluations will result. The German Democratic Republic of today may be compared to an earlier period, for example, 1939, 1946, or 1960. It may also be compared to all nations of comparable size or with comparable natural resources. The GDR might be compared to other members of the Soviet-oriented Council for Mutual Economic Assistance, which share important economic and political principles but differ in many other respects. Or it might be compared to its West European neighbors, which the GDR resembles in terms of culture and prewar level of industrialization, but from which it differs sharply in political and economic principles and international economic relations.

As expected, no nation is truly comparable to the GDR in economic circumstances. Moreover, all efforts to form quantitative comparisons are impeded by incompatible definitions of primary concepts in national accounts statistics (e.g., domestic product, gross investment, public consumption), as well as the lack of sufficient data with which to make transformations into comparable terms. Although foreign economic analysts generally consider GDR statistics to have a tolerably low margin of error, accurate evaluation has become more difficult in recent years as public GDR reports systematically omit important data on balance of payments and the impact of imports on domestic consumption.

The most comprehensive efforts to fashion comparable data have been undertaken by the Research Project on National Income in East

Table 4.1. Gross National Product Per Capita in Eastern Europe and the United States, 1965 and 1982 (in constant 1981 U.S. dollars)

	1965	As % of U.S. GNP per capita	1982	As % of U.S. GNP per capita[a]
United States	$9,344	100.0	$12,436	100.0
German Democratic Republic	6,086	65.1	9,898	79.6
Czechoslovakia	6,356	68.0	9,028	72.6
Romania	2,355	25.2	4,403	35.4
Hungary	4,168	44.6	6,091	49.0
Poland	3,569	38.2	4,866	39.1
Bulgaria	2,413	25.8	3,963	31.9
All East Europe	4,126	44.2	6,159	49.5

[a]Alton notes that calculations based on alternative assumptions yield a GDR per capita GNP of one half to three fourths that of the United States in the early 1980s.
Source: Thad Alton et al., Economic Growth in Eastern Europe, 1965, 1970, and 1975–1982. New York: L. W. International Financial Research, 1983), p. 23.

Central Europe. The project's report offers a comparison of per capita gross national product (GNP) (Table 4.1). By this measure, the German Democratic Republic has the highest per capita GNP of all communist-ruled nations, ranking slightly ahead of Czechoslovakia and the Soviet Union.[16] Among noncommunist states, the GDR has a per capita GNP about three-fourths that of the United States, West Germany, and Japan; roughly equal that of Great Britain; and about one-fourth greater than that of Italy.

The GDR's average annual rate of growth for 1965–1980 was 3.1 percent, about average for Eastern Europe and notably higher than the 2.0 percent recorded in the United States.[17] On the other hand, Japan and several major West European nations achieved substantially greater growth rates in this same period. Clearly, one's degree of satisfaction with these performance indicators depends on one's frame of reference.

Given the general level of East German economic development, it is not surprising that the greatest share of increased GNP comes from the industrial sector, especially in engineering, chemicals, and electronics. At the same time, the highest rates of growth occurred in personal and professional services, construction, transport, and trade. Government administration and public services declined slightly as sources of GNP, while agriculture fell sharply. By 1980 the GNP had acquired the contours shown in Table 4.2.

According to this presentation, which is based on current domestic prices in each nation, the GDR appears to occupy an intermediate position between its East European neighbors, with their heavier reliance on agriculture, and the Western nations, with a stronger service-sector orientation. But Herbert Wilkens of the German Institute for Economic Research (West Berlin) contends that this comparison is misleading, due

Table 4.2. Gross National Product by Sector of Origin for Six Nations, 1980 (in percent)

	German Democratic Republic	Czecho-slovakia	Poland	Federal Republic of Germany	United Kingdom	United States
Agriculture	13.7	16.1	24.4	2.8	2.5	2.8
Industry	43.5	39.7	33.6	40.7	30.6	29.0
Construction	5.3	8.6	6.3	6.0	5.7	4.4
Trade	8.4	8.7	6.3	9.6	8.9	17.9
Transport	8.4	7.1	8.3	6.0	7.4	6.5
Services and other	20.7	19.8	21.1	34.9	44.9	39.4
Total	100.0	100.0	100.0	100.0	100.0	100.0

Source: Adapted from Thad Alton et al., *Economic Growth in Eastern Europe, 1965, 1970, and 1975–1980* (New York: L. W. International Financial Research, 1981), pp. 11–14; Statistisches Bundesamt, *Statistisches Jahrbuch 1982 für die Bundesrepublik Deutschland* (Stuttgart: W. Kohlhammer, 1982), pp. 711–715.

to different price relations.[18] Distortions are introduced by relatively lower East German wages in the service sector and the markedly higher state-fixed prices for East German agricultural commodities. After adjusting for these distortions, a restatement of East Germany's sector origin of GNP shows a much closer similarity to the Federal Republic: The contribution of the service sector rises to about 25 percent, and the contribution of agriculture declines to 4 percent. Such adjustments are critical, if one is to evaluate the GDR's economic performance in terms of the efficient use of capital and labor.

As might be expected, the most detailed analyses of the East Germany economy have involved comparison with the Federal Republic. These comparisons reveal a great many similarities in performance, as is illustrated in Table 4.3. However, U.S. and British observers must be cautious about facile generalizations to their own experience. As suggested

Table 4.3. Use of Gross National Product in Four Nations, 1976 (in percent)

	German Democratic Republic	Federal Republic of Germany	United Kingdom	United States
Private consumption	45	55	60	65
State consumption	29	22	22	19
Investment	25	21	19	17
Net exports	1	2	−1	−1
Total	100	100	100	100

Source: Adapted from Doris Cornelsen et al., *Handbook of the Economy of the German Democratic Republic* (Westmead, England: Saxon House, 1979), p. 97; Statistisches Bundesamt, *Statistisches Jahrbuch 1979 für die Bundesrepublik Deutschland* (Stuttgart: W. Kohlhammer, 1979), pp. 702–705

in Tables 4.2 and 4.3, the structure of the West German economy differs from the U.S. and British in important respects, including a heavier reliance on commodity-producing sectors and a higher annual rate of investment.

Compared to West Germany, the United States, and Great Britain, the GDR devotes a much smaller share of the GNP to private consumption and correspondingly greater shares to state consumption and to investment. As will be shown in the following chapter, the sharply different figures for private consumption require some interpretation, principally an adjustment for the fact that the East German allocations for state consumption include many items that in Western nations are directly consumed through private incomes. The relatively higher East German rates of investment reflect the fact that no significant economic growth is possible through increased employment. Population growth in the GDR is extremely low, and the percentage of that population already holding jobs (the employment participation ratio) is perhaps the highest in the world. Consequently, there is virtually no unused potential labor, and economic planners must rely on increased investment in production capacity, along with improved technology and more efficient organization, in order to achieve growth.

The German Institute for Economic Research estimates that from 1960 to 1975 only 6 percent of East Germany's economic growth was attributable to increases in the size of the work force, extremely low by world standards. Measures to increase labor productivity (output per worker hour) require investment in better machinery and equipment for workers' use. This process of substituting capital investment for labor accounted for about 36 percent of economic growth. The remaining 58 percent of factors contributing to growth is loosely attributed to "technological progress," which can include anything from the application of new production processes to various steps to reduce waste in raw materials, underutilization of workers, and idle time of machinery.[19]

Such a distribution of growth factors is similar to that found in the more developed Western economies. The result is that the GDR has recently achieved increases in both labor productivity and capital productivity (the ratio of produced income to capital assets) that compare favorably to its Western neighbors. But this favorable assessment applies only to rates of change, not to absolute levels. It must be emphasized that the East German economy has long suffered from lower absolute levels in the productivity of both labor and capital, relative to Western industrial economies. Despite notable improvement, the East German system of central pricing and flawed management incentives retains a greater tendency to waste labor and to make inefficient investments.

The overall record of East Germany's economic achievements and shortcomings is a composite of changes effected in interdependent sectors. In addition to attacking general problems of total output, productivity, and organizational efficiency, GDR economic planners have sought to determine and to create the most appropriate balance among the several forms of interrelated activity. A survey of sectoral development[20] illustrates this effort as well as the remaining tasks.

Mechanical Engineering and Vehicles. This sector produces fully 25 percent of the nation's industrial output with only 17 percent of industrial capital assets. The sector includes the production of machine tools, agricultural machinery, chemical processing equipment, and other capital goods. Thus, its performance is decisive for overall industrial production. As in other advanced industrial economies, the GDR has experienced a recent slight decline in capital productivity for this sector, partly due to efforts to introduce too many new products at once. Through the effective use of imported Western technology, the GDR has strengthened its role as the leading supplier of capital goods in Eastern Europe; yet this strategy has allowed it to do no more than maintain its relative position in world markets as a whole. With nearly 30 percent of the industrial work force, this sector remains the largest part of the GDR industry.[21]

Electronics and Electrical Engineering. In recent years the fastest-growing sector, electronics, has surpassed the chemicals industry as the lodestar of East German economic progress. Increasing employment and capital investment have been accompanied by relatively good increases in productivity (at least by East German standards), so that this sector represents a particularly distinguished achievement. Much higher capital productivity might be achieved through more comprehensive shift work, which currently lags behind the average for other industrial sectors. The electronics industry is characterized by especially high rates of female employment; because women are disproportionately burdened with parenting and household obligations, the failure of this industry to provide compensating work-place amenities may hinder efforts to attract more workers to evening and night shifts.

The extraordinary political attention devoted to this sector makes clear the double burden confronting the electronics industry. First, developments in electronics, particularly in microelectronics, are critical in determining the competitiveness of GDR exports. Established markets for industrial appliances, consumer durables, and data-processing equipment are jeopardized by the failure of East German producers to stay abreast of the conversion to miniaturization. More than 50 percent of this sector's output is targeted for export,[22] a major element in combating the nation's trade deficit. Second, the nation's economic planners are counting on the electronics industry to yield enormous benefits during the current Five-Year Plan. By 1985 the nation is supposed to be self-sufficient in the production of microelectronic components, which should permit rapid automation of diverse manufacturing processes and a consequent savings of energy and manpower. Roughly 25 percent of real growth during the current plan is supposed to be derived from the fruits of the electronics industry.[23]

Chemical Industry. In the immediate postwar period, the East German chemical industry was badly underdeveloped. Strenuous efforts, highlighted by the gigantic Schwedt refinery, were early devoted to exploiting this sector's export potential. Self-sufficiency in many forms of pharmaceuticals, chemical fertilizers and pesticides, and industrial chemicals is threatened by rising petroleum costs. Efforts to substitute more abundant domestic chemicals are very expensive, so that some lines of production can be sustained only under conditions of declining productivity. Because of limited funds for investment, the GDR is now electing to skip the earlier stages of some chemical processing and to import semiprocessed chemicals from Czechoslovakia and Poland. This sector enjoyed considerable investment in the 1970s, so that it still makes good economic sense to utilize this production capacity at the highest possible rates.

Metal Processing. This is another sector badly neglected due to the regionally imbalanced distribution of industry in prewar Germany. Consequently, rapid expansion of iron and steel production was necessary to support the first phase of GDR development. More recently, as the import of low-grade steel has become more feasible, the metal-processing industry has shifted toward more specialized kinds of production. Again, this has required new investment and has posed a challenge to keep up with rapid technological innovation. Although the growth of this sector is below the industrial average, its capacity to adapt to modern requirements is a critical factor for the growth of the electronics industry, construction, and consumer goods.

Consumer Goods. Notwithstanding a recent policy emphasis on popular standards of living, the consumer-goods industry has not enjoyed notable growth, despite marked increases in the production of furniture, sporting equipment, and other household items. Investment in this sector has been below average, except in textiles. Because a shift to synthetic fibers has enhanced the export potential of textiles, this industry has acquired some emphasis. A sharp decline in employment has been more than offset by a large increase in automation and a growth in textiles production. Food processing has received some greater attention, as well, and it now records an average annual growth nearly equal to the industrial average—hardly sufficient to overcome long previous years of relative neglect.

Energy. The persistent inability to meet the requirements for power and fuel has been a major factor inhibiting industrial growth. Nearly 80 percent of electrical output is generated by brown-coal plants.[24] Though lower in efficiency and higher in pollutants than most other fuels, brown coal is still relatively abundant in the GDR. Imported hard coal, hydroelectric, and nuclear power stations provide additional electric power. The GDR's nuclear power capacity expanded in the late 1970s to about 12 percent of total electrical output, close to the West European average.[25] Since 1960 the growth of East Germany's electrical output has lagged well behind that of Western Europe and has also failed to meet the growing needs of the nation's industrial production. Power interruptions have meant idle time for workers and machinery, with a consequent decline in productivity. Power generation requires very large investments, and in the GDR the value of increased output has generally fallen below the cost of expanded facilities. Yet these investments must be made, in order to sustain the growth of energy-intensive industry.

A more positive situation characterizes the consumption of petroleum. On a per capita basis, the GDR consumes only about half as much petroleum as Western Europe.[26] This is possible because East Germans do not use oil to generate electricity, because they rely more heavily on coal and gas for heating, and because they rely less on passenger vehicles. As a consequence, the GDR has been damaged less than comparably industrialized nations by increased world prices for oil. On the other hand, the price for imported Soviet energy (roughly 77 percent of energy imports) has risen dramatically. During the 1970s the cost for Soviet petroleum increased more than fivefold; recently it has risen about 20 percent per year. Moreover, long-term contracts now limit GDR purchases to 90 percent of the 1981 oil volume.[27]

Overall the GDR is able to cover 65 percent of its energy requirements from domestic sources,[28] a condition that compares favorably with most Western industrial nations. Ironically, even this situation could be improved with appropriate conservation methods. In 1975 per capita consumption of primary energy was 18 percent higher in the GDR than in the Federal Republic.[29] In fact, along with Americans, East Germans led the world in per capita energy consumption. This is attributable not to wasteful consumers, but to inefficient industry. Paralleling similar observations in the Soviet Union, GDR economists have noted that certain production processes consume as much as 20 percent more energy in the GDR as in the industrialized West.[30] (When compared to other communist nations, higher East German rates of energy consumption are not related to different levels of production efficiency but to the larger role of energy-intensive industry in the GDR economy.) It is not possible to determine how much of this energy waste is due to outmoded production equipment and how much is due to simple mismanagement. In any case, it appears that even though energy supply represents a serious threat to economic growth, it is also an element with considerable potential for improvement.

Construction. Like energy supply, the construction industry is an essential factor in promoting expansion of the commodity-producing sectors. In an early effort to accelerate industrial production, construction was for many years neglected in the GDR. But since the mid-1960s the annual growth rate of investment in construction has generally exceeded the average of all industrial investment. In addition, the construction emphasis for industrial purposes has declined. Significant increases have occurred in construction for agriculture. Housing has declined in relative terms, while construction for government and public services has fallen sharply.

Agriculture. Because of the greater variability of environmental factors, appraisal of performance is much more difficult in agriculture than in industry. But by most measures, East German agriculture has registered remarkable gains. An intensive, largely involuntary drive to collectivization in 1959–1960 resulted in the current distribution of agricultural holdings: 5 percent private, 10 percent state-owned, and 85 percent cooperative.[31] This program was soon linked to altered investment priorities designed to increase the level of mechanization and the application of modern farming techniques. Subsequent changes have involved consolidation of farming cooperatives into larger entities and experimentation with forms of collaboration for improved marketing, research, and support services.

Many changes have occurred in agricultural production, and some East German cooperatives are featured as models for farmers from Eastern Europe and underdeveloped nations. The use of chemical fertilizers is among the highest in the world. Some forms of machinery, especially harvesting equipment, are considered more efficient than those operating in Western Europe. The GDR has created the most productive system of agricultural cooperatives ever developed. Yet an inclusive comparison of capital productivity in agriculture (yield per acre and animal production per stock population) shows the GDR at about 83 percent of West German levels.[32] Labor productivity shows a similar result: high by East European standards, moderate by Western standards. Despite steady improvement, it appears that a segment of the agricultural work force is underemployed, especially the older members of cooperatives who are reluctant to leave the countryside. Natural attrition will gradually lead to improved productivity.

Agriculture successes have been achieved at some social cost. Initially as an inducement to promote collectivization, and subsequently to stimulate modern processes, the East German government fixed agricultural producer prices at a relatively high level while subsidizing lower consumer prices at the market. This, of course, represents a substantial drain on public funds, in some degree resembling the unrealistic food-price distortions that have posed severe political strains in Poland.

Efforts to improve agriculture performance involve new construction, primarily to facilitate care of increasingly sophisticated field equipment and to accelerate lagging mechanization in the production of animal and dairy products. Across the board, East German agriculture provides about 85 percent of the nation's food consumption.[33] Attempts to increase food self-sufficiency would likely be inefficient from the standpoint of the national economy. Instead, further rationalization is needed to release agricultural labor to work in industrial sectors that achieve much higher rates of productivity.

Transportation. In the GDR, the transport of both goods and passengers is heavily oriented to the railway. Track density is high, but only 20 percent of the lines have dual tracks.[34] Diesel power is predominant, and efforts are being made to extend electrification beyond its current 12 percent.[35] By West German standards, GDR use of truck transport and shipping canals is rather low. Truck traffic is impeded by the dearth of multilane, limited-access throughways and by the lack of trucking firms devoted primarily to long hauls. In fact, most trucks are owned by production firms for transporting their own goods in a limited area. By comparison to the U.S. system of long-haul truck lines and independent truckers, the GDR faces underutilization of truck capacity and more double handling, as long-distance goods must be loaded into rail cars. Water transport is limited because canals are linked mainly to the Elbe and the Oder, rivers that are now parts of the GDR's national boundaries. The respective seaports belong to foreign nations. The maritime shipping industry, centered at Rostock, Wismar, and Stralsund, has been developed with considerable investments as a symbol of national prestige and a means for earning foreign currency. This effort has achieved moderate success, despite the absence of major canal linkages to any of these seaports. Efforts to increase the efficiency of the interlocking systems of truck-rail-maritime shipping feature conversion to containerization, which is well under way. Nevertheless, transport bottlenecks are still repeatedly cited as a major cause of idle labor and equipment in many production sectors, most notably in construction.

Passenger traffic in the GDR is about evenly divided between public and private modes. (In the Federal Republic the private share is about 80 percent.[36]) Motorcycles and mopeds are twice as numerous as au-

Table 4.4. Selected Indicators of German Democratic Republic Economic Performance and Plan, 1976–1980 and 1981–1985 (percentage increase)

	1976–1980 Reported	1981–1985 Plan
Produced national income	25.4	28–30
Industrial production	32.2	28–30
Industrial labor productivity	68[a]	28–30
Construction	27	18–20
Transport of goods	25.9	11–12
Foreign trade	40.7	36
Net personal income	20	20–22
Social fund	42	26
Real income per capita	23.7	21–23

[a]For the period 1970–1980

Source: Protokoll des X. Parteitages der Sozialistischen Einheitspartei Deutschlands, vol. 1 [Protocol of the Tenth Party Congress of the Socialist Unity Party of Germany] (Berlin: Dietz, 1981), pp. 52–63.

tomobiles, but the latter are increasingly evident, and urban traffic congestion is quite common during commuter hours. Despite the fact that fares cover less than half the cost of operating public transit, the volume of passenger traffic has remained steady, whereas the use of private vehicles increases annually.

Economic Prospects of the 1980s

The Tenth SED Congress took place in April 1981. As usual, the national economy occupied a central place in the addresses of the major speakers, who summarized the achievements since 1976 and outlined the tasks of the 1981–1985 plan. The economic report of General Secretary Erich Honecker, while subject to considerable data ambiguities, presented a good illustration of official views on the nation's strengths and weaknesses. Table 4.4 was compiled from elements of Honecker's report. These data are not comparable to the data presented earlier in this chapter; they should be interpreted primarily as a political statement.

In the figures presented and in the general tone of Honecker's report, there is an unmistakable sense of moderation.[37] Compared with ostensible recent achievements, most aggregate targets of the next Five-Year Plan are lower. On the other hand, the planned growth rates are considerably higher than the rates recently achieved by developed Western nations and much higher than the GDR's own recent growth rates, as calculated by Western economists.

It is, in fact, remarkable that national income should increase significantly, in view of the very serious constraints on the horizon. Honecker highlighted three major obstacles to economic growth: (1) a temporary absolute decline in the number of skilled workers entering the labor force, presumably a consequence of the political and economic uncertainties of the early 1960s; (2) a virtual end to planned increases in the import of energy and raw materials, due to rising world market costs and to the need to decrease the trade deficit with Western Europe; and (3) the Warsaw Pact decision to sharply increase defense spending in response to comparable North Atlantic Treaty Organization (NATO) developments.[38]

In attempting to resolve this awesome riddle, Honecker placed great reliance on more rational investment strategies and technological innovation, and he did so with great emphasis. Labor-saving investment seemed the highest priority. Automation of industrial processes is the focus of extraordinary expectations. The originally planned increase of nine thousand "industrial robots," observed the general secretary, must be increased forty to fifty-five thousand![39] A key to this dramatic change will be a rapid growth in microelectronics and the production of microcircuitry. No details on the appropriate investment strategy were provided. In any event, it is impossible to imagine such growth in automation without a tremendous increase in the purchase of both Western patented processes and Western automated machinery. This need may be related to the stated goal of sharply reducing raw-materials imports from hard-currency regions.

In general, new investments will be restricted to production that reduces the need for labor, through automation and the transfer of workers to expanded multiple-shift facilities. Outmoded technology will be dismantled, and there will be no more expansion in "green meadows."[40] Raw materials must be conserved as never before. The retrieval of waste metals and chemicals must be perfected in the quest for "closed cycles" of materials. Not only must energy consumption be curtailed, but new emphasis will be focused on nuclear and water power, "bio-gas," and "new electrochemical" power sources.

Great savings can be effected by shortening the time from the initiation of new projects to the stage of actual production. As a rule, suggested Honecker, two years should be the standard expectation. Such rapid shifts to new production are essential, if the GDR is to keep pace with technological change in diverse realms of industry, petrochemicals, and electronics. In addition to continued development of sophisticated production technologies, some of which are sold to Western nations, the East German economy must capitalize on borrowing Western technology in order to produce high-quality goods for East Europe and the less developed nations of the world.[41] In principle, a centrally directed economy with a highly skilled work force should be able to compete effectively with Western capitalist nations on the world market, provided that products and markets are carefully selected and internal bottlenecks are overcome. It is precisely this strategy that has increasingly become the hallmark of East German development goals. Honecker repudiated implicit suggestions that the GDR seek stability without growth: "A stable economic growth is indispensable for socialism; for human needs—the requirements of our socialist society—continue to grow, and only what has been produced may be distributed."[42]

How the wealth of East German socialism is distributed is the subject of the next chapter. But it can be noted that the 1981–1985 plan calls for increased personal income comparable to the preceding plan. The social fund—government spending on goods and services for public consumption—will grow more slowly than in the period 1976–1980, but it will nevertheless contribute to a planned increase in real income.[43]

Conclusion

As in any modern state, the health of the East German economy is the linchpin of national well-being. This fact is made all the more visible by the self-appointed East German role as the "showcase" of socialism. Economic success is the paramount element in the SED quest for legitimacy, and party leaders repeatedly emphasize the GDR's place among the ten most highly industrialized nations in the world.

This considerable achievement is today threatened by unfavorable shifts in the world economy, increasing costs for energy and raw materials, accelerating technological change, and intensified competition for world markets. These transformations are felt most acutely by a nation with few domestic resources other than a highly skilled work force. Flexible adaptation to the international economy offers the only hope for maintaining the East German record of success. Yet internal obstacles, including a declining work force and persistent rigidities in investment and supply structures, place the national economy under severe strain. Nothing less than a qualitative breakthrough to levels of efficiency unprecedented in a centrally directed economy is required.

Notes

1. Manfred Melzer, "The GDR Economic Policy Caught Between Pressure for Efficiency and Lack of Ideas," in Alec Nove, Hans-Hermann Höhmann, and Gertraud Seidenstecker, eds., *The East European Economies in the 1970s* (London: Butterworths, 1982), pp. 45–90.

2. Doris Cornelsen et al., *Handbook of the Economy of the German Democratic Republic* (Westmead, England: Saxon House, 1979), p. 28.

3. Hartmut Zimmermann, "The GDR in the 1970s," *Problems of Communism* 27, no. 2 (1978), pp. 15–18. See also Otto Rheinhold, "Gestaltung der entwickelten sozialistischen Gesellschaft im Lichte des Programmentwurfs [The Formation of Developed Socialist Society in Light of the Draft Program]," *Einheit*, no. 3 (1976), pp. 285–289.

4. Zimmermann, "The GDR in the 1970s," pp. 7–8.

5. Melzer, "The GDR Economic Policy," pp. 88–89.

6. Peter C. Ludz et al., *DDR Handbuch*, 2d ed. [GDR Handbook] (Cologne: Wissenschaft und Politik, 1979), pp. 1091–1099.

7. Cornelsen et al., *Handbook of the Economy of the German Democratic Republic*, p. 111.

8. Konstantin Pritzel, "Die Umweltpolitik in den intereuropäischen und innerdeutschen Beziehungen [Environmental Policy in Inter-European and Intra-German Relations]," *Deutschland Archiv* 13, no. 8 (1980), pp. 834–843.

9. Hannsjörg F. Buck and Bernd Spindler, "Luftbelastung in der DDR durch Schadstoffemissionen [Air Pollution Through Toxic Emissions in the GDR]," *Deutschland Archiv* 15, no. 9 (1982), pp. 943–958.

10. Reiner Raestrup and Thomas Weymar, "'Schuld ist allein der Kapitalmus': Umweltprobleme und ihre Bewältigung in der DDR ['Only Capitalism Is Guilty': Environmental Problems and Their Solutions in the GDR]," *Deutschland Archiv* 15, no. 8 (1982), pp. 832–844.

11. Jochen Bethkenhagen et al., *DDR und Osteuropa: Wirtschaftssystem, Wirtschaftspolitik, Lebensstandard* [GDR and East Europe: Economic System, Economic Policy, Standard of Living] (Opladen: Leske, 1981), p. 155.

12. Zimmermann, "The GDR in the 1970s," p. 23.

13. Cornelsen et al., *Handbook of the Economy of the German Democratic Republic*, p. 235.

14. Ibid., pp. 239–240.

15. Bethkenhagen et al., *DDR und Osteuropa*, p. 188.

16. Thad Alton et al., *Economic Growth in Eastern Europe, 1965, 1970, and 1975–1980* (New York: L. W. Financial Research, 1981), pp. 3, 8, 26.

17. Ibid., p. 26.

18. Cornelsen et al., *Handbook of the Economy of the German Democratic Republic*, pp. 83–93. Wilkens is a coauthor.

19. Ibid., p. 94.

20. Except where otherwise noted, the following sections on sectoral development rely on ibid., pp. 100–159.

21. Zentralverwaltung für Statistik, *Statistisches Jahrbuch 1980 der Deutschen Demokratischen Republik* (Berlin: Staatsverlag, 1980), p. 113.

22. *Protokoll des X. Parteitages der Sozialistischen Einheitspartei Deutschland* [Protocol of the Tenth Party Congress of the Socialist Unity Party of Germany] (Berlin: Dietz, 1981), p. 71.

23. Ibid., p. 72.

24. Wolfgang Stinglwagner, "Die Braunkohlenindustrie in der DDR—ein tragfähiger Brücke ins Atomzeitalter? [The Brown Coal Industry in the GDR—A Durable Bridge to the Atomic Age?]," *Deutschland Archiv* 14, no. 12 (1981), p. 1297.

25. Ibid., p. 1300.

26. Bethkenhagen et al., *DDR und Osteuropa*, p. 64.

27. Siegfried Kupper, "Geplante Stagnation: Zur zukunftigen Entwicklung der Wirtschaftsbeziehungen DDR-Sowjetunion [Planned Stagnation: On the Future Development of Economic Relations GDR–Soviet Union]," *Deutschland Archiv* 13, no. 3 (1980), pp. 225–228.

28. Bethkenhagen et al., *DDR und Osteuropa*, p. 62.

29. Cornelsen et al., *Handbook of the Economy of the German Democratic Republic*, p. 108.

30. Melzer, "The GDR Economic Policy," p. 77.

31. Cornelsen et al., *Handbook of the Economy of the German Democratic Republic*, p. 132.

32. Ibid., pp. 140–141.

33. Ibid., p. 142.

34. Ibid., p. 148.

35. Ibid.

36. Ibid., pp. 157–158.
37. *Protokoll des X. Parteitages*, pp. 51–75.
38. Ibid., pp. 64–68.
39. Ibid., p. 71.
40. Ibid., p. 72.
41. Ibid., pp. 73–74.
42. Erich Honecker, "Address to the Tenth Party Congress of the SED, April 11, 1981," *Deutschland Archiv* 14, no. 6 (June 1981), p. 646.
43. *Protokoll des X. Parteitages*, p. 60.

5
Social Policy

A pronounced characteristic of the Honecker era in East German politics has been the increasing emphasis on social outcomes as the end of economic policy. The "unity of economic policy and social policy" is a firmly established slogan of the current government. Political leaders miss no opportunity to stress that economic growth is not an end in itself, but a means to improved social welfare. The new SED Program of 1976 asserted: "Corresponding to the basic economic laws of socialism, the primary task in the formation of a developed socialist society consists of further elevating the material and cultural living standards of the people on the foundation of a rapid pace of development in socialist production, increased efficiency, scientific-technical progress, and a growth in labor productivity."[1]

After the distortions of the Stalinist period—when the "tonnage ideology" dictated success exclusively in terms of production volume—the current approach ostensibly restores the original Marxist concern with the quality of life. Importance attaches not only to the quantity of production, but also to the conditions of production and the purposes for which output is employed. Consequently, SED policy and government programs focus on "working and living conditions" as the two principal realms of human activity. As objects of public policy, the population is conceived as being made up of producers and consumers. Although conceptually distinct, these two roles are closely interdependent. Except for the very young and the very old, citizens carry out both roles simultaneously. Efforts to better comprehend the interdependence of production and consumption—at both the level of the whole society and the level of the individual—underlay the search for social theoretical breakthroughs in the last years of Ulbricht's rule; this was the thrust of the "cybernetic" model of society, which received so much attention in the late 1960s.[2] A similar, though less pretentious, concern is expressed in current writing on the unity of economic and social policy.

In the East German vocabulary, social policy is an extraordinarily broad concept, encompassing three main elements.[3] First, major attention is devoted to incomes policy, with the aim of providing differential rewards according to one's contribution to the nation's productive goals, while reducing unwarranted income inequality. Of concern here, also, are the tax policies that affect the net distribution of incomes. Second, a host of programs designed to enhance the public welfare are incorporated under the general heading of the "social fund." These state expenditures enhance the incomes of both employed persons and those who, for various reasons, are not presently part of the work force. Included in the social fund are expenditures for income maintenance, family support, health care, housing, education, job training, culture, recreation, and travel. Third, the concept of social policy is concerned with the net effect of income policy and social-fund spending, in terms of insuring satisfactory levels of performance both in the fulfillment of human needs and in the gradual elimination of fundamental social inequities. Success in these terms, it is expected, should also be manifested in higher levels of achievement among the economically active population. And further economic achievement permits a more effective social policy, in a seemingly endless spiral.

Wage Policy

For the economically active portion of the population, about 8.7 million people,[4] income comes chiefly through wages and salaries. In principle, a national wage policy exists to promote the four objectives of remuneration in accordance with actual work performance, reward for the acquisition of higher-skill levels, appropriate distribution of the labor force among economic sectors, and gradual elimination of wage inequalities among social groups. In approaching these goals, a number of practical difficulties emerge.

As with any other nation, socialist East Germany has been unable to devise universal standards of work performance. Consequently, the principle of payment according to performance cannot be rationally applied to harmonize pay rates across economic sectors (e.g., industry, agriculture, public administration). Even within a single production branch, this principle does not provide rational pay differentials between production workers, supervisory personnel, technical staff, and management. As a result, actual rates of remuneration have emerged through an incremental process, beginning with ideologically based adjustments to presocialist wage differentials. These adjustments included the virtual elimination of unearned income, the relative increase of pay for certain skilled labor, and the relative reduction of pay for some categories of professional work. In addition, public ownership removed disparities that had existed among private employers.

Table 5.1. Income Per Employee by Economic Sector, 1955, 1965, and 1978, as a Percentage of Average Income

	1955	1965	1978
Industry	105	103	101
Construction	100	107	104
Agriculture and forestry	74	89	97
Transport	101	105	110
Postal and communications	76	90	90
Trade	87	84	87

Source: Calculated from Zentralverwaltung für Statistik, *Statistisches Jahrbuch 1981 der Deutschen Demokratischen Republik* (Berlin: Staatsverlag, 1981), pp. 109, 137, 152, 169, 217, 232.

Subsequent shifts in the wage differentials among economic sectors cannot be linked to performance standards. The data in Table 5.1 show that, relative to average wages, construction and transport workers have improved their position, and the two lowest sectors, Agriculture/Forestry and Postal/Communications, have moved up much closer to the average. Most probably these changes are related to changes in skill levels. Although the need for skill improvement is great in all sectors, the proportion of the labor force involved in skill development has probably been highest in construction and transportation, corresponding to the increase of construction mechanization and to the growth of air travel. Technical innovation has also been significant in agriculture and communication, so that wage inducements to acquire better skills are appropriate. In addition, these sectors probably reflect a policy concern for reducing wage inequality.

Within economic sectors, especially the commodity-producing branches, wages have evolved through various experiments with incentives for higher achievements. Basic wages are established in agreements between industrial ministries and industrial labor unions. In the period 1960–1976, these rates showed very little change. Worker incomes did increase, however, chiefly through the growth of the "extra-performance wage," which was paid if production targets were reached. Although the extra-performance wage seemed to be a good expression of pay according to performance, it was only weakly linked to actual worker effort. Most often, an enterprise was entitled to an extra-performance wage when its highly effective (and politically well-connected) management was able to secure modest plan targets, large funding for capital investments, and dependable routes around the inevitable supply bottlenecks. In this setting, success bred further success, and the extra-performance wage acquired the character of a permanent component of monthly income, in some industries approaching 80 percent of the basic wage by the mid-1970s. For skilled production workers in privileged industries, the annual wage consisted of about 50 percent basic wage, 40 percent extra-performance wage, and 10 percent year-end bonus.[5]

This situation reflected an important aspect of political power in the GDR. Within the structure of economic planning, past economic performance acquires political significance. Large, high-profit enterprises, especially those in the "structure-determining" industries, have greater freedom to determine their own wage policies. Even though wage policies are subject to review by the labor-union federation, the FDGB, disproportionate influence accrues to the branch unions organized in the more successful industries. An alliance of management and union leaders in the privileged industrial branches secured the gradual expansion of the extra-performance wage at the expense of more comprehensive adjustments in basic wage rates.

In the nonagricultural sectors, this "back door" approach to wage increases has certain discriminatory effects.[6] First, significant wage differentials emerged among enterprises, according to the effectiveness of management, regardless of the efforts of workers. Second, even within the more successful enterprises, certain categories of employees—staff and administrative personnel—participate only marginally in the extra-performance wage. As a result of the shifting practices of wage determination, such personnel suffered a relative loss of income and a diminished incentive to acquire further job qualifications. Finally, because the "extra-performance wage" was not generally applied in sectors not actually producing goods (e.g., trade and services), workers in these areas were induced to seek jobs in industry, resulting in a distorted labor market.

Following the designation of Erich Honecker as SED general secretary in 1971, changes in the labor-union leadership also took place. In 1972 the FDGB formally called for a broad review of wage policy with the aim of overcoming accumulated inequities. Gradual reforms initiated in 1976 have the goal of restoring the basic wage to a level of about 90 percent of the total wage.[7] Within each economic sector, the reformed wage differentials ostensibly incorporate strong incentives to acquire specific job credentials. This policy assumes an approximate correspondence between skills possessed and actual performance. Separate performance indicators have not been abandoned. But the elimination of the extra-performance wage will reduce the variable portion of performance remuneration to 8–10 percent of the annual wage potentially encompassed by the year-end bonus.[8]

Efforts to reduce wage differentials are often inconsistent with the use of wage policy to reward performance and affect the acquisition of job skills and the distribution of the labor force. Nevertheless, the government has adopted a policy of allowing wages for lower-paid workers to rise at faster rates than for higher-paid workers. In addition, periodic adjustments are made in the legal minimum wage, which has been about 42–45 percent of the average wage since about 1967.[9]

Wage discrimination among social groups, especially sex discrimination, is illegal. "Equal pay for equal work" is an expressed principle of GDR wage policy, and there is no evidence to contradict this claim. Nevertheless, women are disproportionately concentrated in lower-paying jobs, and thus their average income is significantly lower than men's. This discrepancy is explained by the persistence of cultural values and child-rearing practices, which inhibit women from selecting certain occupations and from pursuing higher employment qualifications. At most social levels, married couples still give clear priority to the husband's career interests.

A primary measure of wage policy is the distribution of disposable income, that is, take-home pay after payroll deductions for personal income tax and social-security tax. Personal income is taxed at a moderately progressive rate, ranging from 10-20 percent, with some forms of income (bonuses, overtime) exempted or taxed at lower rates.[10] Very small rate reductions apply to married couples and households with dependent children. Higher rates apply to income earned outside the socialist sectors by independent professionals, artisans, clergy, and private shopkeepers. In 1975 the "average effective tax rate on personal incomes in the GDR was 7.2 percent."[11] Except for persons earning the minimum wage, the redistributive effect of personal income tax is slight. The social-security tax on employees is 10 percent of monthly income up to 600 marks, a figure below the average income.[12] For income above 600 marks, the employee may make voluntary additional payments for entitlement to supplementary retirement benefits. About 65 percent of those eligible are enrolled in the supplemental program. Social-security taxes amount to about 6.6 percent of income.[13] Because a portion of higher incomes is excluded from the compulsory program, the social-security tax has an overall moderately regressive effect, typical among industrial nations.

Taken together, deductions for personal income tax and social-security tax reduced the typical East German paycheck about 13.8 percent in 1975. By comparison, income-tax and social-security deductions in the Federal Republic amounted to 27.4 percent of gross pay.[14] In Scandinavia and the United Kingdom, deductions were even higher. Compared to the GDR, all of these countries made greater use of progressive income taxation as a means for reducing income inequality.

Table 5.2. Distribution of Disposable Household Incomes in Quintiles, for German Democratic Republic (GDR) and Federal Republic of Germany (FRG), 1960 and 1974

| | Share in Net Income | | | |
| Proportion of Households | 1960 | | 1974 | |
	GDR	FRG	GDR	FRG
1st Quintile	10.4	8.4	10.9	9.3
2nd Quintile	15.3	12.6	16.2	13.3
3rd Quintile	19.2	16.4	19.8	17.0
4th Quintile	23.4	22.8	23.2	22.1
5th Quintile	31.7	39.8	29.9	38.3

Source: Doris Cornelsen et al., *Handbook of the Economy of the German Democratic Republic* (Westmead, England: Saxon House, 1979), p. 210.

Distribution of disposable income is one step in determining the degree of inequality in the standard of living. Because households are regarded as the primary unit of expenditure in any economy, income inequality is commonly measured in terms of household income. Household income is a product of both the level of wages and the number of economically active persons per household. East German figures for household income reflect the very high rates of female participation in the work force.

GDR data on income distribution are not readily adapted to conventional measures. Table 5.2 shows a computation by the staff of the German Institute for Economic Research. Under perfect equality, each quintile of households would receive 20 percent of personal income. Note that in both nations the percentage shares for the lower quintiles increased slightly from 1960 to 1974, while the shares of the higher quintiles decreased. These changes signify reduced income inequality. As a rough form of comparison, it can be observed that in 1974 the sum of the deviations from perfect equality in East Germany is about two-thirds the sum in the Federal Republic. Since income inequality in the Federal Republic is moderate by the standards of West Europe and North America, East Germany has emerged as a leader among industrialized states in the effort to reduce income inequalities.

But elements in addition to disposable income have a marked effect on the level and equality of economic well-being.

Principle of the Social Fund

In Western capitalist economies, particularly those European nations with highly developed systems of public welfare, the popular standard of living consists of both employment income and a complex of public benefits defined as "social income." In its broadest sense, social income includes money transfers, goods, and services, which are paid for by public funds and consumed by individuals. Thus, social income does not encompass expenditures for purely collective goods and services such as national defense, foreign relations, public roadways, and general administrative costs of government. Specifically included are government contributions to income maintenance (social security, welfare grants), health care, education, housing, and cultural and recreational facilities.

In the socialist states of Eastern Europe, and particularly in the German Democratic Republic, a similar concept—the "social fund"—is employed to indicate public contributions to individual consumption. Compared to the social-income categories of Western Europe and North America, the socialist social fund differs in two ways. First, it is defined very broadly, to include as many forms of public expenditure as can be reasonably included in the general definition. One such important addition is a complex of subsidies to insure low and stable prices for consumer goods. Second, the social fund is not the exclusive concern of government. Although the state provides roughly 75 percent of social-fund expenditures in the GDR, an additional 25 percent is expended from the resources of production enterprises and from social organizations, principally the labor-union federation.[15] This second distinction is a major reason why data given under the two different systems are not comparable, chiefly because social income does not include expenditures by churches, charities, and other public-service organizations.

A major element in the social policy of the Socialist Unity party is the gradual increase in the share of consumption financed through the social fund. As a general principle, consumption by way of the social fund is to grow more rapidly than personal income, although income from employment is to remain the primary means by which economically active persons satisfy both their individual and family needs. In ideological terms, the increasing significance of the social fund lays important groundwork for the gradual transition to the early phase of communist society. The share of the social fund in the total disposable income of economically active households has increased from 24.9 percent in 1960 to 33.4 percent in 1978.[16] For people not part of the statistically standard four-person working household (i.e., pensioners, invalids), the relevance of the social fund is naturally much greater.

The following presentation summarizes the main components of the contemporary social fund.

Income Maintenance

The oldest, most widely implemented form of social policy is income maintenance. The purpose of income-maintenance programs is to replace at least part of a worker's earnings lost due to old age or disability. The first such national program, known as social security, was a German invention of the 1880s. To the present day, social security has been continued and supplemented in several ways.

The East German social-security system is compulsory and nearly universal: 85 percent of the population—those in the socialist economy—are covered by the FDGB (labor union) program; the self-employed and members of cooperatives are under a separate state insurance program.[17] Particularly in the FDGB program, great emphasis is placed upon "self-administration." While full-time FDGB personnel manage the system on a territorial basis, administration in the work place is handled by union volunteers. Disputes over entitlements are arbitrated by special commissions of workers and salaried employees elected by the local unions. Self-administration is intended to promote a greater sense of worker responsibility and class unity, to reduce administrative costs, and (implicitly) to promote a more positive orientation toward the union organizations.

As in most social-security systems, the East German programs link entitlements to the length of employment and the recorded level of income over an extended period. In all cases a basic payment of 110 marks per month is guaranteed; for work experience of fifteen years or more, the minimum retirement benefit is 270–340 marks per month.[18] Under the compulsory program, the maximum benefit is 600 marks. (For purposes of comparison, in 1978 the minimum monthly wage was 300 marks; the average monthly wage was 897 marks.) Additional benefits are paid for death expenses, dependent children and students, and cases of need for special physical care. Since 1971, employees have been able to earn supplemental retirement benefits through voluntary additional social-security contributions from earnings. For war victims, individuals honored for state service, and certain employment categories (miners, scientists, professors), special provisions permit the payment of retirement benefits at somewhat higher rates.

Over the years, the East German social-security system has been the focus of much popular dissatisfaction. Payments for citizens with typical employment records are generally considered too low. For elderly widows, with little employment history, the small pension amount is plainly inadequate to provide for monthly maintenance. In recent years, significant upward adjustments have been made. In 1980 the average monthly pension was 335 marks, or 37 percent of the average after-tax income in the socialist sector.[19]

Given the great variability among nations in terms of their compulsory social-security systems, the availability of nongovernmental retirement schemes, differences in purchasing power with respect to the distinctive consumption patterns of the elderly, as well as deficient data regarding the impact on different categories of recipients, a comparative evaluation is extremely tenuous. Within the industrialized West, significant variations appear between the comprehensive Swedish and British systems and the more modest U.S. system. For our present purposes, nevertheless, the following observations compare East German social security to the standards of other industrial societies.[20]

1. The demographic structure of the GDR is exceptionally unfavorable. Relative to the size of the present work force, the number of elderly pensioners is extremely high: roughly 30 pensioners for every 100 wage-earners. This ratio is about one-fourth higher than for Sweden and West Germany, twice the ratio for the United States, and four times the ratio for the Soviet Union. This heavy demographic burden helps to explain why social-security spending as a share of gross domestic product (about 8 percent) is higher than in all other European states except Czechoslovakia.

2. The extent to which pension benefits make up for loss of income in retirement (the earnings replacement rate) is considerably below the rate for governmental programs in most European states, but comparable to those in North America.

3. In many Western capitalist nations, compulsory government social security is supplemented by nongovernmental retirement schemes, especially for employees with above-average incomes. Such schemes have the effect of both raising the average level of retirement income and increasing the income differentials among pension recipients, relative to the GDR.

4. Despite recent increases in the minimum retirement benefit, the redistributive (equalizing) effect of GDR pensions is not as great as in some wealthier nations. This results from the still considerable range between minimum and maximum benefits and from supplements available to employees in the higher-income range. In other words, the income differentials established during one's working career tend to be preserved in retirement years.

5. A distinctive feature is the recognition given to nonemployed mothers, as performing socially useful work. For the purpose of calculating earnings-related retirement benefits, East German women now receive credit for the time they stay out of the work force to rear small children.

6. About half the cost of GDR social security is paid for by government funds; the remainder is divided almost equally between direct employee and employer taxes. This represents a lower rate of employee contribution than is common in the West, and a lower rate of government support than is typical in Eastern Europe. Government subsidies to the social-

security system represent an increasing share—currently about 18 percent—of the total state budget.[21]

7. Consumption patterns for retired persons typically reveal relatively high shares of household income devoted to food, housing, health care, and travel. The East German government spends considerable money to subsidize the provision of these goods and services, insuring low consumer prices. This practice of price subsidy has the effect of augmenting the utility of modest pension benefits, and thus reducing the generally unfavorable comparison between pensioners in East Germany and in Western Europe.[22]

Unemployment Compensation

All modern capitalist nations maintain unemployment insurance as a means to offset loss of income during periods of involuntary temporary unemployment. Initially, the FDGB social-security system included an extremely small unemployment benefit of around 10 percent of the minimum wage.[23] Unemployment insurance has always been ideologically repugnant and, due to the acute labor shortage, increasingly superfluous. This insurance provision was abolished in 1977.

Of course, current industrial modernization does occasionally reduce the need for labor in individual enterprises. National labor law makes the employer enterprise responsible for retraining displaced workers and/or locating alternative employment. This process is facilitated when the labor union participates effectively in the early stages of modernization planning. Displaced workers are entitled to full pay until alternate employment is provided. If a worker is transferred to a lower-paying job, the previous employer is obligated to cover the loss of income for one year. These progressive measures resemble recent Swedish efforts to deal with technologically determined "structural" unemployment.

Family Allowances and Related Support

East German social policy places great emphasis upon the family as the fundamental unit of social organization and the starting point for acquiring social values. In the face of a declining work force, the government also has emphasized the need for families to produce children. Comprehensive pronatalist policies are designed to overcome a very low birthrate.[24] At the same time, an ideological concern for sex equality, combined with the economic need for maximum female participation in the work force, places a premium on employment for all women—including those of child-bearing years.

In an effort to facilitate the employment of mothers and to reduce the financial strains of family life, the GDR has gradually introduced an advanced program of family allowances and other types of support.

Young married couples under the age of twenty-six are eligible for an eight-year interest-free government loan, equal to about five-months combined income, with which to purchase home furnishings. They may also apply for a second loan of the same amount to buy shares in cooperative housing or to help build a private dwelling. In either case, a portion of the loan repayment is cancelled with the birth of each child; no repayment is due if three children are born in eight years.

Every family receives a grant of 1,000 marks (about one month's income for young couples) with the birth of each child. In addition, the social-security program provides twenty-six weeks of maternity leave at full pay, plus an additional seven-months leave for either parent at 75 percent pay—in the case of the second and subsequent children. From state funds each family receives a monthly allowance, ranging from 20 marks for the first child to 70 marks for the fifth, and an annual clothing supplement of 25 marks for each child.

Additional family support is granted in the form of free lunches for school children, heavily subsidized care for preschool-age children, and after-school care for children of elementary-school age. Only a fraction of these benefits is paid for by government funds; the rest is provided by employers and/or labor unions. As a result, the availability of these services and the level of direct costs to parents is varied. Parents who work for profitable enterprises with effective labor unions derive the greatest benefit.

Working mothers have their workday reduced by forty-five minutes with no pay reduction. Mothers are granted unpaid leave to care for sick children; single mothers receive half pay for this purpose.

In sum, the East German system of family support is among the most comprehensive in the world.[25] Although many other European nations supply family allowances (some considerably more generous), only Sweden endeavors to provide for such a wide range of family needs. Not surprisingly, family-support programs are perhaps the most popular dimension of GDR social policy.

Health Care

East German law regards necessary health care as an entitlement of all citizens, without regard to their financial circumstances.[26] Health care is provided through social-fund expenditures in the form of a national health service. More than 96 percent of all physicians and 82 percent of dentists are employed by state institutions. Nearly 93 percent of the hospital beds are found in public hospitals or medical schools (10 percent); the remainder are in private hospitals, most maintained by religious orders, which receive government compensation for services.

Table 5.3. Medical Personnel and Facilities in Selected Countries, ca. 1975–1977 (per 10,000 population)

	Physicians	Dentists	Hospital Beds
German Democratic Republic (GDR)	19.0	5.0	108
Federal Republic of Germany (FRG)	21.0	5.2	118
Council for Mutual Economic Assistance (Europe)[a]	20.3	3.8	91
European Communities[b]	17.4	4.3	98
United States	16.5	5.1	66
Sweden	16.3	8.8	152

[a]Bulgaria, Czechoslovakia, GDR, Hungary, Poland, Romania, USSR
[b]Belgium, Denmark, FRG, France, Greece, Ireland, Italy, Luxembourg, Netherlands, United Kingdom.
Source: Statistisches Bundesamt, *Statistisches Jahrbuch 1979 für die Bundesrepublik Deutschland* (Stuttgart: W. Kohlhammer, 1979), pp. 675–676.

Citizens pay no subscription or user fee and no fee for prescription drugs.

In general, the quality of medical training and medical facilities in the GDR is comparable to the standards in the world's most developed nations (Table 5.3). Only Sweden can be considered to provide a consistently higher level of care to all citizens. The relatively high percentage of elderly in East Germany places a special burden on the health service, and the relatively high population density permits a more even distribution of facilities than is possible in the United States and the Soviet Union.

The GDR health service performs well on most indicators of health quality. Life expectancy is sixty-nine years for men and seventy-five years for women.[27] These figures lag behind the very high rates for Japan and Sweden, for example, but are comparable to the achievements of most nations in West Europe and North America and better than East Europe. The most common causes of death in the GDR, especially cardiovascular ailments, appear in proportions similar to the Federal Republic and other wealthy European nations.[28] However, in the GDR—as in the United Kingdom and Czechoslovakia—somewhat higher rates of mortality occur from respiratory diseases. As recognized by official sources, this finding reflects the density of industry and the high production of industrial air pollution. On the other hand, the GDR provides excellent care for mothers and children; the nation is a world leader in reducing mortality in childbirth and infant mortality.

Recent efforts to improve the quality of health care highlight concerns also common in the Western industrialized nations.[29] First, the provision of health services is distributed unevenly across regions. In particular, both facilities and physicians per capita are more satisfactory in Berlin and in the slower-growing northern regions than in the industrial south. In other words, medical care has not kept pace with population migration. Within the agricultural regions, there is a sharp difference in available medical technology between urban centers and rural areas. Second, despite the planning advantage of a national health service over market arrangements, the GDR has not entirely avoided a maldistribution of physicians among categories of primary care and specialization. Although the problem is by no means as acute as in the United States, for example, it is still necessary to recruit a much higher percentage of physicians into family medicine and other branches of primary care.

Finally, despite the rather good performance of the health service in statistical terms, there has been much public dissatisfaction with the impersonal quality of care. This complaint flows inexorably from the bureaucratic atmosphere that emerges in the large, integrated "polyclinics." Patients may be abruptly referred from department to department, where their case histories are reviewed *ad nauseum*. With repeated visits, a patient may consult a different physician each time, with no sense of continuing trust. Although this complaint is common in many countries, it is especially severe in national health-service systems.

An additional source of discontent—especially among older citizens—may have been the changing attributes of physicians. In the period before the Berlin border was closed in 1961, physicians constituted a disproportionately large share of emigrants, mainly due to the much higher income potential in the Federal Republic. The urgent need to replace departed physicians under relatively modest pay conditions brought about an influx of women into medical schools. A profession formerly dominated by older males became increasingly populated by younger females. Even in a society supposedly undergoing cultural transformation, the frequent loss of the "fatherly" family physician was undoubtedly resented.

Since the mid-1970s, two remedies have been implemented. First, the medical profession in general—and the primary-care branches in particular—has been made more attractive through increased salaries and special retirement supplements. Second, procedures in polyclinics have been modified to provide, wherever possible, "free patient choice" of physician, with the aim of developing "better trust relationships." Other recent changes include accelerated investment for medical schools, clinics, and training and transport for emergency medical care.

Education and Training

One of the largest components of social-fund expenditures is the "unified system of education and training." In both official sources and commentaries by foreign specialists in education and manpower policies, the East German system has been widely praised. Many of its achievements are indeed dramatic, especially in terms of the extent of reform from the prewar period. Yet conditions in recent years have become somewhat more controversial.[30]

The core of the GDR education scheme is the ten-year general school, beginning at age seven. The present completion rate for this compulsory program is more than 90 percent. (Children aged three to six attend optional kindergartens, which currently serve 87 percent of the eligible population.) In contrast to the prewar system and many contemporary West European systems, the present general school is a *comprehensive* school. There is no segregation of intermediate and secondary pupils into normal, technical, or elite-oriented curricula; instead, all children pursue essentially the same course of study until tenth grade. (Americans are long accustomed to comprehensive schools.) This practice avoids the tendency of segregated schools to reinforce class divisions in society, in which only the children of educated or wealthy parents take part in a college-bound curriculum, while others are "groomed" for the subordinate laboring class.

By delaying the process of segregation according to academic ability ("streaming") until the end of this ten-year program, GDR educators hope to provide students of worker and farm families ample opportunity to overcome cultural handicaps. During the tenth year, teachers single out students likely to succeed in the two-year Expanded Secondary School (EOS). In 1977 only about 9 percent of eighteen- and nineteen-year-olds were enrolled in the Expanded Secondary School (11 percent in 1971). Although pertinent data are incomplete, it is obvious that the EOS is by far the most important channel for entry into the nation's colleges and universities, with the majority of EOS graduates actually matriculating. Consequently, the tenth-year screening process has a profound effect on both the structure of society and the career chances of the individual.

Paralleling the general schools are a limited number of special schools (for physically and mentally handicapped children) and specialized schools (for youngsters gifted in performing arts, sports, foreign language, and science). In aggregate, these schools encompass as high as 4 percent of school children aged eleven to seventeen. In Cottbus and Dresden counties, optional schools provide instruction in the native language of the small Sorb-speaking minority.

For 85 percent of eighteen-year-olds, their major activity includes neither the EOS nor immediate employment. Instead, they enter some form of vocational training. Three-fourths of the vocational schools are attached to production enterprises; the remainder are sponsored by local governments. Most curricula require about two years of classroom and practical study to acquire the *Facharbeiter* (specialist worker) credential. For students who did not complete the ten-year general school (18 percent) and for those seeking the equivalent of the EOS certificate (4 percent), the program requires an additional year. In any case, the vocational school provides more than occupational training; required subjects also include language, mathematics, history, government, and sport. This program is in some respects comparable to curricula offered in many U.S. community colleges.

A higher level of education consists of the 233 technicians' schools, narrowly defined institutions more or less operated by specific economic and government ministries to produce highly skilled employees. In 1977, these schools admitted 51,300 new students, roughly one-fifth the number of vocational school graduates in the same year. The GDR has 5 universities and 48 technical colleges, covering various forms of engineering, commerce, medicine, education, agriculture, and the arts. In 1977, these institutions admitted 32,914 new students, about 9,000 more than the number of EOS graduates, and 12.5 percent of the nation's nineteen-year-olds. (Comparable institutions in the Federal Republic enrolled 13.9 percent of nineteen-year-olds.) It is worth noting that enrollments in both technicians' schools and universities and colleges are down nearly 20 percent from their peak in 1971, when sharp cuts were made to harmonize the educational output with the employment needs of the national economy.

In addition to this essentially integrated system of education and training, the GDR has emulated the Soviet pattern of continuing education for people in the work force who, for one reason or another, had earlier broken off their formal education. Through a combination of correspondence courses and evening and weekend classes offered in the work place, a great many older workers have been able to complete their schooling through the eighth or tenth grade. Some unskilled workers have even earned their *Facharbeiter* credential in this way.

Apart from nominal charges for adult education, the government pays all the costs of education and training. The government also pays living allowances to most students at colleges and universities, as well as to rural students who must go to urban centers to attend an Expanded Secondary School. In the case of workers attending an advanced technicians' school, enterprise and labor-union funds are used for tuition and living expenses.

These high levels of support for education and occupational training are vigorously publicized by the party and government as evidence of the superiority of socialism. Despite the generous state support for education in the United States (the world leader in per capita educational spending) and increasing rates of expenditure in West Europe, it is true that no capitalist nation has equalled the GDR in providing educational opportunity without regard to family income.

The constitution provides to all citizens the right "to proceed to the next higher education level, in accord with the principle of achievement, societial requirements, and with regard for the social structure of the population." In other words, citizen claims on educational opportunity are not unlimited. Beyond the compulsory ten-year school, entrance to educational programs is determined by competition for limited places. The distribution of openings is the result of planned needs for employees with various types of educational and occupational credentials. Extensive career counseling is provided in an effort to harmonize aspirations with real opportunity. Compared with many Western nations, this practice sharply restricts individual choice; on the other hand, it also helps to avoid the penalty for unwise choices—the inability to find employment for which one is properly qualified. From the standpoint of the national economy, effective career planning reduces the waste of manpower resources.

By and large, competition is based almost exclusively on classroom grades and examinations. However, repeated social misbehavior, including public disrespect for school authorities, can be a barrier to advanced study. Church authorities also report that religious practice is a common reason why admission to higher education is denied.

Despite efforts to eliminate unequal educational attainment based on social class, the children of educated and otherwise privileged parents earn a disproportionate share of advanced degrees. In the late 1970s, children of worker-class and farm families, who make up about 86 percent of the population, represented only 60 percent of university and college students. This proportion is a considerable improvement over earlier years, and it compares very favorably to the proportions in most Western nations; yet it is still unsatisfactory to SED authorities. Remaining imbalances are probably attributable to more positive parental attitudes, higher achievement values, and lower need to supplement family income through early employment evident in the intelligentsia class. Consequently, colleges practice mandated "positive discrimination" by adding a class-preference increment to entrance scores of students from working-class and farm backgrounds. The overall effect of these measures is to provide, in East German terms, a highly "democratic" educational system, as a foundation for an increasingly democratic society.

The average level of educational attainment, measured in terms of years of schooling, is very high by world standards, especially for people born after 1945. The GDR ranks first (with Czechoslovakia) among European communist states.[31] Although it lags well behind the nations of North America and Scandinavia, it has surpassed the Federal Republic, France, and other West European nations.

However, in recent years, reservations have been increasingly expressed concerning the *quality* of education.[32] East German educators and politicians have pointed out the inability of research institutions to keep pace with technological innovations in the most advanced nations, as well as the reluctance of administrative staff in economic, government, and social institutions to assume an assertive posture toward problem solving. Following a rush of experiments with "improved" incentives for more autonomous initiative, attention has been focused on the educational system. A frequent criticism has been that studies at all levels have placed a premium on learning specific facts and prescribed responses, to the detriment of student-initiated inquiry.

In some measure this problem stems from the centralized character of the school system, as well as the desire to insure equal education for all. Early concern over the political reliability of teachers was also a factor. The result is a nationally uniform set of instructional material for every subject at every grade level. Schools and teachers are evaluated primarily by their students' scores on tests with narrowly prescribed answers. Rote memorization becomes the dominant mode of learning, regardless of the subject of study. On the whole, students become extremely adept at solving problems for which there are predetermined solutions.

An acute difficulty arises, however, when the tasks of leadership or technological innovation require choices for which there is no obvious precedent.[33] This shortcoming is, perhaps, inconsequential for the average citizen, whose tasks at work and in daily life are more or less routine. But the impact is quite different when the management of an increasingly complex society requires the gradual decentralization of leadership roles. Thus, it is particularly devastating when internal critics denounce universities and colleges for employing "grade school" teaching methods.

Anxiety over the quality of education is hardly unique to the GDR or to socialist states in general. Americans, for example, fret over the discovery of "functional illiteracy." Yet the focus of concern is rather different. In the United States, where elite education is of the highest order, questions arise about the quality and equality of mass education. East Germans, on the other hand, are justifiably proud of their system of mass education, but they confront grave questions about the education of the nation's leaders.

Housing Policy

Despite government claims that its comprehensive housing subsidy constitutes one of the most democratic features of socialism, no element of East German social policy has aroused more public dissatisfaction than housing policy.[34]

On the positive side, it is quite true that household costs for housing are extremely low in the GDR, especially when compared to West Europe and North America. A "typical" household pays only 3–6 percent of its net earned income for rent and utilities, with lower rent charged to those with low income.[35] This is made possible by universal rent controls, plus extensive social-fund (state, enterprise, and labor union) subsidies for construction and maintenance.[36] The subsidies program has the effect of redistributing income in favor of the elderly and other low-income citizens. In this one respect, then, East Germans are spared the infamous "housing squeeze" that affects so many U.S. household budgets.

On the negative side, however, East Germany has long faced an overall housing shortage of very serious proportions. In the immediate postwar period, the availability of housing was good by prevailing European standards—notably better, in fact, than in the Federal Republic, with its greater war damage and higher rates of immigration. But the demands of socialist reconstruction, combined with heavy Soviet-imposed reparations, meant that new construction activity was concentrated overwhelmingly in the industrial sector. Some impressive new housing projects were completed in Berlin and other major cities, but the slow pace of new construction and the niggardly allocations of funds and materials for remodeling meant that the East German housing stock steadily deteriorated.

In simple numbers of residences per capita, the GDR seems adequately supplied, thanks to a stagnant population. However, citizens must reckon with poor quality and poor facilities in the majority of homes, as well as poor distribution by regions and optimal use.

As late as 1971, 52 percent of East German residences had been built before World War I, 22 percent between the wars, and only 26 percent since 1945.[37] (Comparable figures for the Federal Republic were 27, 17, and 56 percent.) Per capita living space (79 square feet) was one-fourth less than in the Federal Republic; it was also the lowest among the European communist states.[38] Despite a sharply accelerated renovation program, in 1977 roughly half of all residences still had no indoor toilet, and nearly three-fourths had no central heating. Such widespread lack of amenities obviously impinges on the quality of everyday life.

Beyond these housing problems, expressed in national averages, mal-distribution of limited resources poses additional problems for specific categories of households.[39] A considerable, though unspecified, share of housing is occupied by elderly individuals or couples with no dependent children; in contrast, there are numerous cases of large families or even two distinct households crowded into a very modest residence. Many of the underutilized residences are suburban private dwellings, whose owners cannot be legally evicted. A slow and only moderately successful approach has been to offer attractive, low-cost retirement centers as an inducement to elderly owners of private homes, whose residences could be made available to large families.

The East German trend toward smaller, nuclear families—an apparently universal attribute of modern societies—clashes sharply with the continuing need for two families to share the same residence. No data are published on the extent of this condition, but the government has promised that "by 1985, in nearly every city and community, each family will occupy its own residence."[40]

This maldistribution of housing according to use is closely related to the poor regional distribution. On the whole, the space availability of housing is best in rural areas and in the "showcase" boroughs of large cities—Berlin, above all. Housing conditions are especially poor in the older communities of medium size. But it is also clear that the shortage of good-quality housing is most acute in the southern metropolitan areas of Halle, Leipzig, Karl-Marx-Stadt, and Dresden. These are precisely the areas undergoing the greatest industrial expansion and thus the greatest need for attracting more skilled labor. Labor-union efforts to counteract the persistent labor shortage visibly foundered on the workers' long-standing complaints of poor housing. Many qualified workers, it seemed, were unwilling to exchange better jobs for poorer residences.

One of the first priorities of the Honecker leadership was to formulate a vigorous response. First, the rate of increase for housing expenditure was doubled, leading to a 100 percent increase in annual expenditure over ten years.[41] Second, increased state credit and enterprise subsidies sharply accelerated the activity of workers' housing cooperatives. Workers buy shares and pay monthly contributions, according to the level of household income and the size of the needed residence. A part of these payments may be in the form of labor. In principle, each cooperative member can expect to own and occupy a new residence within three years. In 1971–1973 the number of new residences constructed annually by cooperatives increased from 17,200 to 32,500 and has increased since that time.[42]

Third, in terms of both credit provisions and materials allocations, the opportunity for private construction of new housing was greatly expanded. This policy reflects not only the urgency of the housing crisis but also the increasing ability of some high-earning households to accumulate sufficient savings to undertake such a large project. As a result the number of new residences constructed by individuals increased from 2,200 in 1971 to 11,200 in 1975. Since then it has held a steady share of about 11 percent of total housing construction.[43] Fourth, direct government (national and local) expenditures for housing have grown steadily, so that the state sector still accounts for about two-thirds of all new construction and remodeling.[44]

In sum, it is clear that housing conditions in the GDR suffered measurably from years of neglect. In the last decade, however, housing policy has undergone a marked transformation. The long-term goal, planned for 1976–1990, foresees the construction or remodeling of roughly 3 million residences, tangibly affecting nearly half the total population.[45] Recent indications are that this plan is proceeding rather close to schedule.

Cultural and Recreational Facilities

One of the basic rights offered citizens under East German social policy is access to cultural and recreational activities. Although cultural activities can be very broadly defined, in this context the chief reference is to such things as museums and the performing arts.[46] Considerable emphasis is placed on a lively repertoire of drama and musical performances, representing not only the achievements under socialism but also the rather considerable achievements of the German nation over several centuries. State subsidies for public admission are ostensibly intended to make artistic culture available to all social segments, thus overcoming the class bias of culture in capitalist nations. Fragmentary evidence suggests that, because of differential rates of participation, cultural subsidies in fact represent a disproportionate benefit to the more highly educated classes. Support for the performing arts is also intended to strengthen a sense of national identity, through greater awareness of German contributions. The vigorous level of cultural activity in Berlin has the added benefit of attracting foreign visitors and much-needed hard currency. Cultural events are subsidized by national and local government funds, following a long-standing German tradition evident today also in the Federal Republic.

The favored position of sports participation symbolizes the GDR's approach to recreation.[47] Thanks largely to the personal commitment of SED First Secretary Walter Ulbricht, the nation launched a drive to sports excellence, which has resulted in extraordinary achievements at the Olympic Games and other international competitions. First conceived as a means to circumvent the nation's diplomatic isolation from many international organizations, this comprehensive program of selection, training, and incentives stands as an unequaled example of a nationally orchestrated sports program.

Although public benefits flow heavily to distinguished athletes, national policy does not neglect the general population. A broad spectrum of competitive and recreational sports is offered to both school children and older people through the auspices of the youth organization and the labor unions. Participation is heavily subsidized, occasionally at 100 percent, with the majority of this subsidy coming from unions or sponsoring enterprises. Again the intent is to minimize class bias in sports participation. However, this particular mode of financing through nongovernmental sources means that the quality of sports programs varies according to the strength of economic activity in the community.

Vacation facilities and summer camps for youngsters constitute an important element of public recreation. Vacation resorts and campgrounds are operated by labor unions or local governments. About half the funding for acquisition and maintenance is provided out of enterprise funds; some large enterprises actually have their own resorts. For the majority of vacationers, lodging arrangements and subsidies are arranged through their union committee. Preference in scheduling the always scarce July–August accommodations is supposedly given to the "best" workers.

Summer camps for youngsters have long been a party priority, especially because of their potential for serving the goal of "socialist upbringing." In their general contours, these one- to three-week camps are recognizable by U.S. and European standards. They are distinguished from scouting experiences chiefly by their lower cost and by their much more explicit emphasis on patriotic and vocational themes.

A notable feature of vacation policy in the last decade has been the growing endorsement of vacations as a family activity. This has been a difficult goal, not only because of the shortage of vacation space but also because of the complexities of scheduling the vacations of two parents through two separate union committees (wherever they have different employers). In recent years the resort facilities at the disposal of the FDGB have been sharply increased. In addition, there has been an increase in the number of independently arranged vacations, especially as more families acquire automobiles and the equipment needed for itinerant camping trips.

It is very difficult to determine a monetary benefit for this segment of social policy, because of the complexities of funding. Official sources estimate that social-fund expenditures (from government, enterprises, and social organizations) for cultural and recreational amenities doubled in the period 1971–1978 to about 2.2 billion marks.[48] This is equivalent to nearly 3 percent of the net earnings for the average household. A comparison with Western democracies is not possible, because data from these countries do not include the very substantial relevant spending by nongovernmental organizations.

Consumption and Standards of Living

Although SED authorities insist that popular well-being is more than a simple matter of satisfying material wants, the nation's general level of consumption and the distribution of material benefits are a constant leadership concern. Government achievements are most often expressed in terms of an increasing standard of living, and those official institutions most directly in contact with the public—local governments and labor unions—find that factors affecting the material conditions of life are the most common source of citizen inquiries and complaints. Like citizens in other developed nations, East Germans tend to credit themselves for their personal material progress and to blame the government when personal achievements do not match expectations. Consequently, the material aspect of social policy represents a prime element in the search of the political leadership for greater popular legitimacy.

In the modern world it is common practice for governments to seek to alter consumption patterns through price ceilings, price supports, excise and value-added taxes, and deductions from income-tax liabilities. Americans, for example, are familiar with agricultural subsidies, price restrictions on natural gas, and taxes on the consumption of fuel, alcohol, and tobacco. Many West European governments engage in similar practices on an even wider scale. Some nations, such as France, derive the greatest share of government revenue from value-added (or turnover) taxes imposed on the value accruing to commodities at various stages of production—ultimately increasing the purchase price. Taxes on sales and production are, in general, regressive; that is, they take a greater share of expenditures of low-income households. Conversely, price subsidies are progressive.

In this context, the GDR and other European communist states are distinguished by the wider scope of commodities affected by such policies, more explicit attention to their effect on consumption, and greater sensitivity to their redistributive impact.

Price-support policies are intended to facilitate the purchase of certain goods and services essential to the maintenance of life and to encourage other nonessential—but socially desirable—consumption.[49] No comprehensive schedule of price supports is available, but some general statements are possible. Subsidies for basic food items, especially bread and potatoes, have risen to about 23 percent of the nominal "unsubsidized" price. Rents for housing (60 percent), heating fuels (50 percent), local transportation (60 percent), and long-distance travel are also heavily subsidized. It is also known that the state subsidizes consumer prices for books, children's clothing, and laundry services. Calculated on the basis of rough official figures, social-fund expenditures "for retaining stable consumer prices" (excluding housing) amount to 17–20 percent of the purchasing power of a typical household. Price subsidies thus represent the largest single component of social-fund expenditures.

On the other hand, the product tax (similar to the West European value-added tax) has a negative effect on the consumption of many other kinds of commodities, including most manufactured household goods, automobiles, and luxury food items. This tax is, in fact, the largest single source of government revenue—about 25 percent of the total.[50] Consumption is altered by the fact that, for the affected goods, an average of 56 percent of the purchase price is tax. Revenue raised by this method is equivalent to more than 40 percent of the average household income. Of course, the "average" household really does not bear the full brunt of this tax, as a disproportionately large share of this tax is paid by households with higher incomes. Ordinary workers are induced to direct a larger share of their spending toward untaxed or subsidized items.

This dual price policy, combining price supports on some goods with taxes on other goods, has three main consequences. First, the essential needs of all are provided for, while the "wasteful" consumption of luxury goods—especially those manufactured goods with a high content of scarce nonrenewable resources—is discouraged. Second, the policy is a significant process for redistributing wealth. One can think of the high product taxes paid by wealthier consumers as providing the revenue for subsidizing essential goods to poorer consumers. Third, the combined policy magnifies the differentiation of consumption patterns according to income classes.

This last effect, the differentiation of consumption, comes about because of the spending consequences of increasing wealth. It is obvious that low-income households direct a high share of their spending to food. As a household experiences a real growth in income, an increased share of spending tends to flow toward more expensive manufactured goods such as fashion clothing, washing machines, stereo equipment, and automobiles. The impact of the product tax is heaviest on these highly desired consumer goods, occasionally more than doubling their purchase price. Thus, a family whose income is climbing into the median range, where the increased purchase of consumer durables should be possible, is suddenly exposed to a sharply higher tax burden. Such "transitional" households find it very difficult to break through to a level of affluent consumption. From the perspective of the whole society, there emerges a marked distinction between those households that enjoy pedestrian modes of consumption and those that have overcome both price and tax obstacles to enjoy the visible amenities of affluence.

Official claims to have successfully implemented a policy of price stability are subject to some reservations. Prices published in support of this claim are those for a sample of commodities from the typical consumer's "market basket," a practice also followed in the West. In any such sample, questions arise about the utility of the "market basket" for comparison over extended periods. Since 1960, the base year for East German price comparisons, consumer preferences have shifted toward increased purchases of manufactured goods not included in the original sample. Even if government subsidies have insured constant prices for basic foods, this does not mean that the East German consumer has escaped price rises.

The policy of stable prices is intended, in principle, to encompass all goods and services. However, exceptions are made in the case of new or redesigned products, or—more recently—in the case of manufactured goods that contain increasingly expensive imported raw materials. Many observers claim that product innovation is a form of "hidden" inflation, in that substantially higher prices are often charged where little or no product improvement is visible. The fact that costs for imported raw materials can alter consumer prices reveals one way in which foreign inflation can creep into a more or less closed economy.

Economists sometimes consider commodity shortages roughly equivalent to inflation, in that both signify inability to satisfy consumer demand. In the GDR and the other European communist states, centrally directed economies lack the capacity of Western market economies to shape and respond to consumer wishes. Consequently, manufacturers occasionally face the problem of disposing of large inventories of unwanted goods. In recent years, for example, some "fashion" clothing was notoriously out of fashion, and washing machines went unsold because they lacked desired convenience features. More common is the problem of shortages, most acutely experienced in the purchase of imported clothing and foods. For example, when the planned production of some furniture designs finds an unexpected demand, the manufacturer is unable—within the context of central planning—to increase output accordingly. The production of personal automobiles is deliberately well below demand, notwithstanding the heavy product tax. The recent import of small numbers of Volkswagen Rabbits did not significantly reduce the waiting lists; it only aroused the indignation of those who lacked the money and privileged position required to buy this West German product.

An indicator of increasing affluence and excess consumer demand is the steady growth of personal savings. When a much-desired product becomes available, an ample number of consumers quickly appear with their savings to buy out the supply. Purchasing some goods is very much a matter of being in the right place at the right time. It is very much an asset to have friends in retail outlets and to have the sort of job that permits "emergency" shopping trips.

Some excess demand is channeled through the Intershop network, a chain of duty-free shops designed to attract the business of foreign visitors with convertible Western currency. Since 1974, GDR citizens are legally permitted to possess convertible currency, usually obtained from West German visitors. This is in addition to various illegal means. Today, an unknown volume of marks of the Federal Republic circulates in the GDR. Such currency is frequently paid for services "outside the economy"—for example, to moonlighting plumbers or house painters. (Incidentally, such exchanges are never reported as declared income for tax purposes and, thus, never enter official statistics on national income.) Without inquiring about its origin, the government permits this currency to be used by GDR citizens for Intershop purchases. Not surprisingly, this practice has produced complaints to newspapers and labor unions that a "two-currency" system has been created.[51] A discriminatory effect is asserted, since some social groups have no regular way of acquiring Western currency. The government has responded by abandoning a planned Intershop expansion.

The continuing problem of shortages of consumer goods is not denied by the government. Official pronouncements on the state of the national economy almost always include an acknowledgment of this state of affairs, as well as promises to put things right. Planned investment increases for this sector and incitements to better market research have not prevented a deepening of shortages since 1978. On the other hand, the long-neglected service sector has demonstrated real, if not wholly satisfactory, progress.

These myriad problems in the supply of consumer goods do not alter the fact that East Germans live rather well by most measures.[52] Food consumption is more than adequate nutritionally. The per capita consumption of various food groups (meat, fruits, and vegetables) resembles that of the wealthier neighboring countries, except that East Germans typically consume larger quantities of potatoes, bread, butter, and milk and smaller quantities of poultry, coffee, and alcoholic beverages. The ownership of radios, televisions, and refrigerators is rapidly approaching 100 percent, and the ownership of other household appliances is only moderately below the level of the Federal Republic. Component stereo equipment is increasingly in vogue. Only in the ownership of private automobiles and, of course, modern housing does the GDR fall well below the West European average. The importance of these two commodities cannot be overestimated.

On the other hand, East German consumption rates are clearly superior to all other European communist states in virtually every conventional category. This applies even in comparison with Czechoslovakia, which enjoyed the highest standard of living through the mid-1960s. It is rumored that East German achievements have been a mild source of friction in relations with the Soviet Union, particularly with Walter Ulbricht's custom of loudly proclaiming the nation's achievements. Since 1971, the circulation of East German pictorial magazines inside the Soviet Union has been sharply curtailed, perhaps because they depict an obviously higher standard of living.

With the considerable volume of tourism throughout East Europe, East Germans have become generally aware of their higher standards of living. But the SED and the government reap few rewards in the form of increased popular support; for the majority of citizens, the primary focus of comparision is not the East European average, but rather the standard of living in the Federal Republic. This focus is central not only because the two nations were once united but also because of the regular continuing exposure to life in the Federal Republic. East Germans make nearly 2 million trips to the Federal Republic each year; nearly 8 million visits are recorded by West Germans (including West Berliners) to the GDR. More important is the fact that well over 80 percent of all East German households receive West German television signals.

The message transmitted by television and personal contact is clear: Despite tangible progress in raising the standard of living, East Germany is falling behind the Federal Republic—and at an accelerating rate. National statistics may show the GDR holding its own in terms of the quantity of most consumer goods, but such data do not reflect the nearly constantly changing fashion and technology. In this most visible manifestation, the GDR is destined to remain the "second German state."

But when comparison is made with East Germany's own past or with world standards, the achievements of the nation's social policy are indeed considerable. A great deal has been accomplished in the way of insuring equity in employment, reducing income inequality, promoting viable families, promoting equal educational opportunity, and providing decent standards of health care for all citizens. Deficiencies are also numerous, most especially the lagging supply of manufactured consumer goods and the scandalous deterioration of housing. Many limitations arise from accumulated distortions in development planning and from the overall stringency of the national economy. The extent to which the system of economic management or of political leadership may act as a brake on material progress is difficult to say. The impact of international political and economic considerations, as well, can be estimated only imprecisely.

The social policy of the contemporary German Democratic Republic stands as a good example of what communist-style socialism has to offer in the way of material benefits and liabilities. Most Western observers will find the GDR wanting; the negative surely outweighs the positive. But from a global perspective, this nation ranks among the world's most developed—both economically and socially. Not surprisingly, it offers many lessons to the people of the world.

Notes

1. "Das neue Programm der SED," *Deutschland Archiv* 9, no. 7 (July 1976), p. 750.

2. Peter C. Ludz, *Parteielite im Wandel* [Transformation of the Party Elite] (Cologne: Westdeutscher, 1968), pp. 294–323.

3. Günter Manz, Gunnar Winkler, et al., *Theorie und Praxis der Sozialpolitik in der DDR* [Theory and Practice of Social Policy in the GDR] (Berlin: Akademie, 1979), pp. 12–20.

4. Zentralverwaltung für Statistik, *Statistisches Jahrbuch 1980 der Deutschen Demokratischen Republik* (Berlin: Staatsverlag, 1980), p. 84.

5. Jürgen Strassburger, "Ein neues lohnpolitisches Experiment? [A New Wage Policy Experiment?]," *Deutschland Archiv* 9, no. 9 (1976), pp. 950–958; Dieter Heibel, "Zur Neuordnung des Lohnsystems in der DDR [On the New Arrangement of the Wage System in the GDR," *Deutschland Archiv* 10, no. 11 (1977), pp. 1226–1228.

6. Hartmut Zimmerman, "In der DDR wird das Lohnsystem reformiert [The Wage System Is Reformed in the GDR]," *Die Quelle* 3, no. 3 (1977), pp. 114–117; Manz, Winkler, et al., *Theorie und Praxis*, pp. 237–238.

7. Manz, Winkler, et al., *Theorie und Praxis*, p. 240.

8. Ibid.

9. Zimmerman, "In der DDR wird das Lohnsystem reformiert," p. 114.

10. Doris Cornelsen et al., *Handbook of the Economy of the German Democratic Republic* (Westmead, England: Saxon House, 1979), p. 205.

11. Ibid., p. 322.

12. Social Security Administration, *Social Security Programs Throughout the World 1981* (Washington, D.C.: U.S. Government Printing Office, 1982), pp. 88–89.

13. Manz, Winkler, et al., *Theorie und Praxis*, p. 368.

14. Cornelsen et al., *Handbook of the Economy of the German Democratic Republic*, pp. 205, 206.

15. Manz, Winkler, et al., *Theorie und Praxis*, p. 250.

16. Ibid., p. 256.

17. Ibid., p. 347.

18. Data for all forms of social-security benefits are from ibid., pp. 362–374.

19. Werner Russ, "Altersrente in der DDR [Retirement Pensions in the GDR]," *Deutschland Archiv* 14, no. 1 (1981), p. 53.

20. C. Bradley Scharf, "Correlates of Social Security Policy, East and West Europe," *International Political Science Review* 2, no. 1 (1981), pp. 57–72. See also International Labour Office, *The Cost of Social Security, 1975–1977* (Geneva: International Labour Office, 1981).

21. Manz, Winkler, et al., *Theorie und Praxis*, p. 363.

22. Ibid., pp. 254–256.

23. International Labour Office, *The Cost of Social Security*, p. 18.

24. Data on family support policies is taken from Manz, Winkler, et al., *Theorie und Praxis*, pp. 126–133, 421–429.

25. Gisela Helwig, "Zum Stellenwert der Familienerziehung in der DDR [On the Priority of Family Upbringing in the GDR]," *Deutschland Archiv* 12, no. 12 (1979), pp. 1311–1315.

26. Peter C. Ludz et al., *DDR Handbuch*, 2d ed. [GDR Handbook] (Cologne: Wissenschaft und Politik, 1979), pp. 474–484 [hereafter, *DDR Handbuch*]; Manz, Winkler, et al., *Theorie und Praxis*, pp. 320–326.

27. Statistisches Bundesamt, *Statistisches Jahrbuch 1981 für die Bundesrepublik Deutschland* (Stuttgart: W. Kohlhammer, 1981), pp. 638–639 [hereafter, *Statistisches Jahrbuch 1981-BRD*].

28. Ibid., pp. 689–691.

29. *DDR Handbuch*, pp. 482–484; Manz, Winkler, et al., *Theorie und Praxis*, pp. 326–331; Konstantin Pritzel, "Konvergenz und Divergenz im Gesundheitswesen der beiden deutschen Staaten [Convergence and Divergence in Health Care of the Two German States]," *Deutschland Archiv* 14, no. 12 (1981), pp. 1284–1296.

30. Except where noted, all data on the system of education and training are drawn from *DDR Handbuch*, pp. 294–316.

31. *Statistisches Jahrbuch 1980-BRD*, app., p. 27. (Page sequence in appendix numbered separately, beginning with p. 1.)

32. Gert-Joachim Glaessner, "Bildungsökonomie und Bildungsplanung [The Economics and Planning of Education]," *Deutschland Archiv* 11, no. 9 (1978), pp. 937–956.

33. Gisela Helwig, "Standhafte Kämpfer heranbilden: Zum Hochschulbeschluss des SED-Politburos [Educate Steadfast Fighters: On the Higher Education Decree of the SED Politburo]," *Deutschland Archiv* 13, no. 5 (1980), pp. 462–463.

34. Except where noted, all data on housing are drawn from Cornelsen et al., *Handbook of the Economy of the German Democratic Republic*, pp. 124–130.

35. Ibid., pp. 214–215; Manz, Winkler, et al., *Theorie und Praxis*, p. 300.

36. Manz, Winkler, et al., *Theorie und Praxis*, pp. 301–302.

37. Ibid., pp. 303–304.

38. Cornelsen et al., *Handbook of the Economy of the German Democratic Republic*, p. 127.

39. Manz, Winkler, et al., *Theorie und Praxis*, pp. 304–305.

40. Ibid., p. 107.

41. Cornelsen et al., *Handbook of the Economy of the German Democratic Republic*, p. 130.

42. Ibid.

43. Manz, Winkler, et al., *Theorie und Praxis*, pp. 315–316.

44. Ibid., p. 312.

45. Ibid., p. 306.

46. *DDR Handbuch*, pp. 632–634.

47. Manz, Winkler, et al., *Theorie und Praxis*, pp. 377–389.

48. Ibid., p. 246.

49. Herwig E. Haase, "Wachsende Finanzielle Belastungen der DDR-Wirtschaft und ihr Ausweis im Staatshaushalt [The Growing Financial Burden of the GDR Economy and Its Impact on the State Budget]," *Deutschland Archiv* 12, no. 8 (1979), pp. 818–838; Maria Elisabeth Ruban and Heinz Vortmann, "Subventionen kontra Investionen [Subsidies Versus Investments]," *Deutschland Archiv* 13, no. 12 (1980), pp. 1277–1281.

50. Cornelsen et al., *Handbook of the Economy of the German Democratic Republic*, pp. 178–182.

51. Hans-Dieter Schultz, "Vor dem Einkauf schnell zur Bank [Quickly to the Bank Before Shopping]," *Deutschland Archiv* 12, no. 5 (1979), pp. 451–453.

52. Cornelsen et al., *Handbook of the Economy of the German Democratic Republic*, pp. 218–223. See also Jochen Bethkenhagen et al., *DDR und Osteuropa: Wirtschaftssystem, Wirtschaftspolitik, Lebensstandard* [GDR and East Europe: Economic System, Economic Policy, Standard of Living] (Opladen: Leske, 1981), pp. 319–353.

6
Integrative Processes

We have seen that East German social policy incorporates a broad variety of means to elevate the general standard of living, distribute more equally the material benefits of society, and remove barriers to life aspirations that derive from differences in income and class background. In pursuit of these objectives, it expresses aims that also are evident in Western nations, most especially in Scandinavia. Compared to these social welfare–oriented systems, the GDR is both more pretentious and somewhat less successful.

But East German social scientists persistently warn against the tendency to regard social policy in exclusively material terms. Human existence far transcends the satisfaction of physical needs: It also includes the intellectual-spiritual *(geistlich)* dimension of life—the need for achievement and self-esteem, for understanding and belonging. In fact, it is precisely in this dimension, it is claimed, that the true superiority of socialist democracy is demonstrated. Even such a strongly antisocialist nation as the United States succeeds rather well, if unevenly, in providing for the material needs of its people. But capitalist success in material terms, it is said, occurs only at the cost of creating deep schisms within the population, between those whose economic privileges permit personal liberty and those whose economic dependency means underdeveloped personalities. East German socialism, by way of contrast, regards economic development and personality development as inextricably intertwined.

Human personalities are multifaceted; they unfold in the context of family life, in the work place, in the course of routine social interaction, and in the exercise of roles in the local and national community. Marxist-Leninist social science accepts Aristotle's view that man is, above all, a "social" creature, who becomes fully human only in the society of other human beings. An essential feature of social policy, therefore, is the destruction of both economic and cultural barriers to human interaction, those trappings of psychological isolation and alienation inherited from capitalist society.

If the tremendous achievements of modern production and modern organization have been achieved through ever greater refinements in the division of labor, in the differentiation of roles, and in the complexity of institutions, there has been a corresponding loss in the sense of solidarity, of human community. Communist-style socialism aims to redeem this loss through the transformation of the modes of social organization, the elevation of collective purposes, and the inculcation of values based on cooperation rather than on conflict. While acknowledging the differences in individual needs and capabilities, SED social policy proclaims the goal of a more integrated society.

Socialist Values

In the early years of the GDR, political leaders commonly spoke of a "socialist cultural revolution," a concerted campaign to supplant bourgeois values (egotism, materialism, social discrimination) with values more conducive to harmonious social relationships. In the spirit of the times, this campaign acquired a sharply belligerent character. It should be recalled that many leading positions in economic management, public administration, law, and even education were occupied by people who had grown to maturity in a bourgeois society; the shortage of a trained socialist cadre necessitated this concession in personnel policy. External forces escalated the stakes in this struggle. On the one hand, agents of the Stalinist Soviet government demanded visible evidence of loyalty to the cause of communism; on the other hand, West German groups openly incited East Germans to repudiate their new government and its political philosophy. Undeniably, the bulk of popular sentiment lay on the side of the latter.

So long as the future of the SED regime remained in doubt, most citizens rejected its claim to rule. Because emigration was difficult and overt opposition was dangerous, rejection of the regime generally meant intense rejection of its officially propagated values. Regardless of any intrinsic merit, socialist cultural ideals were ridiculed merely because they emanated from the Soviet-sponsored political leadership.

In the short run, the highest SED echelons were satisfied with more or less successful efforts to induce citizens to contribute to the cultural campaign through participation in parades and other mobilization activities. Apparently, some leaders too readily interpreted these superficial signs as evidence of a deeper value transformation. They reacted with surprise and confusion to the forceful rebellion that emerged in 1953 and continued in various forms throughout the decade. Only with the permanent closure of the Berlin border in 1961 did the mass of the people begin to accept the durability of the new government, and only then could the culture transformation begin in earnest.

Before and after this turning point, the main points of the value campaign remained essentially the same. First, the new German Democratic Republic represents a dramatically progressive change in the life of the German people, qualitatively different from any previous change. This revolutionary step is made possible chiefly through the intervention—and under the continuing leadership—of the Soviet Union, to whom profound gratitude is due. Second, the socialist revolution is constantly endangered by external enemies, mainly the ruling classes in the Federal Republic and the United States, who employ all possible means to undermine the nation's political and economic stability. Successful resistance to these threats is essential not only to the welfare of East German citizens, but to the maintenance of peace in Europe. Third, the emerging society is founded upon equality of all working people. Collective well-being is inseparable from individual well-being. No one may use economic leverage to exploit another or to damage the collective good.

Fourth, apart from class enemies, all social classes and social segments play positive, essential roles in the creation of the new society. Although the contributions and rewards of individuals may differ, such differences do not impinge upon the equal worthiness and rights of all citizens, regardless of sex, social origin, ethnic origin, or religious belief. Such differences are not the source of social discrimination, but the focus of mutual respect. Fifth, every citizen has the obligation, both to self and to society, to develop his or her talents to the fullest. In particular, personal rewards and social progress depend on the willingness of all individuals to utilize opportunities for education and vocational training in order to become highly productive members of society. Slovenliness and self-indulgence damage one's own character and hinder the achievement of social progress. Sixth, every citizen is morally compelled to assume responsibility for the welfare of neighbors and the nation. Indifference to the fate of others and passivity in the face of momentous national tasks are signs of personal weakness. Taking part in the planning and execution of activities to improve the quality of life for one's employment and residential collective is an integral means to human fulfillment.

Over time, variations have appeared in the relative emphasis placed on each theme. For example, the immediacy with which external threats are portrayed has fluctuated—and generally diminished. The priority accorded Soviet achievements has also been variable; during the later Ulbricht years, in particular, the Soviet role was clearly overshadowed by pride in the GDR's own contributions to the cause of socialist development. Subsidiary themes have also evolved, such as the highly touted "scientific" character of social change (another Ulbricht favorite), the value of such personal virtues as thrift and honesty, the need for strong families, and the dependence of social harmony on the broader ability to understand the different points of view that emerge among people exercising different functions.

Childhood Socialization

The effort to bring about a more integrated society depends on the mechanisms for transmitting appropriate values. Mechanisms of socialization exist in all societies, often without explicit design. A major socialization impact usually occurs in the early years of life within the family context. Children acquire politically relevant values by generalizing from their experience in family authority relations and in imitating the behavior and attitudes of their parents toward the wider world. Obviously, parental participation in this process is, for the most part, unconscious or latent. In a society whose leaders are intent on promoting social change, socialization in the family—whether conscious or unconscious— can be a serious obstacle, especially in those cases where a modernizing political regime confronts a very traditional population. This has occurred most vividly in peasant Russia and in the later Asian communist states. In more stable societies, on the other hand, family socialization is an invaluable asset in preserving social order.

In any society, family socialization is a matter of public concern, since here young people may acquire values that can later lead to socially disruptive behavior. One means for mitigating this negative potential is to encourage or require young people to attend public school or preschool institutions. By thus exposing children to public authorities, the possible negative effects of family socialization can be remedied. To the extent that educators share and practice a common set of values, a degree of cultural homogeneity can be insured for the next generation. In the GDR today, comprehensive teacher training and centrally prepared instructional materials facilitate such a coordinated effort in official socialization. The high rates of participation in kindergartens and nurseries is a further advantage.

The formal curriculum is readily adapted to serve this socialization. The teaching of history and social studies is replete with heartwarming anecdotes about national heroes and ample evidence of the nation's superior capacity to solve problems of the human condition. In this respect, East German practice is not radically different from that even in Western democracies. What is unusual, however, is the extent to which these lessons incorporate heroes and experiences from another country—

namely, the Soviet Union. In addition, other subjects, including mathematics, language, and science, are ingeniously infused with explicit value content. For example, mathematical problems may be used to illustrate how a capitalist calculates the amount of "excess" wages he steals from his employees. Much physical education is presented as quasi-military preparation against an imperialist attack. Although research suggests that in the GDR, as elsewhere, explicit efforts to teach young adolescents prescribed political attitudes are not particularly successful, the cumulative effect of kindergarten and the ten-year general school is presumed to be quite significant.

For most children of ages seven to fourteen, school is supplemented by participation in a Pioneer group. Pioneer activity features patriotic, cultural, athletic, vocational, and public-service themes. It also structures peer expectations by providing a guided collective, which assumes some responsibility for school discipline and the maintenance of school property.

The effectiveness of these officially prescribed socialization experiences is open to question. Even though children clearly learn the curriculum content very well, they show a strong capacity to hold divergent values. In other words, they know how to give expected answers without appropriating the expected values. Knowing the expected answers is important, of course, since it provides a conventional, innocuous vocabulary for use in uncertain public interaction. Children also develop skills in identifying people with real or potential authority (i.e., teachers, leaders of collectives) and in adopting accommodative behavior.

Now that all young parents have themselves grown up under socialism, they too provide crucial guidance to their children, who need to distinguish between public and private values. To be sure, parents in all modern societies, even in liberal democracies, serve a similar function. They have also learned the value of prudent hypocrisy in certain situations—for example, in artful deference toward disagreeable work superiors or polite compliments to incompetent professors. For East Germans, however, the scope of problematic situations is much wider, and the penalties for bad judgment—in terms of damage to one's academic and career aspirations—are potentially much more severe.

Public Media

The relatively high rates of newspaper consumption and nearly universal ownership of radios and television sets make the public media important instruments of social integration.[1] There are thirty-eight daily newspapers, with a total circulation of 8.3 million. Regional and national SED papers (including *Neues Deutschland*) account for about two-thirds of the total circulation. *Junge Welt*, published by the youth organization, accounts for about 10 percent; *Tribune,* published by the FDGB, accounts for 5 percent. Newspapers published by the four noncommunist political parties equal less than 5 percent of the total. In addition, there are more than five hundred monthly magazines and weekly newspapers, ranging from *Für dich,* an illustrated women's weekly, to *Einheit,* a publication for party officials of all levels. Many periodicals focus on the special concerns of various professional groups. The government operates two color television channels, together offering nineteen to twenty hours of daily programming.

The GDR severely restricts the receipt of Western publications, more so than Hungary or pre-1981 Poland, for example. In general, such publications are available only to government, party, economic, and educational institutions. Publications from East Europe and the Soviet Union are freely permitted but rarely purchased, except for aspiring intelligentsia who find it prudent to receive at least one Soviet periodical. The surging interest in Czech newspapers, during the "Prague Spring" of 1968, brought a temporary government embargo.

Electronic media are a different matter. Largely because of the central location of West Berlin transmitters, West German radio and television are received throughout the GDR, except for the southern mountain regions. (Accurate reception of color broadcasts requires a decoder attachment, which can be purchased at Intershop.) As a practical matter, it is not possible to prohibit viewing of Western television—not least because it is a prime source of news and entertainment for the governing elite. (Many are avid viewers of internationally syndicated U.S. programs, which are shown with German-language dubbing by West Berlin stations; crime and Western dramas are most popular.)

Television thus facilitates awareness of the higher standard of living in the Federal Republic. It also provides divergent perspectives on world events. Public surveys have discovered that East Germans are somewhat more familiar with West German politicians than with their own leaders. In the last decade, Western television has become an increasingly pertinent source of news about political and economic conditions in the GDR itself. When television journalists were first regularly permitted in the GDR in late 1971, they gained quick recognition. Some were even approached on the street by East German citizens and asked to do reports on specific issues.

This penetration by Western media places a special burden on SED officials. Both the electronic and printed media continue to practice censorship. For example, certain kinds of economic, social, and military data are not disseminated, and no statements directly critical of either East German or Soviet leaders are permitted. At the same time, many awkward topics are covered, if only in response to Western television broadcasts. Thus, GDR television has gradually moved in the direction of more candid, if still notably biased, reporting. East German television journalists correctly perceive that they are competing for the attention of GDR viewers. Efforts to develop more interesting reporting styles and to be responsive to public opinion are a source of professional pride. GDR reporters are quick to claim higher professional standards than their East European and Soviet colleagues.

Literature and the Arts

In any society, values and national identity may be transmitted through literature, music, and the performing and graphic arts. SED cultural specialists take the position that in capitalist societies such artistic expressions have a profoundly class-based character: The "best" artists are ostensibly appropriated by the ruling class, whereas art for the masses is essentially dulling and escapist. As indicated in the preceding chapter, the socialist GDR has endeavored to make all forms of art available to all segments of society. It also aims to make literature and the arts more relevant to the lives of ordinary people.

The regime's early years were characterized by particularly bitter relations between the party and the nation's creative artists. Following the Stalinist prescriptions of the time, writers and playwrights were enjoined to produce works that would evoke a positive outlook toward the tasks of socialist construction by portraying the extraordinary achievements of ordinary workers. Reacting sharply to this primitive adoption of Soviet "socialist realism," East German writers protested that they could not "create according to plan." Finding most of their work rejected by publishers, of course, many writers did in fact produce "literature" according to the prescribed formula, featuring one-dimensional model citizens, whose temporary troubles were invariably overcome through correct "socialist" action.

Encouraged by the fluctuating Soviet literary policy under Khrushchev, East German writers repeatedly tested the limits of SED policy, with no enduring gain. In 1963–1965 several major works appeared that addressed more candidly the difficulties of life under socialism. Although no formal change in policy occurred, inconsistencies emerged in the practices of relevant publishing boards.

In 1971 Erich Honecker put the stamp of his leadership on cultural policy, when he announced: "If one begins from a firm position of socialism, there can be, in my opinion, no taboos in the field of art and literature." The following year, SED Secretary for Culture and Science Kurt Hager expressed optimism that the nation's creative artists could develop a multitude of styles and forms for expressing the reality of socialism. "As Marxist-Leninists," he said, "we know that contradictions are not a 'blemish' on social development, they are the motor of all social progress." Hager rejected neutral objectivity, preferring "partisan portrayal," which "incorporates people in the coming-to-grips with contradictions mentally and emotionally on a socialist basis— without giving them ready solutions."[2]

The principle of "socialist realism" was thus radically altered. Writers were no longer told what they must write; instead, they should seek to satisfy "differentiated cultural and artistic requirements." Taboos remain, of course, to the extent that literature may not attack the fundamentals of socialism, the nation's current leaders, or its alliance with the Soviet Union.

Subsequent changes in GDR literature show considerable experimentation in forms, as well as more sophisticated encounters with the psychological and spiritual dimensions of life. Career frustrations and sexual complications are richly portrayed. In many stories, the working people either are not "heroic" or are entirely absent. Some stories even have tragic endings. But all say something about the real world, at least insofar as it affects a significant segment of the population. This newest wave of art may not always present an unambiguous version of socialist values, but it does allow more readers to share their common condition. In this respect, it undoubtedly has a far greater integrative effect.

The Risks of Planned Integration

The SED image of an integrated, corporatist society places greatest emphasis on the forms of institutions that are situated between the individual and the society as a whole. Far from being an undifferentiated mass, the population consists of groups, or collectives, each with somewhat different needs and resources. Social integration proceeds in stages, first by creating bonds within the smallest collectives, then by building linkages among similar collectives, and finally by developing a sense of commonality that will transcend occupational and class differences. In practice, this logical sequence of integration is not followed chronologically: Evidence of progress is actively sought at all three levels simultaneously.

Three risks are associated with deliberate efforts to transform society in this fashion. First, those authorities responsible for implementing and evaluating integrative activity are likely to focus overwhelmingly on its most superficial manifestations. The number of farmers who "voluntarily" enter cooperative farms, the number of workers who enroll in evening classes, the number of youth who turn out for neighborhood cleanup campaigns—all such quantitative measures of participation are highly prized by the party cadre. With evident bureaucratization of party work, endless reports must be assembled and forwarded up the hierarchy— ultimately to the departments of the Central Committee and to the Secretariat. The cadre involved with basic collective activity may inflate the numbers in reports or resort to barely veiled coercion to induce compliance. In this way, the entire collective process may become infused with coercion and mistrust, the very opposite of what social theorists intend.

In such a setting individuals seek a personal withdrawal, avoiding any expressions of discontent and consequently disclaiming any responsibility for making their work unit or youth club perform better. Encounters among collectives are characterized by hollow, formalistic language, with no relevance to their cooperative endeavors. This irrelevance and hypocrisy also contaminate broader forms of political and social-service activity. People experience a debilitating schism between their private and public lives, in this extreme kind of repression.

Given their recent experience with the tyranny of the Third Reich, it is not surprising that both group and responsible cadre members often repeated this repressive pattern. In the short run, such repression effectively insured social order and exposed ardent counterrevolutionaries—undoubtedly among the principal goals of many SED leaders and their Soviet advisers. But for the mass of individuals, and for the society as a whole, it also had profound costs.

This process of disintegrating collectives was far from universal, however. In many parts of society, previously established collective bonds proved quite resilient, thus posing a second risk to the new regime. In the face of external demands, the members of such groups could agree to formalistic compliance, while preserving an autonomous group life. Again, this involved considerable hypocrisy, but it was hypocrisy in which collective members provided mutual support.

Although this pattern was more common, it too had costs. Group norms evolved to prohibit any avoidable behavior that might be construed as supporting the new order. For example, students pressured one another into achieving the lowest passing grades in the mandatory study of Russian language and Marxism-Leninism. Work units strove to preserve minimal levels of performance. Nonconforming members of such collectives were ostracized as having "gone over to the other side," a somewhat different sort of repression.

A different result evolved in some of the stronger work collectives, where members of pre-Nazi labor unions formed the core. Here the workers agreed to actively contribute to national reconstruction and to work harder for personal gain, while awaiting the end of the Soviet military occupation and the expected emergence of social democracy.

These were vain hopes, of course. Disillusionment gradually spread in these collectives and erupted in the 1953 strikes.

In both the "minimalist" and "social democratic" collectives, the nominal leading cadre failed in its main task. Some members were active accomplices in the deception; some simply proved incapable of leading, but attempted to conceal this fact from their superiors.

The third risk associated with planned social integration derives from the first two and from what party leaders commonly call "inadequate cadre work." In the absence of truly reliable information from cadre members, the highest authorities are always vulnerable to misreading the real extent of social integration. By *underestimating* the extent to which the population has adopted desired collective values and behavior, SED leaders may maintain an excessive central control over public activity, thus depriving the nation of the individual and collective initiative required to solve complex tasks and promote social progress. The most pessimistic leaders seek to minimize risks by preventing most kinds of social change and by creating large police forces to uncover "hidden" enemies—a highly counterproductive endeavor. This was certainly the pattern of Josef Stalin, whose commitment to social progress was, in any event, suspect. By *overestimating* the extent of social integration, leaders may encourage the open advocacy of irreconcilable demands and in so doing unleash broad social conflict and perhaps endanger the leadership system itself. The Hungarian rebellion of 1956 is the most poignant expression of this sort of error.

East German communists like to congratulate themselves on having found the optimum middle ground, on having determined the correct pace of change. The GDR, it is claimed, has achieved maximum social and economic progress with a minimum of conflict. This boast was asserted most vigorously in informal appraisals of Czechoslovakia's 1968 quest for "socialism with a human face." The SED had no quarrel with humane goals, it was suggested; in fact, the GDR had performed better than its neighbors in avoiding the worst effects of Stalinism. But, regrettably, misguided Czech reformers were jeopardizing their long-term success by attempting "to move too fast."

To be sure, there had been periods of error in SED policy, as well. Among the most obvious signs of this were the confrontations with labor unions throughout the 1950s and the high rates of emigration to West Berlin. By the end of the next decade, however, Walter Ulbricht spoke confidently of "the growing political-ideological and moral unity of the socialist human community."[3] At the time, other party leaders were notably reserved on this issue. Since Honecker's accession in 1971, much greater stress has been placed on evidence of deficient social integration, on the need to gradually overcome "nonantagonistic contradictions" in the "stable community of united classes and strata."[4]

Plan Together, Work Together, Govern Together!

In the contemporary period of what Erich Honecker has termed *"real existierenden Sozialismus"* (real existing socialism), the SED ostensibly formulates its policies on the basis of a clearheaded appreciation of past achievements and present realities. The goal of social integration is pursued with far less pretension. Especially in this realm of endeavor, the previously zealous reverence for science has diminished markedly. Cadre members in the SED and other social organizations no longer are taught the rudiments of cybernetic theory; instead, they focus on personality development and are enjoined to develop more sensitivity in their "work with human beings" *(Arbeit mit den Menschen)*.

Singular attention is drawn to the fact that even the most sophisticated efforts to transmit socialist values—through the schools, the media, and the arts—are quickly destroyed if the practical experience of daily life contradicts those values. The people can hardly accept the state as their own, if they routinely encounter "heartless bureaucrats." Ideals of socialist democracy can hardly thrive, if city officials and factory directors discharge their obligation of accountability by "mere formalism." Workers' aspirations to assume greater responsibility in planning can hardly survive, if their questions are ridiculed and their suggestions rejected without explanations.

Meaningful social bonds are created not merely through study and slogans, but by actually taking part, by assuming and exercising responsibility for some aspect of one's social environment. More than ever, cadre work should do more than strive for large numbers of participants; special effort is required to insure that the *quality* of participative experiences is consonant with socialist goals.

The structures within which East German citizens are asked to "plan, work, and govern together" have remained essentially unchanged for the past twenty years or more. These structures assume three forms: political parties, community organizations, and occupational and interest organizations.

The Allied Parties

The Socialist Unity party has an effective monopoly of political power. It is the linchpin of all other forms of organization and, thus, is qualitatively distinct. Although ostensibly representative of the whole population, membership in the SED is restricted. All other organizations are open to anyone who meets nominal eligibility requirements.

Four other political parties were encouraged as part of the original "alliance policy" implemented in the first years of Soviet occupation. This was an effort to incorporate different social classes into the campaign for national reconstruction under communist leadership. The Christian Democratic Union (CDU) and the Liberal Democratic Party of Germany (LDPD) were continued from the pre-Hitler period. During the militant transition to unambiguous SED control, outspoken leaders of these two parties were systematically excluded. Today, both parties derive most of their membership from among the bourgeois middle class, professional people, shopkeepers, and independent craftspeople—in other words, among people employed outside the socialist sector of the economy. Such people occasionally play important roles in their communities, even though they cannot properly be included in the "party of the working class."

Since the SED closely monitors leadership selection in the CDU and the LDPD, these parties are permitted to present candidates for public office and to articulate the specific needs of their members. They are, in fact, a principal avenue of dialogue. For example, although compelled to endorse the government's 1972 decision to take public control of most remaining semiprivate production companies, both bourgeois parties were consulted on the details of compensation to company owners. The CDU is officially regarded as the political voice of East Germany's Christian communities, and it is credited with securing modifications in legislation concerning school curricula and military service, as well as provisions in the 1974 constitution affecting the rights of religious believers. In 1972, two-fifths of the CDU deputies voted against the new abortion law—the only recorded exception to National Assembly unanimity.[5]

Membership in the LDPD[6] has stagnated at about 75,000. The LDPD has seats in the National Assembly and State Council (granted to all parties), and an LDPD leader is minister of justice. CDU membership has grown somewhat in the last decade to about 140,000. The president of the Supreme Court and the minister of post and telecommunications are CDU members.

The National Democratic party[7] (NDPD) was created to facilitate the social integration of former "small Nazis" and to appeal to nationalistic sentiments among former soldiers of the Third Reich. NDPD membership has gradually declined to about 80,000. An NDPD member heads the State Contracts Court.

The Democratic Farmers party[8] (DBD) is a not entirely successful attempt to elicit political participation among cooperative farmers. The DBD has grown to about ninety-two thousand members, many of whom are actually former city dwellers who have acquired degrees in agronomy or animal husbandry. A DBD member is minister of environment and hydroeconomy.

Community Participation

An important consequence of GDR social policy and of efforts to equitably allocate housing space has been a visible breakdown in the former patterns of residential segregation according to income classes. Apart from certain small elite groups, families from a variety of social and occupational backgrounds today live in the same neighborhoods and share the same apartment buildings. Neighborhood associations, therefore, offer an opportunity to create integrative linkages.

District committees of the National Front (see Chapter 2) are supposed to insure that each neighborhood and apartment complex has a voluntary representative. Ideally, this should be a person without full-time employment and without official responsibilities in a political party or other social organization. A neighborhood association is created, which—like all social institutions—is formally charged with looking after every conceivable need of the residents. However, its actual functions are rather limited. The neighborhood association usually makes some effort to clean up and decorate for the annual National Day (October 9), and it promotes candidate appearances and voter turnout in elections every five years. Other activities vary considerably among communities. Where large housing complexes operate their own childcare and recreational facilities, the association exercises a custodial role. In neighborhoods with many elderly residents, the association may coordinate efforts to monitor their health and social needs.

On the whole, neighborhood associations have done little to promote social integration. This may be because most citizens experience more than enough collective activity in work-related groups and prefer to spend their spare time in less structured ways. High rates of female employment mean that evenings and weekends must include household chores. Most significantly, people spend increasing amounts of leisure time viewing television.

A more meaningful form of community participation occurs in the citizen commissions of local government.[9] Each city, city-borough, and town creates eight to ten commissions concerned with various public policies. Each commission consists of local government and party officials (SED and others) responsible for relevant policies and substantial representation from affected occupational and residential categories. Those commissions dealing with specific social policies are the most active: housing, retail trade, health, schools, youth and sports, culture, and transportation.

Most commissions meet at least quarterly to evaluate efforts to satisfy public needs. Although some pompous formalism is inevitable, both the GDR media and foreign observers report that criticism of public officials is not uncommon. Since the topics under discussion do not involve the integrity of the regime (e.g., basic principles of socialism, SED rule, foreign relations), discussion is frequently rather candid. Responsible officials are induced to acknowledge shortcomings and to promise remedies. Citizens are generally aware of the restraints that government centralization places on local officials, so great attention is focused on the *sincerity* of official efforts to respond to public needs. An official who repeatedly fails to win public confidence can be replaced; in this event, much depends on the attitude of the mayor and the local SED first secretary and on the availability of a qualified replacement.

Participation in citizen commissions is far from universal. A good deal of self-selection is involved. Almost by definition, these participants are "above average." Most are distinguished in their jobs, and many have advanced education. Nevertheless, commission activities contribute substantially to the sharing of community responsibility, and they are perhaps the most recognizable of East German efforts to develop a form of what Westerners accept as political democracy.

A distinctively communist form of community participation occurs in the administration of justice. The GDR clearly exemplifies the Marxist-Leninist principle that socialist law serves a profound educative function. The general European tradition of code law is followed, but considerable flexibility in the application of law is permitted in the interest of preserving the state and strengthening the socialist order. As a result, each judicial proceeding includes an explicit "instructional" component, in which a connection is drawn between the specific case and the broad social purposes concerned.

Citizen participation is insured through the institution of Social Courts, modeled after the Soviet Comrade's Courts. Social Courts were first instituted in 1953, in the form of Conflict Commissions, to deal with labor disputes. Since 1963, Social Courts have also been established in rural areas, and their competence has been extended to include a wide range of misdemeanors: minor civil disputes; worker claims over wages, bonuses, and improper dismissal; and assorted other regulations, such as school truancy. Work-place assemblies or residential communities elect Social Courts from their peers, who receive orientation from the Free German Labor Union Federation (FDGB) or the Ministry of Justice. Meeting as a group of eight to fifteen lay citizens, the Social Court convenes in a public hall without the direct participation of trained judicial personnel.

In a loose analogy, East German Social Courts perform a function similar to that served by U.S. justices of the peace in an earlier day, when justice had a more rudimentary, populist character. The Social Courts apply community standards as defined by a proper socialist standpoint. Avoiding formalistic rules of procedure, the lay panel asks whatever questions are necessary to determine the facts of the case, the motives of the accused, and other factors relevant in determining penalties, including work record and class background. Work associates and neighbors are frequently consulted. Possible penalties include public reprimand, restitution, public service, and fines—but not incarceration.

The Social Courts are closely supervised by legal professionals. The Supreme Court plays an active role, issuing explicit guidelines on how certain classes of cases should be handled. The district courts are an avenue of appeal. Most importantly, a highly centralized system of state attorneys monitors all findings of the social courts, and the local state attorney is empowered to initiate appeals, order hearings, and even negate Social Court results. Early experiments with the Social Courts determined frequent examples of "excessive leniency" toward "class enemies." Today, the state attorney is more likely to alter outcomes in favor of the accused, citing Social Court reliance on unverified allegations or inattention to mitigating circumstances. Social Courts are repeatedly warned of the damages of alienating citizens and are urged to stress ways for building collective support for people who have only temporarily offended the public order.

For all participants, the Social Courts seem to be an effective means for integrating citizens into a generally recognized set of public values.

Occupational and Interest Organizations

It is useful, for certain purposes, to regard the East German population as divided into classes or, alternatively, into territorial constituencies. However, a far more salient perspective is one based on functional differences. In a corporatist concept of society, functional differences describe the kinds of contributions that each social segment makes to the performance of the whole. Unlike conservative corporatist philosophies, Marxism-Leninism seeks to reduce functional differences and negate their most obvious psychological ramifications. Yet, at any given stage of social development, functional differences do exist. The SED's policy of social integration incorporates existing functional differences as a primary basis for social organization.

As befits the Marxist view that productivity is a defining element of human existence, the most important social organizations are formed on the basis of employment. The largest of these is the Free German Labor Union Federation, intended to encompass all working people in the public economy and public service.[10] Only cooperative farmers, self-employed persons, and those in active military service are excluded. Total membership is more than 8.2 million, roughly 97 percent of those eligible. Unlike some European and U.S. unions, the FDGB is organized according to economic sector rather than by trades. Thus, there are eight industrial unions, plus additional unions for food and retail trade, government and public services, state-owned agriculture, health, education, science, art, and civilian employees of the military.

Each union is supposed to represent all employees, including management, professional staff, office workers, supervisors, and laborers of various skill levels. Such a structure is intended to overcome differences among occupational strata within a given enterprise or institution and encourage a cooperative, collective consciousness. In the early days, this structure was supposed to counteract the "bourgeois" arrogance of nonmanual employees, but today, a status hierarchy remains, as will be pointed out in the following chapter.

Because the FDGB is ostensibly "the interest representative of all working people," its tasks are enormous. An *abbreviated* list includes the following things it is to do: (1) promote the broadest possible participation of all employees in improving production, reducing waste and inefficiency, and discovering new resources; (2) familiarize all employees with the production plan and, through joint management-worker committees, take part in the formation and evaluation of annual plans; (3) lead work collectives in "socialist competition" to achieve higher levels of performance; (4) insure adherence to wage and bonus regulations; (5) guarantee management's attentive handling of workers' suggestions and the payment of appropriate financial rewards; (6) insure worker discipline and prevent arbitrary management behavior; (7) promote worker training and career advancement; (8) enforce laws regarding labor safety; (9) help determine expenditures from the culture fund and the social fund; (10) advocate the housing and consumer needs of employees; and (11) administer the social-security system. The FDGB provides important linkages to other social and political institutions. Representative assemblies at all levels of government include a substantial union contingent. Every SED executive committee at every level includes an FDGB representative.

In light of the SED's self-definition as "the vanguard of the working class and all working people," the very existence of the FDGB as "the interest representative" of its members is something of an anomaly. Despite the fact that FDGB officials at nearly all levels are simultaneously SED members, the history of the GDR (and virtually all other communist states) reveals an intermittent antagonism between the unions and the ruling party. In recent years the FDGB ostensibly has been elevated above the status of other social organizations. The new constitution affords the unions special rights. The 1976 wage reform was legally authored by the "Central Committee of the SED, the Executive Committee of the FDGB, and the Council of Ministers of the GDR"—implying a sort of party-union-government triumvirate.[11] For the time being, there is no reason to consider these changes as anything more than nominal. Yet the FDGB does seem to present unique opportunities and problems in the scheme of social integration.

Alongside the unions there exists a host of other occupation-based organizations. The Chamber of Technology[12] (KdT) is a formally separate organization, whose 270,000 members are drawn from several FDGB branch unions. Their purpose is to foster technological innovations within and among production enterprises. Because a majority of KdT members hold university or technical-college degrees, they probably constitute a semielitist subgroup within their respective local unions.

Other social organizations devoted to the professional intelligentsia include the Jurists' Union, the Association of Journalists, the Association of Theatrical Producers, the Association of Composers and Musicians, the Association of Film and Television Producers, and the Writers' Association. These organizations play a special role, because their members work in relatively independent circumstances and because the products of their work are critical to the SED program for cultural change. Particularly with respect to creative artists, the SED leadership permits more organizational autonomy than with other social groups. The result is an occasionally discordant dialogue between these associations and SED cultural specialists.

The second-largest social organization is the Society for German-Soviet Friendship (DSF).[13] Presumably a great many of its 5.5 million members have joined in the belief that this affiliation may have a positive effect on the academic, professional, and political advancement to which they aspire. Organized mainly in the work place, DSF groups have the dual functions of publicizing the achievements of the Soviet Union as the leader of world socialism and the benefits of the GDR-USSR alliance and of exchanging experiences with similar groups in the Soviet Union. This second function includes both studying Soviet publications and traveling to visit "fraternal worker brigades" in the Soviet Union.

The Free German Youth (FDJ)[14] is an extraordinarily important organization, both for social integration and recruitment to political leadership. The FDJ has about 2.2 million members, roughly 70 percent of the population aged fourteen to twenty-five. The participation rate is especially high in the fourteen to sixteen age group (96 percent) and in the army (86 percent). Rural youth are seriously underrepresented, and participation in the universities, although nominally very high, has little practical consequence. It is universally recognized that a record of active FDJ membership is a prerequisite for admission to the expanded secondary school and subsequent educational institutions.

The FDJ has developed an increasingly diverse and attractive range of activities. Its basic purpose is, of course, to provide a peer context that promotes desired socialist values as outlined at the beginning of this chapter. Its principal activities include sports competition, cultural and political training, career counseling, summer camps, and public service. FDJ groups are very visible participants in patriotic celebrations, and they can be counted on to remind citizens to vote on election day. The FDJ leadership represents youth in the work place (52 percent are workers or apprentices) and in local government. The FDJ is credited with the increasingly "realistic" approach to sexual mores and with the growing availability of discotheques and other contemporary forms of entertainment.

The Democratic Women's Federation[15] (DFD) encompasses 1.4 million members, about 16 percent of the female population. Although it has concentrated its recruitment efforts among the unemployed, fewer than one-fifth of the nation's housewives have joined. In the last decade, DFD leaders have been rather outspoken about the need to respond to the special burdens of working mothers, an issue also emphasized by the women's committees of the FDGB. The DFD has recently begun offering social services of its own, including premarital and divorce counseling.

Three other interest organizations deserve mention. The German Gymnastics and Sports League[16] (DTSB) promotes a wide variety of participation sports, including football (soccer), gymnastics, swimming, fishing, horsemanship, and auto racing. It includes 2.8 million members, about half of whom are under the age of eighteen. Not all DTSB activities can be considered recreational; much of the league's effort is devoted to promoting international-grade competition. The Culture Federation[17] (KB) is an association of around 210,000, which promotes appreciation for, and participation in, the performing and graphic arts. Urania[18] is a society of technical intelligentsia. Its 360,000 members are devoted to popularizing the physical and social sciences through magazines, television, and public lectures.

Hierarchy of Participation

The preceding survey of integrative processes and organizations does no more than indicate the efforts of East German social theorists and political leaders to construct the framework of an integrated society. The actual impact of these efforts on the population is much more difficult to appraise. However, observations of the patterns of political and social affiliations tend to support three generalizations.

First, although the total membership of all the organizations mentioned is extremely large—in fact, larger than the total GDR population—this does not mean that everyone is a substantive participant. On the contrary, most of this total membership is accounted for by subsets of the population who carry multiple affiliations. For example, a male book illustrator will probably belong to both the FDGB (Arts Union) and the Society for German-Soviet Friendship. Because he seeks fulfillment beyond his occasional routine job, he may join the Culture League and the CDU. If he is articulate and respected for his work, his local union may help secure for him a position on the Culture Commission of the city assembly. His extra activities not only provide personal satisfaction; they also indicate his civic orientation, an asset in the quest for a job promotion. Similarly, a young construction worker might belong to the FDGB, the Free German Youth, and the sports league. In a more unusual case, a female laboratory technician in a chemicals firm might hold simultaneous membership in the FDGB, the Democratic Women's League, the Chamber of Technology, and the Society for German-Soviet Friendship. She could also be a member of the union's Women's Committee and a leader of the "socialist competition" in the lab. As a highly trained worker and model citizen, she might even be a member of the SED as well.

Second, in a great many cases, membership involves only minimal participation. For people with multiple affiliations, practical limitations of time require that some membership obligations be neglected in favor of others. Yet there is no incentive to formally terminate membership in any group; in fact, to do so will invite unpleasant inquiries. People originally join such organizations to gain benefits, to satisfy job expectations, or to help out a recruiter who is a personal acquaintance. Members fall away, when the rewards are few. However, their names will be retained by group leaders, who wish to demonstrate evidence of success. The extent of purely nominal membership cannot be gauged, but it is undoubtedly greatest in the largest organizations.

Third, there is strong evidence of a kind of hierarchy of participation, closely associated with social status and mobility. Virtually everyone belongs to one of the two "foundation" organizations, the FDGB or the FDJ. People with aspirations of upward mobility are required to assume some leadership role at this basic level and urged to join an additional social organization—at minimum the Society for German-Soviet Friendship. Further status advancement requires, at each stage, the acquisition of additional affiliations, each more specialized and more demanding. This progression in organizational affiliation is linked to career advancement: Stagnation in one will mean stagnation in the other. This may occur voluntarily or involuntarily. In either case, the individual retains his or her organizational affiliation—although it will gradually lose much substantive content.

It was once fashionable for Western scholars to view this network of overlapping organizations primarily as a mechanism through which strategically placed SED cadre members could keep a watchful eye on the population. In the early years of the GDR, this image of organized control had considerable validity. However, the success of three decades of childhood socialization has sharply diminished the control aspects of social organizations.

Today, the social organizations exist to provide the intrinsic rewards of participation and to provide channels of dialogue between the party-government leadership and specific social segments. But most important, the *network* of organizations—the hierarchy of participation—exists to allocate social status and rewards. While it may not be completely true that every citizen has an equal opportunity, it is true that the majority of citizens can acquire positions of influence only by working their way through this hierarchy. At each level, many people are shunted to the side—some with contentment, some with a profound sense of failure. Only the few acquire significant influence even within their local communities.

Sociologists describe similar status hierarchies and mobility ladders in liberal democracies, but social mobility in the GDR differs in important ways. Unlike more pluralistic systems, the GDR does not offer alternative paths to social advancement; education, employment, and social and political participation all play a part in an interwoven network. In effect, there is only a single path. Most East Germans embark on this path early in life and proceed as far as they can. When the demands become too great, people settle into a comfortable social niche. For them there is rarely an alternative path, rarely an opportunity to later pursue a real change in life.

Integration and Selection

Integrative processes in the GDR are comprehensive and thorough. By means of schooling, the public media, and self-conscious use of the arts, young East Germans easily adjust to the prevailing values of society. Practical experience, both directly encountered and transmitted by parents and peers, nonetheless insures that the prevailing values do not precisely coincide with the "socialist" values expressed by representatives.

The effort to promote integration by participation in political, occupational, and interest organizations has been successful only in insuring that most citizens now hold a common understanding of the rules of social mobility and the advantage of personal advancement. To be sure, many people can advance without some of the barriers common in capitalist societies, particularly those of inequities deriving from the status and wealth of one's parents. Yet this system has not promoted significant social integration beyond the smallest collectives.

The GDR has adopted the Leninist principle for the distribution of rewards under socialism: "From each according to his ability, to each according to his contribution." As SED authorities freely acknowledge, this principle—commonly called the "achievement principle"—produces its own form of social differentiation. In the effort to create a developed socialist society, all are called, but few are chosen.

Notes

1. Peter C. Ludz et al., *DDR Handbuch,* 2d ed. [GDR Handbook] (Cologne: Wissenschaft und Politik, 1979), pp. 372–376, 858–860 [hereafter, *DDR Handbuch*].

2. Volker Gransow, *Kulturpolitik in der DDR* (Berlin, West: Volker Spiess, 1975), pp. 266–267.

3. Quoted in Hermann Axen, "Die DDR schreitet zuverzichtlich vorwärts [The GDR Strides Confidently Forward]," *Deutsche Aussenpolitik* 14, no. 12 (1969), p. 1404.

4. Otto Rheinhold, "Gestaltung der entwickelten Sozialistischen Gesellshaft im Lichte des Programmentwurfs [The Formation of Developed Socialist Society in Light of the Draft Program]," *Einheit,* no. 3 (1976), pp. 286–287.

5. *DDR Handbuch,* p. 926.

6. Ibid., pp. 665–666.

7. Ibid., pp. 761–762.

8. Ibid., p. 247.

9. Ibid., p. 445–446.

10. The discussion of the labor unions is drawn chiefly from C. Bradley Scharf, "Labor Organizations in East German Society" (Diss, Stanford, 1974), pp. 169–227. See also *DDR Handbuch,* pp. 351–362.

11. *DDR Handbuch,* p. 697.

12. Ibid., pp. 576–577.

13. Ibid., pp. 467–468.

14. Ibid., pp. 362–367.

15. Ibid., pp. 249–250.

16. Ibid., pp. 258–259.

17. Ibid., p. 626.

18. Ibid., pp. 1110–1111.

7
Social and Political Differentiation

Any major SED statement on the nature of the present "developed socialist society" is likely to feature the long-standing commitment to "gradually overcome the essential differences between city and rural life and between intellectual and manual work," as well as the "assimilation of all classes and strata on the foundation of the Marxist-Leninist world outlook of the working class."[1]

The preceding chapters have described many GDR programs and party policies, which aim at effecting this fundamental social transformation. This chapter summarizes the social and political differences that still characterize East German society in the 1980s. This survey begins with the three main Marxist-Leninist categories: cooperative farmers, laborers and employees, and intelligentsia. Overlapping these three categories is the subclass of lower-level "functionaries," those people who assume a particular leadership role in their work place or community. An overarching set of small elites enjoys special status and privileges. Alongside this hierarchically arranged structure, two other social categories—religious communities and political dissidents—deserve special mention.

Cooperative Farmers

Cooperative farmers constitute about two-thirds of East Germany's agricultural work force (down from three-fourths in 1965).[2] The remainder are mostly workers and employees of publicly owned farms or state services for feed, fertilizer, machinery, animal care, and plant quality. These public employees are organized in the agricultural union of the FDGB, have the approximate status of industrial workers, and thus are regarded as part of the working class.

The first cooperative farms were formed in the land reform of 1945–1949, when many farmers acquired "ownership" for the first time. For some, the collective sharing of meager resources was the most reasonable path to survival. The introduction of modest financial inducements during the next decade brought only a small increase in the rate of collectivization. Finally, in 1959–1960, the SED ordered an intense drive to collectivization, accomplished chiefly by denying independent farmers access to seeds and animal feed. Naturally, many crops were not planted, and starving animals had to be slaughtered. Although East Germany avoided most of the violence and physical suffering associated with Soviet collectivization, the shock of this period remains a vivid and bitter memory to most farmers.

Cooperative farmers today live a more secure existence. Their fluctuating incomes still depend on their shares in the cooperative profits, yet they are guaranteed a minimum wage on a par with industrial workers. Basic earnings from cooperative employment are significantly below those for urban workers.[3] However, household income occasionally exceeds the national average, because of supplemental earnings from animals and crops raised on private plots (three-fourths to one acre), auxiliary employment in the towns, and small shares paid to former owners of land willingly contributed to the cooperative.

Despite these improvements, collective farmers frequently voice complaints. Price supports have meant that cooperative income has generally been sufficient to gradually increase investment in machinery and equipment, but there is rarely enough money for construction. Buildings are urgently needed to protect new equipment from the weather. Cattle stalls, storage barns, and common buildings are in disrepair. Working hours are often very long: Some cooperative farmers average three hundred hours of overtime per year.[4]

Most cooperative farmers live in private homes. Though often more spacious than urban dwellings, they generally lack modern amenities. Extended families are common, with older members notably unwilling to leave the land. Collective farmers do not enjoy the cultural and recreational benefits available to labor-union members; they also receive less favorable retirement pensions. Shortages of consumer goods are more common in the countryside, yet nearly universal television ownership permits ready comparison of divergent living standards.

Younger people, most of whom have visited Berlin on FDJ excursions, are especially aware of differences between urban and rural life. Many aspire to find jobs in the city, but the more gifted experience great difficulty in gaining advanced education anywhere except in an agriculture institute, from which they are expected to return to the countryside as architects of modern farming. On the other hand, those who do make the transition to urban employment are not likely to suffer the kind of social discrimination commonly reported in the Soviet Union.

Cooperative farmers are the object of obvious political discrimination. Although partly the result of farmers' preferences, the cooperatives are seriously underrepresented in the SED membership and in the Central Committee. Even the highest government and party officials responsible for agriculture are noted for their lack of personal experience in the countryside. Rural political and economic leadership reflects the cumulative effects of SED cadre policy, which has often relegated less competent cadre members to the farms. It is not surprising that many cadre members try to mask their deficient skills by extreme arbitrariness. High SED spokesmen have acknowledged these shortcomings and have given assurance of better training for collective farm leaders.

The 1977 reform of the general law on cooperative statutes ostensibly provided greater leadership accountability and membership participation. It also promoted further specialization in work tasks and countless modes of collaboration among different forms of agricultural units. Apparently, a great deal of time and fuel is consumed in transporting specialized workers from one site to another. Farmers complain that frequent meetings establish nothing, except that interdependent work units find it very easy to evade responsibility for shortcomings in production.

Laborers and Employees

A difficulty in describing East Germany's social structure derives from the conventional language employed by SED politicians and sociologists. According to ideological presumption, there are no fundamental social distinctions between manual workers (*Arbeiter*) and nonmanual workers (*Angestellte*), a category that includes those in skilled and unskilled service jobs and office workers ("white collar" employees). Thus, much potentially useful information is highly aggregated; for example, data concerning household consumption lumps "laborers and employees" under a single heading. Since the category of "laborers" includes both skilled and unskilled manual workers and "employees" is essentially a residual category of many disparate occupations, this convention obscures interesting social divisions.

In the last decade East German social scientists have undertaken limited research into the working and living conditions of this broad "social class"—occasionally even noting differences within this class. Since about 1975, however, the *publication* of such research shows a clear trend toward less explicit data, as well as a reluctance to draw any general conclusions that are not wholly in agreement with established policy. This change probably results from Honecker's assertion that scientists—especially social scientists—had become too involved with non-Marxist theorizing and too divorced from the party's practical political concerns in "real existing socialism."[5]

Nevertheless, by combining published sociological research with a variety of other sources (press reports, literature, observations by foreign visitors), one can reach tentative conclusions about this most numerous class.

Official sources include more than 7.7 million people in the class of laborers and employees, roughly 89 percent of the total work force. If we subtract from this the members of the intelligentsia, this share drops to about 6.3 million, or 73 percent. Of these, more than 40 percent have completed the "specialist worker" curriculum.[6] Although the acquisition of this credential is highly touted in the official press, no available evidence suggests that it regularly plays a part in defining one's social status.

Much has already appeared in earlier chapters about this amorphous social class. Laborer and employee households are, after all, the "typical" households for whom most social policies have been created and the ones who receive the "average" benefits. And it is they who form the vast membership of the large social organizations, especially the FDGB.

Some significant differences arise within this class, depending upon one's family circumstances, employment situation, and career progress. All of these factors help to shape people's priorities and their choice of means for coping with competing demands on their time.

East German sources depict the typical family as having two employed parents and one or two children. There is no evidence of discrimination against couples who elect to have no children, but this is not an approved life choice. If homosexual households exist, they are not acknowledged in demographic studies. Single adults are always presumed to be widows or divorcées. Marriage and child rearing are strongly encouraged by cultural norms, as well as by official policy.

The increasingly evident educational and career concerns of women, together with modern birth-control methods, have gradually postponed the time when couples first have children. Children make a profound impact on life-styles. Parents will sometimes change jobs in order to secure better housing for their children or access to better child-care facilities. Young parents are acutely aware of the importance of educational achievement and a good "social record" (i.e., FDJ participation, no trouble with police) to children's life chances. They seek ways to maximize their time with children, for example, taking advantage of statutory child-care leaves. At the same time, most people believe that young people's chances for educational advancement or for overcoming minor difficulties with public authorities is generally affected by their parents' social position. So parents try to maintain a good record of work-place and FDGB participation, at least partly to aid their children.

This dual imperative—to give more attention to children and to give more time to work and public activities—can be very stressful. The normal work week is forty-two or even forty-four hours in some occupations, despite recent statutory revisions designed to reduce this obligation.[7] The shortage of time is also aggravated by inadequate provision of the many time-saving amenities people in Western "consumer" societies take for granted. There is considerable demand for more convenient food shopping: The government's earlier emphasis on large, centrally located supermarkets slowly is being supplemented by the resurrection of smaller neighborhood grocery retailers. There is also great demand for more prepared foods and labor-saving household appliances. Long waiting times for laundry services and repair services is a legendary complaint. Since the mid-1970s, the government has acknowledged the critical contribution of private enterprise in meeting these needs, and the policy of further reducing the number of independent markets and service establishments has, for all practical purposes, been abandoned.

As long as children are in school or college, parents are responsible for financial support—even though children's allowances, free tuition, and college stipends mitigate this burden. Once children are regularly employed, they may continue to live at home for a few years, but life changes for parents. It is now much easier to take advantage of travel opportunities, even if travel is normally restricted to the fraternal socialist countries. And it is time to relieve grandparents as caretakers of the family garden. (It is an old German tradition to have small gardens in otherwise unused spaces: at the edges of parks, along railroad rights-of-way, and so on.)

But life at this time can easily become a relatively unchanging routine, particularly as the majority of people in this situation long ago reached a career plateau. Work promotions go to younger, more qualified people. Although employers must provide adult-education programs, there is little reward for taking part. Since parental status has little effect on the life chances of mature offspring, parents lose the incentive to assume extra duties at work. This sudden and simultaneous diminution of both parental and employment pressures can be stultifying. At the age of forty, many people find that their lives are mostly behind them. It is not surprising that they often display bitter disenchantment with their own lives, as well as resentment and envy toward those who are more successful and privileged.

To the extent that these speculative generalizations are valid, one would expect them to apply equally to laborers and to other categories of employees. In some respects, however, production workers carry a special burden. For example, many laborers are exposed to health hazards on the job. Since the late 1960s, the labor unions have pursued this problem with some vigor, so that accident rates in some industries are now lower than in West Europe.[8] Nevertheless, East German laborers suffer more from polluted air, excessive noise, and toxic chemicals than do other citizens. Time is also a special problem for production workers. Not only do they work two to four hours longer per week than office employees, they also experience more pressure to take part in union and production meetings held after work hours. In addition, about 1 million workers are engaged in double- or triple-shift production.[9] Although shift workers usually have a slightly shorter workday, this is inadequate compensation for the extent to which normal family life is disrupted. Finally, production workers do not have the advantage—exploited by many office workers—of being able to occasionally leave work for short shopping errands. This may seem like a small benefit, but it can be helpful in reducing the burdens of running a household and in acquiring the often scarce consumer product.

In discussing East Germany's working class—that is, the class of laborers and employees—it is important to emphasize the extent to which incremental differences in the quality of life are directly linked to career achievements and the extent to which careers depend upon education and training and upon appropriately visible acceptance of social responsibility through some form of organizational participation. Most important is the fact that the entire occupation structure acts as a giant screening process in which the odds of moving from one level to the next are not favorable.

During the earlier Stalinist era, people had to contend with the possibility that false accusations or accidental associations could bring arbitrary and harsh intervention by the State Security forces (the "Stasi") and the destruction of career aspirations. The State Security apparatus still exists—quite visibly—and people still get into trouble with it and with other public authorities. But today they do so willfully, generally aware of the limits of permissible behavior. The random character of such damaging encounters is sharply diminished.

Today people know what they must do, and what they must *not* do, in order to succeed, at least in the material dimensions of life. As a result, people who weaken their career chances—by failing an exam, neglecting their work, or pointlessly challenging some public authority—are likely to blame themselves. Much psychologically oriented East German fiction addresses itself to this syndrome. The sense of failure is sometimes profound; it is believed to be associated with alcohol abuse, marital infidelity, divorce, and suicide.

For people whose career prospects have become bleak, there are very few choices. An unrepentant encounter with the Stasi is more or less permanent. Lesser problems, such as conflicts at work, can be handled by seeking other employment. But this is not always easily accomplished, and its benefit lies more in relieving tension than in resuming one's career advancement. And it is very rarely that people ever make a transfer to an entirely different kind of work.

As a point of comparison, it is quite true that Western liberal democratic societies are also career-bound and highly achievement oriented. Although Western governments do not incessantly propagate the "achievement principle" as a matter of public policy, the cultural norms of materialistic accumulation and the de facto distribution of political influence and social prestige may have the equal effect of creating homogeneous standards of success and failure. East German socialism certainly has no monopoly on the disruptive psychological consequences of career frustration, yet important differences remain. Unlike East German society, liberal democracies offer a wider variety of occupations and social institutions through which people can earn some respect and self-esteem and—discounting movements such as America's "moral majority"—fewer penalties for those whose life-styles depart from the accepted norms.

SED commentators would respond to this by claiming that diverse life-styles exist in capitalist liberal democracies only because differences in inherited wealth and social privilege enable certain individuals to evade socially useful roles. The GDR, they would argue, is made up predominantly of people who are engaged in socially constructive activity and who embark on their careers under essentially equal circumstances.

If one concentrates solely on the East German working class of laborers and employees, as presented in this discussion, there is some validity to the SED's claim of "equal opportunity." There are, however, some noteworthy exceptions to this general claim. The disadvantageous position of the cooperative farmers has already been mentioned. We now turn to the intelligentsia and the lower "functionaries," and the advantages they possess.

Intelligentsia

In contemporary East German usage, the term "intelligentsia" is not a synonym for intellectual; it does not describe one's reasoning abilities or one's approach to life. It merely describes the set of individuals who have earned a university or college degree. In light of the traditional—and contemporary—German tendency to attribute considerable prestige to such credentials, members of the intelligentsia have some characteristics of a distinctive social grouping.

SED sources contend that the intelligentsia is actually part of the working class, because it has the same relationship to property as do the laborers and employees. However, the intelligentsia is commonly referred to as an identifiable social stratum, a subset of the working class. In 1983 the intelligentsia encompassed about 1.5 million people with educational credentials and corresponding job titles, including scientists (physical, economic, social), physicians, teachers, engineers, artists, and writers.[10]

In the first postwar decade, the East German intelligentsia was almost exclusively of bourgeois origin. During the period of the open border to West Berlin, the intelligentsia contributed disproportionately to the westward emigration. In an effort to enlist the support of these highly qualified people, the GDR provided high salaries and privileged access to new housing. This pattern of material preferences is continued today; members of the intelligentsia commonly earn three times the average income for the ordinary working class. Although the intelligentsia is not formally entitled to housing preferences, the network of personal contacts developed within this stratum is sufficient to insure favored treatment in the acquisition of housing and scarce consumer goods.

Although the intelligentsia and the working class are employed in the same enterprises and institutions, and though they often belong to the same work collective, there is little socializing between the two groups apart from the work place. Nevertheless, the urban working class is very conscious of the notably higher standard of living enjoyed by the intelligentsia. This difference is evident in the way that homes are furnished, in the ownership of private cars, and in the quaint country cottages—the weekend retreats of the intelligentsia—visible to any who pass through the suburban countryside. A thrifty worker might find it possible to go to an elaborate restaurant or cabaret once a year. There he will find the intelligentsia, for whom such recreation is common.

Working-class resentment at the privileges of the intelligentsia is mitigated somewhat by the generations-old presumption that a better way of life is "naturally" due the nation's intellectual leaders. But SED teaching has gone far toward undermining this type of "bourgeois" thinking. Few workers fail to appreciate the irony of their inferior status in a "workers' state."

SED authorities argue that the benefits that accrue to the intelligentsia are not evidence of elitism. The intelligentsia, it is claimed, is nothing more than the best product of the working class. In terms of social origin, it is true that much of today's intelligentsia comes from working-class families. In the official view, there is no discrimination involved, when exceptional rewards flow to those who exercise exceptional responsibilities in the management of society.

Of course, other interpretations are possible. There is good evidence that the criteria for entry into the intelligentsia once again favor the children of the intelligentsia. Through their greater skills and resources these parents provide a home atmosphere more conducive to learning and to securing places in the best kindergartens and schools. Mothers find it much easier to get part-time jobs, permitting more time for child rearing. The affirmative discrimination preferences offered working-class students in university admissions has only marginally reduced the intelligentsia share among the student body. Among those students enrolled, children of the intelligentsia record a higher rate of graduation.

In a society where all are exhorted to ever-higher levels of achievement, it may be that working-class resentment is nothing more than envy directed at those who have achieved what all have aspired to. But when decisions concerning who is admitted to the expanded secondary schools and the universities turn on very small margins and occasionally subjective assessments, the differential rewards for those who "make it" and those who do not are indeed rather large. One is also entitled to question the values of a "worker's state" in which success is measured by one's ability to escape being a worker.

Functionaries

A number of different connotations can be attached to the term *functionary*. In common European usage, it simply refers to any official or anyone who carries out an official function. A similar SED concept is "cadre," which denotes people who, "because of their political abilities and occupational expertise, are active as leaders, officials, and specialists in all areas of society."[11] As noted in Chapter 3, a primary function of the party is to locate potential cadre members in all walks of life and to insure that they are properly trained and placed in responsible positions throughout governmental, economic, educational, and all other major social institutions. In one sense, this amounts to a desire to see that society is managed by capable people. Because it is so comprehensive, the cadre category overlaps all other social categories; because of the importance of expertise, the majority of the intelligentsia is necessarily designated as cadre.

For the purpose of the present discussion, I wish to make a subjective and problematic distinction between two types of cadre. On the one hand are those leaders who are essential to the functioning of any complex society. These are the people who assume management responsibilities—who direct the production enterprises, the enterprises of product distribution, the schools and universities, the army, the police, the labor unions, and the many administrative units involved in collecting public revenue and providing public services. For the most part, these cadre members—the "managing" cadre—have, through training and experience, acquired the substantive knowledge and decision-making skills necessary to lead people in production of specified goods and services.

Notwithstanding shortcomings in information and incentive systems, the managing cadre members are accountable for their leadership. For example, the effectiveness of an enterprise director can be observed by government and party officials, by employees, and by consumers. The quality of the work environment and the quantity and quality of the goods produced, as well as many other dimensions of effective management, are all subject to some sort of measurement. Likewise, it is possible to hold a hospital director accountable for the quality of health services, or labor-union leaders can be held accountable for their success in promoting safety or work-place amenities.

It may well be that, in practice, little is done to exploit these opportunities for accountability. But this defect does not alter the fact that, by the nature of their jobs, managing cadre members are responsible for some tangible outcome.

In contrast, one can identify another type of cadre member, whom I call "functionaries"—with a decidedly pejorative connotation. Functionaries may be defined as those people whose *primary* purpose is to promote an integrated society by instilling in others a sense of solidarity in the work-place collective, pride in the community, and loyalty to the nation. Functionaries are found in virtually every sort of institution. Some are easily identified, such as an enterprise union leader for culture or a city party second secretary for propaganda. Others hold less obvious titles, such as deputy enterprise director or hospital director of public information.

What all functionaries have in common is an evident detachment from the defining activity of the enterprise or institution. They are rarely involved in the production of goods and services. Instead, they produce slogans and coordinate meetings on raising morale, on the necessity for better work qualifications, or on the relevance of SED resolutions for the immediate tasks of socialist construction. Some of what functionaries do may indeed have a beneficial effect, but there is no way to determine whether their activities have any positive effect on social integration.

A word of caution is in order here. It should be evident that the task of social integration is not reserved exclusively to functionaries. Managing cadre members often contribute to this task, either as a by-product of their primary activity or as a deliberate adjunct duty, such as making public speeches. Ordinary employees, of course, may promote social integration by their approach to any kind of collective activity. What separates functionaries from the managing cadre and ordinary workers is the nature of their primary or defining activity. In effect, they are professional "cheer leaders."

Another feature of the functionary role is that the supposed results of the activity can scarcely be measured. To be sure, one can count placards on the walls or attendance at enterprise meetings, yet these are poor indicators for the fundamental goals of spreading patriotism and commitment to socialism. As a result of this shortcoming, functionaries cannot really be held accountable for the products of their work. Thus, their job security and promotion depend mainly on their ability to convince superiors in the appropriate propaganda division of the SED and FDGB that they are performing well.

It is small wonder that fellow workers regard functionaries as sycophants. It is widely believed that people who become functionaries are rather poor workers, who attempt to gain by "boot licking" what they could not hope to gain by merit. Most workers consider functionaries as a simple fact of life, a phenomenon to be tolerated. Some employees claim to have created a wholesome socialist collective, despite the existence of functionaries. Overt opposition to functionaries is to be avoided, since they can create obstacles to career advancement.

At one level, functionaries can be considered a resource to be exploited or merely a nuisance. But occasionally they are the object of deep resentment, because of the benefits they reap. Despite marked differences in actual responsibility, many functionaries occupy employment positions formally on a par with managing cadre. As such, they are designated as carrying special societal responsibilities, and they receive additional wage increments. Not only are these wage benefits perceived as undeserved, they also constitute a burden on the wage fund of the employing institution and a drain on the entire national economy.

Elites

Beyond the specification of three main social classes—cooperative farmers, laborers and employees, and intelligentsia—and the overlapping subgroup of functionaries, further refinement of the status hierarchy is extremely speculative. The East German press and authorized literature reveal little about the nation's highest elites; social scientists deny their existence altogether. Yet private conversations and personal observations confirm the existence of a very small and especially privileged set of elites—encompassing perhaps no more than five hundred leaders and their families. Precise description is impossible, so the following picture is offered as an "educated guess."

The most important segment of the East German elite is, of course, the *party-government elite.* As a rough estimate, this segment should include most of the 213 members and alternates of the SED Central Committee, above all the SED Secretariat and the leaders of prestigious Central Committee departments, most members of the Council of Ministers, and the first secretaries of the regional SED committees. As noted in Chapter 3, disagreement within this elite is to be expected, as individuals advocate different priorities in public policy corresponding to their own areas of specific responsibilities. Different perspectives also arise between those in Berlin and those in the regions. On the whole, however, membership in the Central Committee is a widely recognized mark of status. Those who occupy this position have a common interest in preserving their power and privileges.

The Central Committee always includes at least nominal representation from each of the other elites. But it is appropriate to give the other elites separate mention, since most of the members do not belong to the Central Committee.

One can estimate an *economic elite,* consisting of perhaps 40–50 directors of the major economic enterprises, primarily the large industrial combines. A *military-security elite* probably includes 30–50 of the highest officers in the National People's Army and the State Security Service. An *academic-scientific elite* would probably include the 150 full members of the Academy of Sciences. The nation's 40–50 best-known writers and performers would constitute an *artistic elite.*

Were it practical to conduct a thorough sociological study of these elites, the following observations would probably be supported.

1. Entry into any of these elites is achieved through a combination of merit and personal connection (patronage), with a decided emphasis on the latter. Disaffected intelligentsia claim that certain of the highest SED officials, not noted for their personal brilliance, must have achieved elite status *exclusively* through patronage. The most extreme illustration of personalistic recruitment is provided by Erich Honecker, whose wife is minister of public education, whose brother-in-law is head of the Central Committee Department for Foreign Information, and whose father-in-law became an FDGB representative for relations with Western countries.

2. Patronage networks exist within each elite, extend down from each elite into the ranks of the intelligentsia, and often link several elites together. Of course, network linkages to people in the party-government elite are the most useful. Top SED officials apparently gain personal satisfaction in following the careers of writers or academics, occasionally

seeking direct contact and even personal friendships. The recipients of this interest find such party contacts enormously valuable when one of their artistic or scholarly works comes under criticism from some other official.

3. The interaction of elites probably differs between Berlin and the regional centers, but it would not be unusual to find representatives of several different elites together at a public or social event. One might even discover a high SED cultural official sharing cocktails with an innovative writer, whose latest novel the official had criticized in the party press. The point is that, despite internal differences, the GDR elites constitute a somewhat closed community.

4. This "community" character is made possible, in part, because the GDR experiences what sociologists call a slow "circulation of elites." A great many people who rose to prominence in the early transition years are still professionally active. For example, novelist Stefan Heym has belonged to the artistic elite for about as long as Kurt Hager has been SED secretary for science and culture (since 1955). Over the years, these two men have clashed many times, through many changes in literary policy. Undoubtedly, they have learned very well to anticipate each other's behavior. Although a concerted effort by top SED officials can eventually cause an individual to lose elite status, people such as Stefan Heym demonstrate the durability of the elite system, as well as the utility of combining talent with protective patronage.

5. A common attribute of all elites is an extraordinarily high standard of living. Personal incomes are many times the national average. In addition, members of the elites typically have received one or more public honors—orders for service to the state, prizes for outstanding professional achievement—with a financial bonus of 2,000 to 20,000 marks.[12] Those in the artistic elite normally receive the highest incomes, mainly through royalties. Except for self-employed performers and writers, elite members hold high official posts in party, government, or other public institutions. Official rank entitles them to a host of free personal amenities, such as domestic servants, access to specially reserved retail outlets for food and consumer goods, and exclusive use of cultural and recreational facilities. Special housing is available in guarded residential enclaves. Moreover, the elite citizens seem to be immune to other problems that complicate the lives of ordinary citizens, such as customs regulations, traffic laws, and routine administrative restrictions. In many cases, they are able to extend these privileges to their children. At the very least, children of the elite enjoy advantages in school. They also are able to build upon established networks of all-important personal connections.

6. Finally, it should be clear that the elites make the rules for East German society. They wield enormous power over their aspiring successors, having the ability to give careers a vital assist or a grievous setback.

Overview of the Status Hierarchy

An overview of contemporary East German society reveals a very small elite exerting predominant influence over an essentially three-tiered class structure. An amorphous category of intelligentsia, less than one-fifth of the people, constitutes what might be called the upper-middle class. Nearly three-fourths of the population are aggregated into the lower-middle class of laborers and employees. The small group of cooperative farmers is accurately described as the lower class. For most purposes, employees of public farms and the handful of remaining private farms are roughly equivalent to the lower-middle class. The self-employed, some 1.6 percent of the work force,[13] do not form an identifiable social category, since this designation ranges from the marginal shopkeeper to the affluent writer.

The GDR differs from most Western liberal democracies in the shape of its social structure. In the first place, a wealth measurement shows less distance between the top and bottom classes. A class of destitute poor, such as America's migrant workers, does not exist. At the same time, the GDR has nothing comparable to the West's "super rich." Even the highest elite enjoys a level of consumption scarcely beyond the reach of many U.S. middle-class families. As a result of this compressed class structure, there are fewer identifiable gradients at the margins of each class, and the life-style differences between classes seem to be more abrupt. Mature citizens with no opportunity to alter their basic social status also find it extremely difficult to effect marginal improvements in their standard of living and thus to draw nearer to the next-higher class. In contrast, Americans generally find that the next rung on the status hierarchy is not far away. Perhaps the increasing shift of GDR employment toward more specialized occupations in the service sector, indicated by the growing class of intelligentsia, may lead to a refinement of the status hierarchy and the recognition of more intermediate levels.

The avenues of social mobility—advancement from one class to the next—are rather rigidly prescribed in East Germany. All modern societies rely heavily on educational attainment as a requisite of social advancement, but the GDR has gone further than liberal democracies in reducing the linkage between educational attainment and class background. Only in the very limited case of elite families can East German youngsters use inherited status to compensate for shortcomings in schooling. People who elect to become "functionaries" may enjoy marginal improvement in personal privileges, but this is rarely converted into actual upward mobility. Virtually all changes in a person's social status occur as a result of screening that takes place between the ages of fourteen and thirty. A setback experienced in this period—poor school grades or conflict with public authorities—is permanent.

The farther up the status hierarchy one progresses, the more privileges are provided. Since most privileges are tied directly to one's employment, especially among the intelligentsia, there is great incentive to avoid any action that might jeopardize one's job. This situation creates a profound dilemma for those who are called upon to exercise initiative in approaching problems in production or administration, since initiative may involve implied criticism of one's superiors—those with the power to take away material privileges.

Religious Communities

Religious communities do not represent the same sort of social differentiation as the classes and strata discussed so far. In fact, the larger churches form a sort of vertical linkage that cuts across class divisions. Thus, churches may be regarded as institutions of both differentiation and integration. This is certainly the case in the GDR.

Westerners commonly think that Marxism-Leninism is fundamentally antithetical to any sort of religion. Even though there is much in the history of church-party relations to support this view, it can be seriously misleading. Clarification is necessary at both the philosophic and practical levels.

It should be noted that Marxism emanated from a European Christian culture. Many of Marx's humanistic goals have obvious roots in the humanistic dimension of Christianity; much of Marx's description of the future society—one of equality, fraternity, solidarity—is very reminiscent of early Christian communities. Marx's antagonism was directed not against these religious values, but rather against the organized church of nineteenth-century Europe, which encouraged passivity among the impoverished masses and urged them to accept their condition as "God's will."

In the twentieth century, the relationship between communist parties and organized religions has been partly a function of two elements: the degree of mysticism and fatalism in church doctrine and the willingness of the church to accept the secular authority of the state and to reject temporal sources of divine authority, such as the pope in Rome. The fate of churches in postwar East Germany is not merely a matter of SED reluctance to antagonize the church-affiliated majority of the population; it is also a product of the prior disposition of the churches and their compatibility with specific goals and needs of the new state.

It is, therefore, highly significant that the major churches in East Germany are among the most "secularized," socially activist churches. The Evangelical (Lutheran) church has long been the home of social-reform advocates and the sponsor of manifold social services. And it long ago came to terms with secular authority. At the same time, Lutheran leaders have sometimes spoken out sharply against specific government practices, producing many martyrs on behalf of resistance to Nazism. Unlike church leaders in the East European states, German Lutherans could not easily be accused of collaboration with fascism. To a similar extent—though less visibly, perhaps—these same points apply to Roman Catholics in the GDR, except that certain applications of papal authority have spawned sharp government reaction. Taken as a whole, it can be said that organized religion has enjoyed more freedom and autonomy in the GDR than in any other communist state—with the possible exception of the Roman Catholic church in Poland.

In the GDR today,[14] there are an estimated 7.9 million members of the Evangelical (Lutheran) church. This equals about 46 percent of the population and 86 percent of all church members. As with the other major churches, Evangelical membership is declining at the rate of about 2.5 percent annually. This represents a rather pervasive element of church-affiliated citizens. Although SED members, functionaries, and other cadre members are rarely church members, many of their friends and relatives are. In its own way, the church is a very normal part of life in East Germany; its presence is felt in most segments of society.

The Evangelical (Lutheran) church operates fifty-one hospitals and hundreds of convalescent centers, retirement homes, campgrounds, and nurseries. Their patrons include a great many SED members. It has more than fifteen thousand employees in these institutions and in parishes. Sunday morning services have been broadcast by radio since 1946, and television has been added since the 1960s. Since 1978, the church has been permitted broadcasts of special events, as well as a monthly program of news and commentary. This level of religious media access represents an earlier, and far more positive, church-state accommodation than in any other East European state. There are five weekly Evangelical newspapers. With very few exceptions, church use of the media is not subject to censorship. Of course, there is no censorship of the content of religious services or of the bishop's letters occasionally read to congregations.

Church social services are subsidized by public funds, although the construction of new facilities is not. The poorly paid pastors of small congregations receive government income supplements. The national labor code includes a special section written by the church for its own employees. Each of the five major universities has a theology faculty for training new ministers, without a tuition fee.

The Evangelical church retains title to much land, unaffected by the early land reform. In recent years, land for new churches has been acquired by exchanging agricultural church land for public land in urban areas. Public funds have been used to restore to use several old churches designated as national landmarks.

Church revenue comes from voluntary church "taxes" on members (unlike the government in the Federal Republic, the GDR government no longer collects taxes on behalf of the church); from government subsidies for social services, pastoral education, income supplements, and construction; and from rents on land leased to agricultural cooperatives. A substantial additional source of income is contributions from "sister" churches in the Federal Republic, which often exceed one-third of the total income. These outside contributions are actually welcomed by the GDR government, since they boost the national economy through hard-currency transfers.

Taken as a whole, the above arrangements portray a rather prominent social profile for the Evangelical (Lutheran) church and a relatively accommodative government posture toward this institution outside the SED-sponsored network of public organizations. This picture also reflects a position of privilege, when compared to churches in other communist states and even to smaller churches in the GDR.

For the purpose of regulating church-state relations, there exists a Community of Christian Churches in the GDR, which encompasses the Evangelical (Lutherans), Methodists (thirty-seven thousand members), Baptists (thirty thousand), and six smaller churches. The Roman Catholic church, with more than 1.2 million members, has observer status in this community. The Russian Orthodox church has a very small, but unspecified, membership. Somewhat curiously, in 1960 Berlin was designated the seat of Russian Orthodox leadership for all of Central Europe.

As in many other nations, the tiny community of Jehovah's Witnesses has no legal standing in the GDR, chiefly because it rejects secular authority. Jehovah's Witnesses are not systematically persecuted, but members of this community are occasionally prosecuted for refusing even noncombatant alternatives to compulsory military training.

The Jewish community is very small and well on the way to extinction, having dwindled from 3,100 in 1946 to only 750 in 1981. Despite official GDR denunciations of "Zionism," the government practices no overt discrimination against Jews. Many receive social-security supplements as "victims of fascism," and state funds have recently been used to rebuild several synagogues and to construct two new ones. But there is no rabbinical school and, since 1969, not a single rabbi.

The development of church-state relations has consisted primarily of a dialogue between the SED Department for Religious Questions and Lutheran and Roman Catholic leaders.[15] Like the Lutherans, Roman Catholics are very active in providing social services, and together they share a great many perspectives on dealings with the SED. This dialogue frequently has generated bitter conflict over four main issues.

First, despite much evidence of accommodation, long-term SED policy foresees the eventual obsolescence of religious communities. This decline should result from the gradual secularization of daily life and the spread of "scientific" culture—similar to processes occurring in other modern societies. But the SED has also taken deliberate steps to hasten this process. Throughout the 1950s, the government gradually abolished the former German practice of providing religious instruction in the schools. Church-sponsored youth clubs were shut down, and youth and parents were pressured to abandon christenings, confirmations, and church weddings and funerals in favor of analogous state-sponsored ceremonies. Religious instruction for youth is permitted if conducted in church facilities. A limited scope for other religious activities for youth, such as summer camps, has reemerged in the last decade.

A certain degree of stability now exists in this contest over secularization of life. But the early years were full of conflict, frequently leading to defiant protests, arrests, and emigration.

Second, the GDR leadership has continuously fought both Lutherans and Roman Catholics over the issue of church authority and territorial boundaries. For many years Western governments followed the lead of the Federal Republic in denying to the GDR the legal status of a sovereign state; the GDR was, in this view, merely "the Soviet Occupation Zone." Consequently, in its struggle to win international diplomatic recognition, the GDR government demanded that the East German Lutheran church become formally separate from the West German church organization and that Roman Catholic diocesan boundaries be brought into conformity with the national boundaries of the GDR. Not until 1969 did the East German Lutheran church agree to organizational separation, in exchange for an expanded scope for religious activity within the GDR itself. The Roman Catholic church has been even more reluctant to comply with government demands. In 1972 the Berlin bishopric was finally removed from the authority of the Polish church, and Silesia was formally recognized as Polish territory. But the Holy See still administers church affairs in the western GDR through West German authorities. The continuing high visibility of Rome's authority over East German Catholics, combined with unresolved disputes over the territorial question, irritates

GDR officials. As a consequence, Roman Catholic leaders have less freedom than their Lutheran counterparts. Catholics are especially subject to government interference with their efforts to meet with Catholics from other nations.

The third major area of conflict concerns allegations of government discrimination against members of religious communities. In one sense, discrimination is obvious with respect to recruitment to positions of public leadership. With few exceptions, public posts routinely go to SED members; both the party and the religious communities generally believe that SED membership is incompatible with active church membership. In a broader sense, the issue of discrimination is subject to dispute. Some church leaders claim that young people who take part in religious education are systematically excluded from advanced secondary and higher education. There have been a few reports of successful legal challenges against educational authorities on the grounds of religious discrimination. But discrimination can be subtle and very difficult to prove. In August 1976, a Lutheran pastor committed public suicide by self-immolation as a protest against "suppression of youth." The church delivered a sharp indictment of the SED leadership. This was followed by extensive party-church consultations, Erich Honecker's repeated assurances of equal opportunity for all citizens, and a highly publicized plan for accelerated construction of churches and church-related social-service facilities.

The fourth issue involves an emerging role for the church as a critic of public policy. Partly as a result of expanded church rights and a regular pattern of church-SED negotiations, some religious communities—especially the Evangelical (Lutheran) church—have attained the status of a "loyal opposition." The unprecedented meeting between Erich Honecker and Lutheran Bishop Albrecht Schönherr in March 1978 may be interpreted as a tacit acknowledgment of this position. While stressing the active cooperation of the "church in socialism," many Lutherans seek to preserve a "critical distance" from the ruling SED, a posture that occasionally leads to public criticism of party policies. In recent years, church leaders have expressed reservations about the new abortion law and the militaristic emphasis in public education. Both issues evoked an SED willingness to discuss church concerns. In 1980, pastoral letters and church media mentioned Soviet involvement in the Afghanistan war as an example of a threat to world peace. On this issue the party leaders showed no tolerance. Church newspapers were censored, and a church delegation was refused permission to attend a West German convocation.

Despite such confrontations, both sides appear determined to build a stable *modus vivendi.* The church is thoroughly engaged in the life of the GDR, and it is likely to take full advantage of its opportunities for social criticism. The SED authorities have accepted the church as an indisputable fact of life, and they are willing to seek common ground wherever possible. At the same time, the extensive privileges granted to the church provide the party leaders with a host of sanctions, to be applied whenever church leaders step beyond the bounds of tolerable opposition.

Political Dissidents

East German's political dissidents cannot be identified as a distinctive social category for several reasons. First of all, it is not at all clear what attributes or behavior actually constitute dissidence. In the GDR, as in almost any society, it is not possible to neatly separate antisocial acts from antigovernment acts. For example, is vandalism in the schools a sign of political dissidence, because it damages state property? Should an assault on a public official always be construed as a political act, or might it sometimes be merely the effort of a social deviant to gain notoriety? Second, to the extent that political dissidence can be identified, it assumes radically different forms. A treatise by Professor Robert Havemann challenging the Marxist credentials of "real existing socialism" is hardly comparable to a slogan painted on a public wall (Russians go home!) or a teenager wearing a T-shirt reading "U.S. Naval Academy." Finally, since such disparate political dissidents generally have no knowledge of one another's existence, they cannot be described as a group in a sociological sense.

Nevertheless, it is quite useful to identify as subcategories of the principal social divisions those individuals who have consciously adopted a posture of dissent from the tenets of SED rule. In addition to the self-conscious "critical distance" exemplified by some opinion leaders of the religious communities already noted, political dissidents are evident in three other settings: youth, writers and intellectuals, and frustrated aspirants to higher social status.

Youth

Although a great many East German young people acquire achievement values and group norms in school and FDJ activities and busily embark on an approved path of occupational and social mobility, some become disaffected with social and political rules rather early in life. Two kinds of youth are especially prone to dissident orientations: those who are permanently screened out of the contest for advanced education by early academic failure and the rather different group of children from privileged families who easily perceive the extent to which antiintellectual "functionaries" seek to manipulate the mass of citizens. For both groups, the widely recognized disparity between their own material and recreational amenities and those available in the Federal Republic is an acutely felt aggravation.

Youth dissidence is often expressed in unstructured ways. For example, many young citizens eagerly emulate U.S. and West German styles in music, clothing, and colloquial speech. This trend cannot readily be interpreted as a decided preference for Western social or political systems; it is more likely a simple effort to stay up-to-date or to demonstrate defiance of adult norms.

In the 1970s, dissident GDR folksinger Wolf Biermann acquired a large youth following, with his songs about the false promises of modern society. In 1975–1976 youth discussion groups—some using church facilities—were reported in several East German cities. These groups dealt with dissident literature and prohibited political treatises by East German and Soviet Marxists and Social Democrats. When some groups drafted letters protesting the treatment of Wolf Biermann, their leaders were accused of an antistate conspiracy and "voluntarily" exiled to the Federal Republic.

Young people are occasionally involved in spontaneous public disturbances. The most visible such event took place during the National Day celebration in 1977. When a public rock concert was closed down prematurely by police, protesting youth became violent, destroyed holiday propaganda signs, and shouted anti-Russian sentiments. Smaller clashes with police have been reported in subsequent years.

Writers and Intellectuals

Over the years, dissidence among East Germany's writers and intellectuals has been a recurring, but somewhat fragmented, phenomenon. The most common protest concerns gratuitous and restrictive interference by inexpert SED officials in the establishment of literary standards and academic research emphases. During certain political phases, these protests have culminated in dialogue and bargaining between officials of the SED Secretariat, on the one hand, and the Writer's Association or segments of the Academy of Sciences, on the other. Such a bargaining phase was very evident in 1972–1975, the early Honecker years.

At other times writers and intellectuals have gone beyond the narrow problems affecting the exercise of their professional roles. They then articulate a more inclusive criticism of the GDR's political and social system, an activity that more properly qualifies as open dissent. Such criticism is usually diverse. Some dissenters attack the contemporary system from the standpoint of a "more authentic" or a "more humane" Marxism; others crystallize antibureaucratic or anti-Stalinist sentiments.

Two catalytic events of the mid-1970s helped to shape this critical mood into a recognizable dissident movement.[16] The first was the GDR's acceptance of the Final Act of the Conference on Security and Cooperation in Europe, signed at Helsinki in August 1975. The act includes significant provisions concerning civil liberties and the reunification of families, especially pertinent to East German citizens. The second event was the Berlin Conference of Communist Parties in June 1976. This conference was notable for the assertive posture adopted by several West European communist parties, their thinly veiled attacks against remnants of Stalinism in East Europe, and the inability of the participating delegations to adopt even the facade of unity in the concluding conference documents.

East German intellectuals seized these two events as justification for demanding unhindered exercise of civil liberties and for proposing a course of GDR political development more consonant with the "Eurocommunism" of their Western counterparts. A great many advocates of these claims were SED members in good standing. Authorities in the SED Secretariat tried to mute this wave of dissent by depriving the most outspoken protesters of their public forums and their positions in artistic and academic organs. Each such attempt produced a spate of protest and a further consolidation of dissidents into an identifiable group.

Robert Havemann and Wolf Biermann reemerged as focal points of dissent. Havemann is a Marxist philosopher who was deprived of his Humboldt University professorship and expelled from the SED in 1964, following a series of lectures in which he claimed that socialism did not exist in the GDR. "Socialism," he said, "cannot be realized without democracy."[17] Wolf Biermann similarly had been deprived of an audience for his Marxist critiques in poetry and song. For twelve years, both Havemann and Biermann maintained an East German following by publishing in the West German media.

In November 1976, Wolf Biermann began an officially approved concert tour of the Federal Republic, during which he was deprived of his GDR citizenship.[18] A host of writers and intellectuals, including Havemann and several award-winning novelists, vigorously denounced this perfidious and illegal government action. Havemann was placed under house arrest. Several writers were expelled from the SED and from the Writers' Association. The few who intensified their organized opposition were arrested. Others who barely stayed within legal bounds were "encouraged" to emigrate to the Federal Republic.

Incarceration and exile were not entirely suitable weapons, however, for most of the nation's renowned writers, artists, composers, and actors had participated in these protests to one degree or another. The SED leaders were unwilling to suffer the embarrassing loss of an entire generation of prominent intellectuals. Consequently, SED cultural authorities have undertaken a bewildering and somewhat contradictory policy of granting privileges to certain less obstreperous dissidents, while prosecuting and/or exiling others.[19] The frequent policy of compulsory emigration is clearly unwelcome to many dissidents, who consider themselves good Marxists and loyal citizens. But emigration has the ironic effect of enabling dissidents to disseminate their views to a wide GDR audience through the use of West German media.

After the initial post-Biermann outburst, the SED troubles with internal dissidents was fueled by two further incidents. In the summer of 1977, SED member Rudolf Bahro successfully published a sophisticated political study through a West German firm.[20] His work, *Die Alternative*, is a pointed, but scholarly, critique of "real existing socialism" in the GDR and the USSR.[21] Bahro was sentenced to prison for "propagating hatred against the government." In January 1978, a West German news magazine published the "Manifesto of the League of Democratic Communists of Germany."[22] The anonymous authors portrayed themselves as an underground camp of East German dissidents. The "Manifesto" included denunciations of corruption, the remote rule of the "Politburocracy," and the repressive effect of Soviet interference.[23]

By 1980 the most vocal expressions of intellectual dissent had subsided. Although high SED sources sharpened their verbal attacks against ideological and military threats from the West (as part of the general deterioration of East-West relations), most dissenting intellectuals had regained their former professional status. Rudolf Bahro emigrated to the Federal Republic, after having been released from prison in the amnesty of October 1979. In 1980, two more writers were prosecuted for attempting to publish "hostile propaganda" in the West German press.[24] Emigration is still occasionally offered to dissidents who wish to leave. But most intellectuals and writers now avoid direct and open dissent, choosing instead to focus on exploring the limits of freedom within their respective professions.

Frustrated Ordinary Citizens

An accounting of political dissidents is not complete without mention of the unknown number of ordinary citizens who turn against a political system that, they feel, has turned against them. Westerners can find numerous unofficial accounts of East Germans whose efforts to forge successful careers have been sabotaged by arbitrary action on the part of political "functionaries" and other public authorities. These confrontations are not random, and citizens have an opportunity to elect their own responses.

For example, a professor on academic exchange to a foreign country may be asked to assist the State Security Service, or a citizen may be asked to drop a complaint against a corrupt police officer. The prudent citizen knows what is expected in the way of "cooperative" behavior. But citizens are not always prudent. As a result, they find their career aspirations damaged. At this point, according to numerous case histories, one is confronted with a choice: to accept one's fate with resignation or to intensify one's protests. The latter course can lead to outright political opposition and, eventually, a prison term.

There is no way to determine how many people follow this glamourless path to political opposition. They make only small waves, and they never make the headlines of the Western press. Amnesty International estimates 3,000–7,000 political prisoners in the GDR.[25] In October 1979 more than 21,000 prisoners were released in a general amnesty; of these, perhaps 1,500 were political prisoners, according to the nongovernmental West German "August 13 Working Group." Many former political prisoners are eventually permitted to emigrate to the Federal Republic, as part of a humanitarian program heavily financed by the West German government.

Of course, the majority of citizens never even approach the state of political dissent. They have learned to regard the somewhat pretentious aspirations of the party and government leadership with a good deal of cynicism. And if the unequal distribution of privileges falls far short of SED promises, most citizens find congenial and politically acceptable ways to express their frustrations. In the last analysis, the East German people can find much that is good in life, they can note that social progress is slow but tangible, and they can console themselves with the thought that a certain amount of self-aggrandizement and hypocrisy characterizes government in virtually all nations of the world.

Notes

1. "Das neue Programm der SED," *Deutschland Archiv* 9, no. 7 (1976), p. 761.

2. Jochen Beth Renhagen et al., *DDR und Osteuropa: Wirtschaftssystem, Wirtschaftpolitik, Lebensstandard* [GDR and East Europe: Economic System, Economic Policy, Standard of Living] (Opladen: Leske, 1981), p. 96.

3. Ibid., p. 99.

4. Doris Cornelsen et al., *Handbook of the Economy of the German Democratic Republic* (Westmead, England: Saxon House, 1979), pp. 136–143.

5. Quoted in Otto Rheinhold, "Gestaltung der entwickelten sozialistischen Gesellschaft im Lichte des Programmentwurfs [The Formation of Developed Socialist Society in Light of the Draft Program]," *Einheit*, no. 3 (1976), p. 287.

6. *Protokoll des X. FDGB-Kongresses* [Protocol of the Tenth FDGB Congress] (Berlin: Tribüne, 1982), pp. 43–44.

7. Ibid., p. 29.

8. Ibid., p. 16.

9. Ibid., p. 21.

10. Günter Erbe, *Arbeiterklasse und Intelligenz in der DDR* [The Working Class and the Intelligentsia in the GDR] (Opladen: Westdeutscher, 1982), p. 90.

11. Günter Erbe et al., *Politik, Wirtschaft, und Gesellschaft in der DDR* [Politics, Economy, and Society in the GDR] (Cologne: Westdeutscher, 1979), p. 100.

12. Peter C. Ludz et al., *DDR Handbuch*, 2d ed. [GDR Handbook] (Cologne: Wissenschaft und Politik, 1979), pp. 115–127 [hereafter, *DDR Handbuch*].

13. Zentralverwaltung für Statistik, *Statistisches Jahrbuch 1980 der Deutschen Demokratischen Republik* (Berlin: Staatsverlag, 1980), p. 86.

14. Data for all churches are taken from *DDR Handbuch*, pp. 586–596.

15. Gisela Helwig, " 'Wir müssen und wollen Flagge zeigen': Zur derzeitigen Situation der evangelischen Kirchen in der DDR ['We Must and We Will Show the Flag': On the Current Situation of the Evangelical Church in the GDR]," *Deutschland Archiv* 14, no. 4 (1981), pp. 345–347.

16. Karl Wilhelm Fricke, "Zwischen Resignation und Selbstbehauptung [Between Resignation and Self-Assertion]," *Deutschland Archiv* 9, no. 11 (1976), pp. 1135–1139.

17. Robert Havemann, "Über Sozialismus und Freiheit [About Socialism and Freedom]," *Deutschland Archiv* 9, no. 8 (1976), p. 1105.

18. Manfred Jäger, "Das Ende einer Kulturpolitik: Die Fälle Kunze und Biermann [The End of a Cultural Policy: The Cases of Kunze and Biermann]," *Deutschland Archiv* 9, no. 12 (1976), pp. 1233–1235.

19. Harald Kleinschmid, "Die geistige Auseinandersetzung in der DDR findet im Westen statt [The GDR's Intellectual Confrontation Is Taking Place in the West]," *Deutschland Archiv* 10, no. 10 (1977), pp. 1011–1017.

20. Ilse Spittmann, "Der Fall Bahro [The Bahro Affair]," *Deutschland Archiv* 10, no. 10 (1977), pp. 1009–1011.

21. Manfred Hertwig, rev. of *Die Alternative: Zur Kritik des real existierenden Sozialismus* [The Alternative: On a Critique of Real Existing Socialism], by Rudolf Bahro, *Deutschland Archiv* 10, no. 10 (1977), pp. 1093–1098.

22. Peter Bender, "Episode oder Alarmzeichen für Honecker?: Anmerkungen zum 'Spiegel-Manifest' [Incident or Alarm for Honecker?: Observations on the 'Spiegel Manifesto']," *Deutschland Archiv* 11, no. 2 (1978), pp. 113–116.

23. "Das Spiegel Manifest und die Reaktion der DDR [The Spiegel Manifesto and the Reaction of the GDR]," *Deutschland Archiv* 11, no. 2 (1978), pp. 199–219.

24. Harald Kleinschmid, " 'Fehler sind Natur': Zur Kulturpolitik der DDR im zweiten Halbjahr 1980 ['Mistakes Are Natural': On the Cultural Policy of the GDR in the Second Half of 1980]," *Deutschland Archiv* 14, no. 1 (1981), pp. 39–44.

25. *Amnesty International Report 1980* (London: Amnesty International, 1980), pp. 269–272.

8
National Security and Foreign Relations

Citizens in many Western liberal democracies—especially in the militarily and economically dominant nations, such as the United States—have long been accustomed to regarding foreign relations as quite removed from the ordinary conduct of politics. For most Americans, foreign policy could be reduced to the relatively single-minded task of "safeguarding the free world." Because this task depended heavily on the complexities of military technology and the secret world of intelligence and espionage, Americans came to depend on the advice of experts and the principle of "bipartisanship" in devising appropriate policies. But more recently, extensive citizen participation in the Vietnam War and the increasingly tangible effects of dependence upon a fluctuating global economy have taught Americans the lesson learned long ago by the citizens of smaller nations: Foreign relations are not a detached realm of activity, but an integral part of any society's endeavor to provide peace and well-being for its people.

Historical Background

Nowhere is the intertwining of foreign and domestic policies more palpable than in the German Democratic Republic. Here, in a way that most Westerners would find impossible to comprehend, vital questions concerning the legitimacy of the state and the people's way of life depend upon a precarious balance of somewhat contradictory principles of foreign relations.

East German foreign policy must concern itself with three high priorities: (1) strengthening the legitimacy of SED rule and acceptance of the GDR as a sovereign socialist state (a concern with both internal and external dimensions); (2) security against the threat of almost certain destruction in the event of overt warfare between Europe's two military blocs; and (3) assuring economic growth and improved popular well-being through an expansion and rationalization of foreign trade. Speaking generally, of course, a great many nations face a similar array of foreign-policy goals. What distinguishes the nations of East Europe—and the GDR, above all—is the degree to which the world's political and economic alignment creates dilemmas in the pursuit of basic goals.

This point can be illustrated by contrasting the circumstances of the two German states. For at least the first two decades of its existence, the Federal Republic was able to pursue its quest for legitimacy, security, and economic development within the context of wide-ranging U.S. military, economic, and political hegemony. This orientation was dictated by the circumstance of military occupation and greatly facilitated by the population's reserve of pro-American, anti-Russian sentiments. Although the process unfolded slowly in the beginning, the West Germans found ample rewards in adopting a dependent position within the U.S. sphere of influence. By accepting the U.S. military presence as the defining element of national security, by implementing economic policies congenial to U.S. capital investment, and by instituting political reforms in the American image, the new Federal Republic enjoyed the strong support of the considerable diplomatic leverage of the United States. This support made it possible to acquire international recognition, the intimidating might of U.S. modern armed forces and nuclear weaponry, and such economic advantages as Marshall Fund financing for industrial reconstruction, easy access to the vast U.S. market for the export of German consumer goods, and partnership in the far-flung Western network for the transfer of raw materials from the underdeveloped nations to the manufacturing centers of the United States' allies.

None of this should be interpreted to mean that the Federal Republic became merely a U.S. "satellite" or that the Bonn government somehow violated the interests of the German people; present hindsight suggests quite the opposite. What should be most evident, however, is that the tremendous resources of the United States allowed West Germany to satisfy all of its basic foreign-policy goals within a single alliance system. The U.S. alliance posed no profound dilemmas, no incompatibility of goals. The early leaders in Bonn did not have to sacrifice economic gain in exchange for military security; they did not have to jeopardize internal legitimacy in return for international prominence.

A starkly different picture emerged for the new government of the German Democratic Republic. Apart from the obvious limiting effect of the Soviet military occupation, the lessons of history required that East German military security could be attained only under Russian hegemony. Poland's tragically repeated experience of dismemberment at the hands of competing empires was sufficient to rule out the prospect of Swiss-style neutrality. This conclusion grew all the more obvious as U.S. influence was consolidated in the Federal Republic.

The GDR's unavoidable security dependence upon the Soviet Union brought with it a number of very great costs. In the first place, historic popular antipathy toward the Russians was especially virulent in the aftermath of war. Earlier tales of Soviet mistreatment of their own German-speaking minority were supplemented by reports of barbaric handling of the Red Army's German war prisoners. In addition, many Germans felt that the Russians had undertaken unwarranted destruction of German cities during the last stage of the war. In the face of desperate conditions of human survival, the repressive occupation policies of the Soviet military command seemed excessive. And the practice of transporting dismantled German factories to the Soviet Union and appropriating the entire output of some remaining factories for Soviet use was extraordinarily punitive and wasteful.

In the popular view, the Soviet alliance brought manifest sacrifices but no tangible benefits. From the standpoint of the SED leaders, the Soviet alliance meant a trade-off between national security and internal legitimacy. In other respects, too, the Soviet alliance was poorly equipped to respond to the GDR's foreign-policy needs. Moscow's diplomatic leverage, limited to a handful of client states, was no match for the United States. As a result, by 1950 only eleven nations had official diplomatic relations with the GDR; as late as 1968, this number had risen to only thirteen.[1] Throughout most of this period, the Federal Republic and the United States had confronted most nations of the world with the choice of conducting trade and diplomatic relations with either German state, but not with both. Obviously, most nations preferred the economic advantage of dealing with the Federal Republic. In this way, the Bonn government secured international legal sanction for its claim to "speak for the entire German nation."

In the absence of broader diplomatic recognition, the GDR was relegated to the status of the "Soviet occupation zone" or the "so-called GDR" in most international forums. Some West German institutions flaunted their diplomatic advantage. For example, GDR citizens who tuned in televised news broadcasts from the West were treated to a weather map of "Germany" in its boundaries of 1939—as if the GDR simply did not exist! Especially frustrating was the inability of the Soviet alliance to secure GDR participation in international organizations. Beginning in 1956, East Germans were permitted to participate in the international Olympic Games, but only in the degrading role of affiliates to the West German team. Only in 1972 were East German athletes finally allowed to compete as an independent delegation under their own national flag.

The GDR government was well aware of the lack of support within its own population. Therefore, the search for external recognition became a means to promote internal legitimacy. Though the leaders' resources were few, they reacted sharply to outside forces that denied them legitimacy. Because the Federal Republic was the most prominent of those forces, the GDR government utilized the most effective weapon at its disposal—control of surface routes between West Germany and West Berlin—to punish Bonn for acts prejudicial to the GDR's international position. On occasion, Soviet support was enlisted in this cause. But Soviet resources, too, were limited, and Soviet support was not always constant.

If the Soviet alliance had a sharply negative impact on the drive for legitimacy, its effect on economic goals was more ambiguous. The reparations period, of course, severely undermined the GDR's industrial reconstruction. But since 1954 the GDR has found mutual economic benefit within the Soviet sphere. In particular, the Soviet Union has proved to be a reliable supplier of raw materials and energy for the GDR's manufacturing sectors. Throughout the 1960s, these supplies were generally obtained at prices below world market levels. In return, the Soviet Union represented a large and secure market for East German finished goods, even when their quality lagged behind the level of products available from the Western industrial economies. On a considerably smaller scale, GDR trade with the other Soviet-bloc states (except Czechoslovakia) followed a similar pattern.

This assured role for the GDR as the prime manufacturing center for Eastern Europe has contributed significantly to economic progress and to East Germany's achievement of the group's highest standard of living. It also has entailed what economists term a high "opportunity cost." That is, by committing a major portion of its production of exportable goods to long-term deliveries to the Soviet Union and other East European partners, the GDR loses the opportunity to try to sell those goods in Western markets, where they could earn convertible Western currency. Such currency could be used to accelerate the purchase of Western machinery and technology, which in turn could raise the efficiency of East German industry. In effect, the present system of GDR economic integration into the Soviet alliance provides protection from the competition and fluctuations of the world market while precluding the possibility of higher levels of economic development.

As early as 1963, prominent GDR economists argued that the nation had much to gain by seeking more extensive participation in the Western market economies. Yet Soviet preferences, and the political judgment of the GDR's own leaders, have prevented any major redirection of trade. Above all, East German leaders are sensitive to the fact that trade between two nations of different economic strength can become a political weapon in the hands of the government with the larger national economy. Both the Federal Republic and the United States have demonstrated a willingness to use trade as a weapon against dependent trading partners. (The Soviet Union has used similar tactics within its own alliance system.) Despite the evident economic rationality in expanded Western trade, the GDR is reluctant to expose its economy to this sort of manipulation.

Unlike the Federal Republic, therefore, the GDR faces acute dilemmas in the fulfillment of foreign-policy goals. Although the essential requirements of national security can be met only in close alliance with the Soviet Union, the very nature of that alliance undermines the nation's pursuit of internal and external legitimacy. The continued development of the national economy can be best achieved by the acquisition of modern technology and expansion of trade into stronger markets, both of which are most readily available in the U.S.–West German alliance system. But closer relations with that system involve trade vulnerability and possible threats to security. The German Democratic Republic finds itself at the juncture of two opposing military and economic alliances— simultaneously attracted to, and repelled by, both.

A Socialist Foreign Policy

Official SED sources define East Germany's foreign policy almost exclusively in terms of its position within the "socialist state community." Taken together, the Soviet Union, the GDR, Poland, Czechoslovakia, Hungary, Bulgaria, Romania, and Mongolia represent a "completely new type of alliance."[2] In all public statements the alliance with the Soviet Union is elevated above all others as "a great revolutionary achievement," which is "indestructible for all time."

The Soviet alliance is the foundation of an ostensibly uniform socialist foreign policy, which aims at preserving and strengthening the achievements of existing socialist states and promoting conditions that are favorable to the creation of socialism in other lands. In no way do the foreign policies of the socialist-state community foresee aggressive use of military force. To be sure, it is presumed necessary to maintain extensive and modern armed forces, but only to deter the aggressive impulses of the capitalist imperialist nations. Such impulses are allegedly most evident in the United States and the Federal Republic, where influential voices advocate armed intervention in less developed nations, in order to stamp out spontaneous popular movements for liberation from the economic and political restraints of worldwide capitalism. Even more dangerous is the perceived temptation of Western capitalists to employ economic leverage and implied military threats to seduce East European nations onto a path of "neutrality" leading to renewed subordination to the capitalist sphere of influence. In other words, the GDR and other Soviet allies see themselves as engaged in military deterrence; they seek military power sufficient to nullify the military power of the West. Within the context of the resulting military stalemate, the natural processes of socialist development are expected to occur peacefully, without armed intervention. In this view, socialist armies would never be used to propagate socialism, but only to protect socialism wherever it has already taken root.

Outside observers find it difficult to accept this official rationale for socialist foreign policy. All too often, it seems, the deployment of manpower and weapons by socialist nations, including the GDR, exceeds the requirements of equalizing the world military balance. The Soviet alliance seems bent on achieving superiority, not simple equality. A more candid appraisal would have to take into account two additional factors. First, armed forces in most nations serve the dual functions of defense against external threat and preservation of internal order. Compared to the nations of West Europe and North America, East European governments face a more palpable threat of serious internal disturbances. Consequently, a significant increment of their military forces must be viewed as having a domestic police function—thus, one explanation for their having somewhat larger military forces. Second, in the contest for socialism in the less developed nations, the Soviet allies are well aware of their relatively limited economic leverage. To a certain extent, therefore, the Soviet alliance must count on military strength not only to provide for defense but also to compensate for the lack of economic influence over the evolution of world affairs.

In this general perspective, it is noteworthy that we find no evident differences between the foreign policies of the GDR and the Soviet Union. In fact, it is not unusual to find major GDR foreign-policy statements that consist of nothing but quotations from recent Soviet pronouncements. To a considerable extent, this identity of foreign policies springs from a genuine similarity of basic interests. On the other hand, the GDR has evidently found benefit from adopting a public role as the most loyal to Soviet allies. There is reason to believe that Moscow from time to time insists on this overt compliance in exchange for unspecified concessions.

Visible expressions of consonant foreign-policy objectives have not always characterized Soviet-GDR relations. As Edwina Moreton has amply demonstrated,[3] these two nations have frequently differed over the questions of four-power responsibility for Germany and the residual limits on East German sovereignty, as well as over how to deal with the Federal Republic. These questions are reviewed in the following descriptions of the GDR's relations with major foreign nations.

The Warsaw Treaty Organization

The military dimension of the German Democratic Republic's security policy revolves around participation in the Warsaw Treaty Organization (WTO).[4] The WTO was created in May 1955, following West German entry into the U.S.-sponsored North Atlantic Treaty Organization. Eight months later the GDR formally joined seven WTO members: the USSR, Albania, Bulgaria, Czechoslovakia, Hungary, Poland, and Romania. (Since 1961, Albania has ceased to be an effective member.) This action concluded the extended period during which the Soviet Union repeatedly suggested that the two German states might become united within the context of an all-European security system.

Henceforth, the GDR would be sovereign in all its foreign relations except those matters affecting Berlin, in which case the four-power agreements assured Soviet responsibility. Since the eastern sector of Berlin has become the de facto capital of the GDR, this exception was very significant. In addition, the GDR was regarded differently from the other signatories in the mutual-defense provisions of the Warsaw Treaty; whereas in the event of armed conflict the other member states would decide for themselves the appropriate level of response, the nature of the GDR's response would be decided by the WTO as a whole. This subsidiary role was underscored by the fact that, in contrast to all other East European states, the GDR had no bilateral defense treaty with the Soviet Union until 1964. Comparable bilateral treaties were finally concluded in 1967 with Poland, Czechoslovakia, Hungary, and Bulgaria. In the wake of Romania's success in establishing diplomatic relations with the Federal Republic, these new bilateral treaties were part of an East German effort to consolidate allied support in the confrontation over the status of Berlin and other outstanding German issues.

A rather weak treaty with Romania was finally signed in 1972. This remains the only major agreement between the two states. East German defense interests were incorporated in a net of bilateral treaties with the Soviet Union (1975) and with Poland, Czechoslovakia, Hungary, and Bulgaria (1977). With limited success, the GDR has repeatedly endeavored to employ a united Warsaw Treaty Organization as a weapon, both to put pressure on West Germany and to obstruct "irresponsible" internal experiments in other East European states. Thus, GDR leaders were among the most outspoken critics of the 1968 Czechoslovak reforms and the 1980–1981 labor union reforms in Poland.

The German Democratic Republic has armed forces of about 167,000 (army: 116,000; air force: 37,000; navy: 14,000). This is roughly one-third the size of the West German military.[5] Among WTO members the GDR ranks fifth in the ratio of military personnel to total population. In 1962 compulsory military service was introduced, with an eighteen-month term of enlistment—shorter than all other WTO states except Romania. With about 4.5 percent of the total WTO population, the GDR contributes only 3.3 percent of the total military personnel.

What it lacks in numbers, it contributes in quality. The army features a highly mobile and well-trained infantry. The navy has mostly newer warships, the second-largest fleet in the alliance. The air force is small, but more than adequate to defend the nation's compact territory.

The presence of Soviet forces contributes immensely to the GDR's external and internal security.[6] The Soviet Armed Forces Group in Germany includes an estimated 380,000 personnel. (There are about 80,000 Soviet military personnel in Czechoslovakia, 65,000 in Hungary, and 40,000 in Poland.) The total of Soviet and East German forces is thus slightly smaller than the total of West German, U.S., and other NATO forces in the Federal Republic. When all forces in the Central European theater are added, however, the WTO nations enjoy a marked numerical advantage in manpower and conventional weapons. The Soviet group exercises extensive control over the GDR's military forces, which—unlike those of other alliance members—are fully integrated into the WTO Supreme Command at all times.

The Council for Mutual Economic Assistance

East German efforts to promote economic development through foreign relations are dominated by participation in the Council for Mutual Economic Assistance[7] (CMEA), established in 1949 by the USSR, Bulgaria, Czechoslovakia, Hungary, and Poland. Albania was a member from 1949 to 1962. The GDR became a full member in 1950, Mongolia in 1962, Cuba in 1972, and Vietnam in 1978. Yugoslavia has an associate status comparable to its linkage with the West European Common Market. North Korea, Angola, Ethiopia, Mozambique, and South Yemen play very limited, consultative roles. The heart of CMEA is those seven nations who are also members of WTO—the basic "socialist-state community."

In the early postwar years, the East German trade orientation was strongly affected by political considerations. In addition to the heavy reparations and the Soviet desire to gain economic benefit and diplomatic leverage through access to the GDR's industrial production, discriminatory trade practices by the U.S. alliance also caused abrupt trade discontinuities. But beyond this initial shock, GDR trade with the socialist-state community has grown more and more on the basis of economic rationality. In other words, the present high volume of trade with the USSR and other CMEA neighbors makes a great deal of economic sense.

In the late 1950s, the Soviet Union accounted for more than half of the GDR's total trade turnover.[8] After declining to about 30 percent in 1974, the Soviet share now exceeds 40 percent; much of the increase is accounted for by rising costs for Soviet oil. (In 1981 purchase of Soviet oil absorbed one-third of GDR revenue from exports to the USSR, up from 8 percent in 1970.) The two nations are each other's most important trading partners; the GDR represents about one-sixth of total Soviet foreign trade. This situation persists in large measure because of the high degree of complementarity between the two economies: Within the socialist bloc the GDR is the leading producer of high-technology industrial goods, and the USSR is by far the largest source of raw materials. Each provides what the other most needs.

Although the Soviet Union's larger economy generally means a less immediate dependency on external trade, the Soviet-GDR partnership is very much one of mutual dependence. It would be difficult for East Germany to find reliable alternative sources for the large volume of raw materials currently purchased from the USSR: hard coal, coke, ferrous and nonferrous metals, oil, natural gas, cotton, meat, and vegetable fats. By the same token, the GDR is the major foreign supplier of many Soviet needs, including agricultural machines, toolmaking equipment, data-processing equipment, scientific instruments, railway cars, ships and cargo gear, chemicals, and synthetic fabrics. A disruption of this partnership would mean a severe shock in trade and consumption for both countries.

Czechoslovakia, Poland, and Hungary are, respectively, East Germany's third, fourth, and fifth most significant trading partners; together they account for more than one-fourth of the total trade.[9] (The Federal Republic is the second, as will be discussed later.) Trade with Bulgaria, Romania, and Cuba, though not insignificant, equals only about 5 percent. In most of these cases, trade follows a pattern similar to the GDR-USSR exchange of industrial products for raw materials. Notable in these exchanges are the significant imports of Polish coal and Hungarian food, as well as the slowly increasing role for imported vehicles and machinery products from both Poland and Hungary.

The GDR-Czechoslovak trade partnership differs from all the others because of the very similar structure of these two economies. Within each commodity category (raw materials, capital goods, consumer goods, and agricultural products), East Germany and Czechoslovakia sell a comparable volume to each other. This reflects a more refined division of labor and a more sophisticated effort to determine comparative advantage in Berlin and Prague. Thus, this partnership is able to benefit from the same kind of authentic specialization that characterizes the intensified trade among Western industrial economies.

On the whole, the Council for Mutual Economic Assistance has fallen far short of East German expectations. Despite a strong Soviet initiative in 1960, CMEA has never made the transition beyond an interrelated series of bilateral and multilateral agreements for consultation in plans and standardization of limited product lines. Thus, it has acquired none of the supranational attributes of the (West) European Communities.

The GDR, in particular, has been disappointed by the failure of projected specialization agreements. These agreements were intended to restrict the production of certain goods to those few countries that enjoyed a comparative advantage in production efficiency. Thus, a highly industrialized GDR would promise to expand its output of finished goods in exchange for a promise by other nations not to undertake production of competing goods, but instead to contract to buy more of the GDR's output. In principle, the GDR could then reduce costs through longer production runs, and other nations would benefit by importing these products at prices lower than the cost of new domestic production.

Although the specialization concept was intended to apply to any CMEA country, most early agreements assigned specialization prerogatives to the GDR and/or the USSR. The less developed CMEA states, led by Romania, objected that such agreements would simply perpetuate existing differences in levels of development. Although some specialization agreements do exist, they have not resulted in the dismantling of any inefficient production facilities. Nor is there any evidence that these agreements have materially affected the investment decisions of any CMEA member.

Romanian protests over this issue eventually established the rule that CMEA cooperative measures would be effective only for "interested parties." In other words, member states could individually select those group arrangements they wished to support. This lack of unanimity greatly weakened steps toward organized integration. Such CMEA affiliates as the International Bank for Economic Co-operation (1963) and the International Investment Bank (1970) have never fulfilled their potential, as even their most enthusiastic originating states—including the GDR—have not fully met their obligations for initial capital contributions. In large measure, East Germany's waning support is due to disenchantment with Soviet preferences for channeling International Investment Bank investments primarily toward the less developed CMEA members, including Cuba and the large underdeveloped regions of the Soviet Union itself.

Today, East German officials continue to express unqualified public support for further CMEA integration. Substantive efforts at integration, however, take rather narrow forms aimed at resolving specific problems. For example, GDR has several cooperative arrangements with Poland involving issues such as the employment of Polish workers in East German factories, the cooperative use of Baltic seaports, and even a jointly operated textile mill in Poland. Integrated product arrangements, involving the assembly of components from two or three countries, exist between the GDR, Czechoslovakia, Poland, and Hungary. Many such arrangements have been set up between the GDR and the USSR. It must be emphasized that the resulting level of integration is almost insignificant in contrast to the multifaceted integration achieved in the (West) European Communities or that achieved by U.S. transnational corporations.

Since the mid-1970s the Soviet Union has spearheaded a movement toward greater mutual dependence by means of joint investment projects arranged outside the structure of formal CMEA bodies. To date, the GDR has been the major non-Soviet participant in such projects, most of which involve the production of Soviet semifinished goods or the development of Soviet energy reserves. One of the largest such projects is the Orenburg natural-gas pipeline completed in 1979. East Germany and other East European investors are guaranteed a future share of the output of all such projects. In an era of deteriorating terms of trade for the GDR—as the costs of imported raw materials rise faster than the price of exported finished goods—such joint investments represent a rare path to future economic stability.

On the other hand, the immediate need for capital investment in future deliveries places an added burden on the present East German economy. In particular, the productivity of industry must be sharply increased in the short run. Throughout the 1970s, the East German strategy has been to increase productivity by importing Western technology. This technology is financed by a combination of expanded consumer-goods exports to the West and by credits from the Federal Republic and other Western sources. Expressed in rather simplified terms, successful execution of this strategy requires that the greater share of the repayment of Western debts be delayed until the fruits of the joint GDR-Soviet investment projects begin to arrive in the form of low-cost raw materials and energy sources. From Moscow's standpoint, this strategy amounts to having East European nations borrow Western money, which in turn frees capital for the development of the Soviet Union's natural resources.

Nearly all East European nations have engaged in this strategy to some degree. In the cases of East Germany, Romania, and Poland, imported Western technology has brought a significant increase in industrial productivity. But on balance the East Germans have recorded the best overall success. This success is measured not simply in terms of increased productivity (Romania and Poland have greater productivity increases), but in the relationship between productivity and accumulated debt. In other words, the value of increased East German output from imported technology seems to be nearly keeping pace with the obligation to repay accrued borrowing; in contrast, in the cases of Romania and— most especially—Poland, the relatively higher rates of borrowing have resulted in repayment obligations far exceeding the value of increased production. This latter situation can lead, of course, to some form of bankruptcy. As is now apparent, Western creditors are evidently unwilling to allow a nation like Poland to go bankrupt. Thus, they undertake extraordinary steps to reschedule these debts. At the same time, the Soviet Union also fears the bankruptcy of its smaller allies; so it, too, takes steps to relieve Poland's economic pressures.

As we have seen, attempts to rescue Poland have come only after profound social upheaval. East German leaders are most eager to avoid such internal disturbances. In effect, they are gambling that their economists have correctly calculated the margins in this present strategy of investment and development. An especially serious problem arose in the failure to anticipate rapidly rising interest charges on the large volume of GDR debt to Western banks. A financial catastrophe was narrowly averted by the abrupt reduction in the import of Western consumer and capital goods during 1981–1982, despite the inevitable consequent decline in the East German standard of living.

Other Integrative Measures

Apart from the very visible aspects of military and economic interdependence, the GDR engages in several other activities designed to promote integration with its East European neighbors. Most prominent is the encouragement of tourism. Since 1972, citizens of the GDR, Poland, and Czechoslovakia may travel among the three countries without visas, thus permitting the kind of easy movement that West Europeans have long enjoyed. A surprising upsurge in day visits produced an unanticipated demand on restaurants and retail stores. In particular, Polish shoppers in the GDR abruptly distorted the domestic supply of consumer goods in several East German cities. Consequently, limits have been placed on the volume of private purchases that may be carried across the border on each visit, and speculative bulk buying is prohibited. Additional "temporary" restrictions were imposed during Poland's crisis in 1982–1983, for both political and economic reasons.

Overall, East Germans are by far the most active foreign tourists of the socialist community, annually recording nearly 75 trips per 100 population.[10] About three-fourths of these trips are to the "fraternal" states, with Czechoslovakia and Poland the most favored destinations. Official policy encourages such tourism as a means to weaken the traditionally Western focus of the German people. Although East German visitors play a significant role in the local economies of their Slavic neighbors, these neighbors occasionally resent what they perceive to be excessive East German affluence and a tendency toward arrogance. In all, East Germans make more than 9 million trips each year to socialist countries, compared to roughly 8.5 million visits from those same countries.

Academic exchanges represent another important integrative measure. Each year about sixty-five hundred people from other socialist states study in the GDR, with a comparable number of East German students in exchange. About two-thirds of East German students abroad are at Soviet institutions.[11] These exchanges are supplemented by a broad range of faculty exchanges, academic conferences, and collaborative research undertakings. In addition, labor unions, friendship societies, and youth organizations facilitate exchanges of work experience and general tourism.

The cumulative effect of these various modes of interaction is difficult to evaluate. One might expect that perceived common interests have grown considerably in the last two decades at both the national and personal levels. An increasingly significant proportion of the East German population is familiar with the degree to which all member nations of the Soviet alliance share a common fate. Yet it is hardly axiomatic that this realization will produce the cultural blending and emotional solidarity so optimistically portrayed in official pronouncements as "socialist internationalism." East Germans, in particular, may well be capable of regarding this necessary interdependence with cold pragmatism. The history of contemporary multiethnic states and multinational communities shows that proximity does not always reduce cultural barriers; it may actually enhance them.

The uncertainty of integrative efforts is especially problematic where East German citizens are concerned. The relative lack of international legitimacy arouses defiant assertiveness among some East Germans, as is manifest in their pride in national achievements. Economic prowess and athletic supremacy are occasionally interpreted as tangible evidence of a presumed cultural superiority over the Slavic nations. Equally important, these successes can be cited to prove that East Germans are "just as good as" West Germans.

This persistent role of the Federal Republic as a point of reference—even, occasionally, a standard to be emulated—is perhaps the major impediment to more successful GDR integration into the socialist community. The GDR's eastward orientation has never been exclusive; for both the political leaders and the people, the Federal Republic and West Berlin have always been primary objects of concern and interaction.

The Federal Republic and West Berlin

The evolution of the relationship between the German Democratic Republic and the Federal Republic of Germany has proceeded at several levels and through several stages, each revealing peculiar nuances and ambiguities.

Prior to the legal creation of the two states in 1949—and extending to the formal acquisition of foreign-affairs sovereignty in 1954—this relationship was technically conducted through the offices of the four occupying powers. Although political leaders in the respective occupation zones occasionally expressed views of the prospects and conditions for eventual reunification, these views carried little immediate significance. But as the lines of cold-war confrontation grew more rigid, the leaders of each German state attempted to gain legitimacy by portraying the other state as an undemocratic tool of a foreign power. The social reforms and the new constitutions of the GDR and the Federal Republic were each put forward as the foundation for a new democratic order for all of Germany.

Except for limited amounts of necessary trade, the flow of people and communications was virtually cut off between the two states. But the circumstances of Berlin presented a unique problem. Located within the territory of the GDR, more than ninety miles from the Federal Republic, Berlin retained the temporary status of an occupied city. Access to the city was formally controlled, but movement between the western and eastern sectors of the city was not. As the eastern sector was gradually transformed into the de facto capital of the GDR, the city itself became the primary avenue of extensive emigration. Between 1949 and 1961, more than 2.6 million people left East Germany, most by way of West Berlin.[12] Some were victims of political or religious discrimination; some were seeking to escape economic hardship; others were attempting to rejoin their families or simply looking for better career opportunities. There is no way to determine the mixture of motives that led people to leave. But the vast emigration was a sure sign of the low legitimacy of the SED rule.

Given the obvious deficit in both internal and external legitimacy, the GDR's position in the inter-German war of words was decidedly defensive. By 1957, as the USSR effectively abandoned its concern with German reunification, the SED's Walter Ulbricht proposed the formation of a German federation, to be constructed through consultations between the two German governments. Because of Ulbricht's emphasis on preserving the social and political achievements of socialism, Bonn rejected this proposal as merely a symbolic gesture aimed at securing legal recognition of the SED leadership as the legitimate representative of the East German people.

Acting with the full support of the Warsaw Pact nations, the GDR forcefully closed the border between East and West Berlin in August 1961. The Berlin Wall not only ended the drain on the East German labor force (emigration was averaging more than twenty thousand per month); it also provided new leverage for the GDR in dealing with the Federal Republic.

Although West Berlin was governed by a semiautonomous senate under four-power supervision, the Federal Republic had developed far-reaching economic and political links to the city. These links, like the GDR's own assimilation of the eastern sector, violated the principle of the temporary postwar agreement. Because of the location of West Berlin and the city's symbolic role in appealing to East German citizens, the GDR perceived the intense Federal Republic–West Berlin connection as an infringement of East German sovereignty. Now this connection became more of a vulnerability for Bonn, as the GDR proceeded to employ its control of the Berlin border and the surface routes between West Berlin and the Federal Republic as weapons in the struggle.

Acting with apparent Soviet support, the GDR pursued its primary aims: full legal recognition of the GDR in the international community and formal independence for West Berlin. Subsidiary, and sometimes conflicting, aims included development of trade between the two German states, a nuclear free zone for all of Germany, the positive settlement of financial claims against the Federal Republic for postal and transit services, and the support of "democratic" reforms in West German government.

In the wake of the 1962 crisis over Soviet missiles in Cuba, both the United States and the Soviet Union seemed eager to reduce the potential for superpower conflict. A high priority was some degree of "normalization" in Berlin and Germany. Consequently, both the Federal Republic and the GDR were compelled to abandon their most aggressive postures and to begin some sort of dialogue.

With the decline of Chancellor Konrad Adenauer and the rise of Willy Brandt, the shift in West German politics permitted the gradual demise of Bonn's putative claim to speak for all German people and the emergence of a corollary economic offensive toward the East. By offering economic and diplomatic concessions to the Soviet Union and Eastern Europe, West Germany's new "eastern policy" frankly aimed at weakening Warsaw Pact support for East German demands in the imminent inter-German negotiations. The Federal Republic–Romania treaty of 1967 demonstrated how a socialist ally could denigrate GDR diplomatic claims in exchange for West German economic benefits. The SED perceived an even greater challenge in 1968, when Czechoslovakia's political and economic reforms were linked to improve trade relations with the Federal Republic.

Following the WTO invasion of Czechoslovakia, the Soviet Union effectively enforced foreign-policy coordination within the alliance (except for Romania). But as a price for this new solidarity, the GDR found itself compelled by events to assume a more accommodating position on major issues of inter-German dispute.

Following Brandt's elevation to chancellor in September 1969, events moved quickly. Brandt met with GDR Prime Minister Stoph in Erfurt (GDR) in March and in Kassel (West Germany) in May 1970. A temporary Postal Agreement between the two governments was concluded in April. In August the USSR signed a major treaty with the Federal Republic (with appropriate economic inducements). And as West German–Polish treaty talks entered their final stage, the first high-level negotiations between the two German states began in November 1970.

At year's end, the insistence of West German politicians on holding major party conferences in West Berlin again produced GDR protests and the temporary closure of transit routes. In January 1971, direct telephone lines were opened between East and West Berlin for the first time in nineteen years. But inter-German talks stagnated, as diplomatic attention shifted to the new four-power negotiations on the status of Berlin. GDR-Soviet disagreement over the resolution of the Berlin problem and the demand for full diplomatic recognition for the GDR was evidently one of the issues resolved with the resignation of SED First Secretary Ulbricht in May.

In September the four powers concluded a new Treaty on the Status of Berlin; the Soviet Union had failed to meet the earliest East German demand that any such agreement should be contingent on prior diplomatic recognition for the GDR. Now the GDR was deprived of a major element of leverage. Federal Republic–GDR negotiations resumed, leading to the Transit Treaty (December 1971), the broad Foundation Treaty (December 1972), and the reciprocal establishment of permanent diplomatic representatives with a status just short of the highest diplomatic accreditation (March 1974). Although the Federal Republic did not abandon its intent to work for the eventual unity of the German people, it did drop its claim to speak for all of Germany. This crucial concession, so long in coming, brought a flood of new diplomatic recognition from around the world, including the first recognition by NATO members (Netherlands and Luxembourg, May 1973) and eventual diplomatic relations with the United States (September 1974). Both German states were granted full United Nations membership in September 1973. By 1981 the GDR had established diplomatic relations with 131 nations.

In most respects, "inter-German" relations have remained stable since 1974. The range of cooperation between the two governments has expanded slowly, producing some resolution of outstanding boundary ambiguities, expanded communications between East Berlin and West Berlin, agreements on joint investments for improved land and water transportation, accreditation of journalists, and numerous other issues. The principal result of all these agreements has been to provide a foundation of cooperative stability with sufficient momentum to survive disputes in other areas.

Recent matters of dispute between the FRD and the GDR fall into three broad categories: problems arising from the bipolar Soviet-American contest, matters directly affecting intercourse between the two German states, and matters of human rights and political stability in East Germany.

Superpower Influence

Because both German nations play decisive roles within their respective alliances, it is inevitable that their interaction will immediately reflect the course of relations between the United States and the Soviet Union. From time to time, the status of Berlin and other German disputes have themselves been a prime issue in Soviet-American rivalry, as in the Soviet efforts to impede German rearmament in the mid-1950s. For the most part, however, the German setting has demonstrated considerably more stability than other arenas of East-West confrontation, such as the Caribbean, the Middle East, Southeast Asia, and Southwest Africa. Consequently, inter-German relations have occasionally become more acrimonious as a secondary effect of some geographically remote problem. Perhaps the most dramatic example was the enhanced military activity in Berlin in the aftermath of the 1962 missile crisis in Cuba.

In recent years, the linkage between superpower relations and inter-German relations has had positive effects, as well. U.S. commitment to détente and Soviet determination to win formal acceptance of the European status quo via the Helsinki agreements were instrumental in removing obstacles to improved Federal Republic–GDR relations.

With the present elaborate structure of inter-German contacts, some observers have imputed to Soviet leaders a concern that the two German states may develop a somewhat special relationship, based on common concerns not always consonant with Soviet interests. In both German states, but particularly in the Federal Republic, there is an evident desire to sustain the momentum of the 1970s. Despite U.S. denunciation of the Soviet Union's involvement in Afghanistan, the West's boycott of the 1980 Moscow Olympic Games, and the vigorous Reagan government concern over Soviet military capability, a Federal Republic–GDR summit meeting was scheduled for early 1981. Twice postponed because of mutual wariness over the Solidarity-government collision in Poland, the meeting between Erich Honecker and Helmut Schmidt finally took place in December, on the very eve of Poland's declaration of martial law. At that time Honecker asserted that inter-German relations would be affected by U.S. and West German attitudes on missile reduction in Europe. He also acknowledged Soviet apprehensions by denying that GDR–Federal Republic relations could be "an island of détente."

Direct Inter-German Relations

Apart from complications arising from their respective alliances, the two German states face numerous questions of direct dispute. Plainly unsatisfied with the lax implementation of the 1971 Four Power Agreement on Berlin, the GDR insists on a strict interpretation of the provision that the Western sectors of Berlin "continue not to be a constituent part of the Federal Republic, and not to be governed by it." Thus, certain political activities in West Berlin, such as conventions of the West German parties, meet with strenuous objections. By the same token, the GDR is at pains to complete the formal integration of the Eastern sector, as manifest in the unprecedented direct election of National Assembly delegates from East Berlin in June 1981. This action violates Western interpretations of the Berlin Agreement, which includes no specific statement on East Berlin, but as a whole applies to all of Berlin.

Another serious issue, which Honecker has declared an obstacle to improved relations, is the West German law on citizenship. Applying a pre–World War I statute, the Federal Republic today recognizes all German residents of the GDR as citizens of West Germany. Not surprisingly, East Germany regards this law as an infringement on its national sovereignty and a symbol of Bonn's refusal to establish relations of full equality.

A more positive dimension of inter-German relations is the realm of trade and related economic matters. Based upon the Berlin Commercial Treaty of 1951 (revised 1960), trade with the Federal Republic has always been a major component of East Germany's foreign economic relations.[13] Except for brief declines in the early 1950s and early 1960s, inter-German trade has shown relatively stable growth. Despite occasional stagnation in periods of domestic East German economic difficulty, trade with the Federal Republic has kept pace with the GDR's overall rate of trade expansion. For more than a decade trade turnover with West Germany has remained about 10 percent of East Germany's total foreign trade, second only to the USSR.

Although trade with the Federal Republic far exceeds trade with any other capitalist country, it falls far short of a potential based on simple economic criteria. The GDR imports substantial quantities of coal, organic chemicals, light industrial machinery, machine tools, and clothing. Exports to the Federal Republic include soft coal, semifinished metals, plastics, machine tools, and a variety of furniture, household appliances, and other consumer goods. At one time a triangular trade, comprising West Germany, the GDR, and West Berlin, was essential for supplying necessities to the enclave city. But changes in West Berlin's economic structure, combined with more secure routes to the Federal Republic, have sharply reduced the city's role in overall inter-German trade.

Given the considerable similarity in economic structures between the two German states, the potential exists for a relatively refined system of comparative advantage and a radically expanded trade in most major commodity groups. The volume of trade has been restricted by rigidities in the GDR's system of centralized management, by the low market appeal of some East German products, by the GDR's chronic shortage of convertible currency, and by the West German preference for balancing trade within commodity groups.[14] The much-heralded East German goal of reducing economic dependency on its "antagonistic" neighbor was evident in the campaign to "eliminate disturbances" (*Störfreimachung*) of the early 1960s. Since that time, however, this goal has apparently receded, as the GDR seeks ways to expand imports from the Federal Republic.

To some extent inter-German trade has been facilitated by the GDR's exemption from the import tariffs generally imposed on goods entering the European Common Market. This privilege derives from the early common market concessions to the Federal Republic, which regarded inter-German trade as domestic commerce. (Ironically, the resulting East German economic benefit conflicts with the insistent demand that relations between the two states be conducted as between two independent and sovereign nations.) In addition, the Federal Republic provides the GDR with an interest-free credit ("swing"), which in a given year equals 10–14 percent of total inter-German trade.[15] The government of Chancellor Schmidt introduced a variety of political and humanitarian requirements into the 1982 negotiations on renewal of the "swing" credit. Because some of those requirements were not accepted by the GDR, the Federal Republic imposed a gradual 30 percent reduction in interest-free credit through the end of 1985. The March 1983 transfer of power in Bonn to the Christian Democrats aroused East German concern over a further worsening of inter-German relations. Trade between the two states continues to grow, however, in part facilitated by a new 1 billion mark loan to the GDR (June 1983) by West German banks with Federal government guarantees.[16]

Human Rights

The third area of inter-German dispute concerns the status of political freedom and human rights in the GDR. Of course, the East German government prefers to regard these as internal matters, not subject to discussion in international relations. While this perspective may be technically correct, it does not take into account the immediate personal stake many West Germans feel for the well-being of relatives in the East. The most visible problem concerns personal contact between citizens of the two states. Since the 1971 Four-Power Agreement and the subsequent inter-German treaties, a number of favorable changes have been implemented. West Berliners are now accorded the same rights of entry into the GDR as are citizens of other Western states. (Such rights are, in fact, less restrictive than those for tourists from CMEA states.) In addition, telephone contact between West and East Berlin has been restored, transit controls on Federal Republic–Berlin traffic have been simplified, and greater effort has been devoted to reuniting families. As a result, the number of visits from West Germany and West Berlin has more than tripled, to about 8 million in 1980.[17]

Although the GDR economy benefits from the increased influx of West German currency, this expanded personal contact increases the burden on East German security forces and inhibits the general regime goal of infusing the population with a separate national identity. One official response was to enact legislation prohibiting East Germans in "sensitive" occupations from personal contact with "possible foreign agents." Since both the designation of sensitive occupation and the classification of possible agents were defined very broadly, large numbers of GDR citizens became subject to harassment. In October 1981, the GDR also introduced a sharp increase in the minimum amount of currency that visitors must exchange on entry. In part, this measure was intended to reduce the influx of GDR marks purchased at unofficial rates in West Berlin banks, a potentially disruptive form of currency speculation. More importantly, it had the additional effect of reducing the number of one-day visits. (For multiday visitors the minimum exchange is not necessarily restrictive, since it is less than the amount normally expended for meals and lodging.) In the Federal Republic, the minimum exchange requirement is a much publicized issue that threatens to interfere with other areas of discussion.

West Germans are also concerned for the civil rights of GDR citizens, especially those who suffer job discrimination or imprisonment because of political dissent or efforts to emigrate to the West. Apart from official prisoner exchanges involving convicted spies, the Federal Republic has secured the release of political prisoners in exchange for cash payments. Because the GDR has demanded secrecy as a condition for a continuation of this process, few details are known. Unofficial sources estimate that these "ransom" transactions involved more than one hundred thousand dollars annually. This unsavory business, along with the grotesque facade of the Berlin Wall and the barbed wire and mine fields along the state borders, represents the worst face of present inter-German relations.

But current realities should be cast in a larger perspective. The changes effected in GDR–Federal Republic relations may be considered the most constructive developments in East-West relations in the last decade. The negative consequences of historical anachronisms have been substantially ameliorated, tensions have been reduced, the welfare of real human beings has been improved, and a network of relationships between two pivotal states has been firmly established. More than being simply a stumbling block or an object of East-West confrontation, the two German nations may have acquired the potential for positive autonomous contributions to stability in Europe.

The Neutral Nations of Europe

From the earliest years of formal sovereignty, the GDR has looked to the neutral nations of Europe as a means for replacing destroyed trade patterns and as an avenue for circumventing the NATO-imposed diplomatic isolation.[18]

Although Finland was the first noncommunist nation in Europe to conclude a formal governmental trade agreement with the GDR, Finnish trade has never exceeded .6 percent of the East German total. Moreover, Finnish receptiveness to East German overtures did not extend to granting diplomatic recognition before NATO countries had done so. To date, Finland has been distinguished only by having concluded a general treaty with the GDR (December 1972) and by extending most-favored-nation trade status (March 1976).

Austria, remaining most attentive to West German concerns, has been even more reserved. Early trade developed very slowly and only through semiofficial channels. Along with Switzerland and Sweden, Austria was the first Western nation to establish diplomatic relations with the GDR— on the very day on which the Federal Republic–GDR Foundation Treaty was signed. Austria has subsequently engaged in joint investment projects in the GDR, but the overall level of economic involvement remains quite modest. In November 1980, Austria became the first Western nation to receive SED leader Honecker. East German authorities consider this visit a great achievement, because of the consular agreement recognizing separate GDR citizenship and because of the portent of multiple cultural exchanges.[19] Relations with Sweden and Switzerland remain rather distant, despite a gradual expansion of trade. Switzerland, in particular, has demanded East German compensation for Swiss property seized in the socialist takeover.

In sum, the GDR has devoted a great public-relations effort to creating warm relations with these four nations, as models for other nations to follow. In the cases of Finland and Austria, some modest results have been achieved. But the general strategy has fallen far short of its goal.

The United States, NATO, and Japan

For the most part, all nations of the Western alliance network have hewn closely to U.S. and West German preferences in dealing with the GDR.[20] Great Britain and France (except for a fleeting Gaullist gesture of independence) have been especially enthusiastic supporters of Bonn and harsh critics of the East German regime. Most nations followed a pattern of denouncing East Germany more severely than any other communist government, while gradually permitting the expansion of economic exchange through semiofficial channels. Today, Great Britain and France have become the GDR's ninth- and tenth-largest trading partners, respectively, each accounting for nearly 2 percent of East German trade. The Netherlands and Italy each account for more than 1 percent of East German trade.

Following the signing of the Foundation Treaty with Bonn (December 21, 1972), the first NATO states to extend diplomatic recognition were Belgium, the Netherlands, and Luxembourg. Canada, in August 1975, was the last. Many of these nations have been slow to establish embassies in East Berlin, and few have yet concluded consular agreements, chiefly because of conflict over definitions of German citizenship. For the GDR, the citizenship issue is of great importance, both as a practical matter and as leverage for eventually achieving full legal equality with the Federal Republic.

Perhaps more important is the East German desire for a radical expansion of trade with the industrialized West, the end of discriminatory tariffs (i.e., the granting of most-favored-nation status), and credits for the import of industrial technology. Quite clearly, the United States has become the GDR's main target in this general strategy, as manifest in careful courting of David Rockefeller and other prominent financiers and in the selection of a foreign-trade expert as ambassador to the

United States. Modest success has been achieved in the increase of food purchases and in the creation of long-term contracts with chemical and petrochemical firms. By 1980, the United States ranked as East Germany's thirteenth-largest trading partner. In that year soaring grain imports yielded a GDR trade deficit of U.S.$516 billion. Concern over potential U.S. use of trade leverage led East Germany to drastically curtail these purchases over the next two years.

Nevertheless, Washington continues to withhold the coveted most-favored-nation status. The U.S. government has demanded indemnity payments for Jewish Americans who fled fascism in the territory currently governed by East Berlin and compensation for seized U.S. property. Along with Canada, the United States has also pressed for emigration rights for East Germans wishing to join relatives in North America. Some progress has been achieved in reuniting families, but indemnity offers have been rejected as too low.

Japan's tremendous economic significance has made it another of the GDR's prime targets. Although diplomatic relations were established in mid-1973, Japan still accounted for less than .03 percent of East German trade. In November 1977, Politburo economist Günter Mittag went to Tokyo to conclude a series of agreements on trade and cultural exchange. From 1976 to 1979, trade with Japan increased eightfold. Japan has invested in East German hotels and chemical plants and has provided loans for the purchase of high-technology equipment. Erich Honecker visited Tokyo in May 1981, his first visit to a major U.S. ally. Japan did not endorse the GDR's position on the citizenship issue, but an important breakthrough occurred with the grant of most-favored-nation status.[21]

On the whole, East Germany's efforts to make inroads into the heart of the capitalist alliance have produced mixed results. In Europe, the Benelux nations (an intergovernmental union of Belgium, Netherlands, and Luxembourg), along with Great Britain and France, have become important suppliers of producer goods, but they remain firm in refusing political concessions. Despite obvious business interest, the United States and Canada are most adamant in placing preconditions on improved relations. On the other hand, Japan, possibly seeking enhanced economic flexibility and more avenues of diplomacy, has been considerably more receptive to East German overtures.

From an economic standpoint, the results have been positive. While accumulating a precariously large debt to Western creditors (including West Germany) of more than U.S.$8 billion,[22] the GDR has secured a continuous flow of investments and technology, as Western commercial interests press their governments to underwrite their marketing efforts. So long as high unemployment imperils the Western economies, East German planners can probably count on further credits. At the same time, the GDR is preparing more active marketing initiatives of its own: A 1981 reorganization of trade institutions is designed to encourage more flexibility in the search for hard currency sales.[23]

The Middle East and North Africa

The German Democratic Republic has been formally recognized by about one hundred developing nations, yet its significant contact with these regions is considerably more limited.[24] Moreover, the GDR's interest in the less developed states is widely differentiated. Three groups of states deserve particular attention, beginning with the Middle East and North Africa.

East German relations with this region, as in most of the Third World, have closely followed Soviet initiatives. After the Soviet Union extended military and economic assistance to several key members of the anti-Israel (and thus anti-U.S.) constellation, the GDR was able to provide limited economic assistance in exchange for some international visibility. In the case of Egypt, this contact blossomed into a fairly stable pattern of trade and quasi-governmental relations. For many years Egypt was the GDR's major trading partner in the underdeveloped world; it now ranks second, despite a sharp decline in political relations.

East German willingness to overlook the harsh treatment that some governments inflicted on domestic communist groups permitted the growth of cultural and economic exchanges throughout the region. This persistence was rewarded in mid-1969, when Iraq and Syria became the first noncommunist nations to extend diplomatic recognition. More recently, in addition to undergirding the Soviet quest for a strategic position, the GDR has sought to develop export markets and alternative sources of petroleum. Since the Soviet Union has proved unable to keep pace with East German consumption, Arab nations (mainly Iraq and Syria) now supply roughly 10 percent of GDR petroleum imports.[25] Small purchases of petroleum are also made from Algeria and Libya, yet these two nations have not been willing to develop closer relations, apparently preferring diplomatic autonomy and stronger economic relations with Western Europe.

The Third World Independents

For a nation of only modest size, the administrative costs of maintaining foreign economic relations are considerable. Consequently, the GDR has elected not to pursue every conceivable trade partner, but rather to concentrate on those nations that offer the greatest potential for trade growth in the medium term.[26] Such nations are identified by five main characteristics: (1) a relatively stable political system; (2) a growing economy in need of modern production technology and expanded networks of transportation and communications; (3) a middle-income class large enough to absorb consumer durables; (4) the capacity to export food, raw materials, and semiprocessed goods; and (5) a willingness to demonstrate a degree of political and economic independence from the major capitalist nations.

Since the late 1950s, India has typified this category of Third World nation, and the GDR, along with other Soviet-bloc nations, gradually has built the foundations of mutually beneficial trade with this South Asian power. In the 1960s, Brazil also chose to diversify its trade relations, a move that coincided with the GDR's first major program of trade expansion. Today, Brazil and India are East Germany's third and fifth most important trading partners in the Third World, together accounting for .8 percent of the total. In some years, East German sales of vehicles, machinery, and chemical fertilizers are sufficient to produce a positive trade balance and vital hard currency revenue.

During the 1970s, other successful developing nations have grown more receptive to East German contacts, partly as a result of internal changes and partly in response to the end of the GDR's diplomatic isolation. Argentina, Peru, and Colombia have all established modest trade relations with the GDR. And in September 1981, Mexico received a visit from Erich Honecker, amid festive pronouncements of lasting friendship, common opposition to the arms race, and a bright future for mutual trade—featuring East German investment in Mexico's agriculture and possible Mexican investment in East German oil refining.[27]

In no case do these relations with Third World "independents" signify any political gains for the world socialist movement. In fact, East German authorities are exceedingly pragmatic in this regard. Visiting dignitaries and the GDR media are quite facile in identifying every glimmer of "progressive" social policy in these nations, while ignoring evidence of internal economic exploitation and continued heavy dependence on foreign capitalist nations.

Impoverished Africa

Economic benefit does not always play a decisive role in the GDR's foreign-relations priorities.[28] Despite considerable financial cost, East Germany is engaged in a Soviet-directed strategic and ideological offensive in southern Africa and the western Indian Ocean.[29]

In the wake of Soviet misadventures in the Sudan and Somalia, the GDR has devoted economic aid and personnel to Ethiopia and the Democratic Republic of Yemen, two nations lying along the entrance to the Red Sea and providing port facilities for Indian Ocean traffic. Yemen, in particular, has become something of a special project for the GDR. Thousands of East Germans provide training for police and military forces, management of hospitals, and planning and implementation of agricultural projects. The extent of political penetration in Yemen is unprecedented for the GDR, with East German advisers even claiming credit for having fashioned the 1979 constitution.

Farther south, the GDR has also developed intensive relations with the two former Portuguese colonies of Angola and Mozambique. Together with Zambia, these two nations form a belt dividing the southern half of the continent. There the Soviet Union, Cuba, and East Germany offer a coordinated set of services: The Soviet Union provides the bulk of economic and military aid, Cuba provides military personnel, and the GDR again concentrates on the nations' administrative and economic infrastructures.

These two pairs of nations may be considered as strategic and ideological "bridgeheads." All have undertaken a panoply of political, economic, and cultural links to Soviet-bloc nations, complete with the trappings of Marxist-Leninist language. For the GDR, the benefits of these extensive undertakings are chiefly symbolic. Above all, they are tangible evidence of support for Soviet foreign policy. Because Yemen, Ethiopia, Mozambique, and Angola have an average annual per capita GNP of only U.S.$280, they offer little economic return. East German goods and services are financed by long-term, low-interest credits, which may never be repaid. Persistent social and political instability prevents systematic development of even the few energy and mineral resources available there.

Summary

The last decade has seen remarkable changes in the foreign relations of the German Democratic Republic. The end of the period of diplomatic isolation has not produced a measurable increase in the SED's internal legitimacy, but it has facilitated much more extensive contact with foreign governments and commercial interests, expanded trade with the economically significant developing nations, and improved access to Western credits and technology. The web of agreements with the Federal Republic has not fully satisfied the GDR's demand for complete equality; it has, in fact, aggravated disagreement over certain issues. In some respects, inter-German relations now support better contact for families affected by the national division. But the consequent further impediments to the creation of a distinctive GDR identity have led to a further restriction of some civil liberties. Perhaps most important, the new civility of dialogue between the two German states provides a moderating influence against occasional increases in Soviet-American tensions—and, thus, an additional measure of security.

If East German foreign-policy interests generally complement those of the Soviet Union, the obligatory support for Soviet interests in such far-flung regions as Cuba, Vietnam, and eastern and southern Africa may well constitute an unwelcome burden—the more so since these areas offer little economic or diplomatic advantage. Along with the Soviet military presence in the GDR itself, these overseas adventures are part of the price to be paid for inclusion in the Soviet alliance.

Notes

1. Peter C. Ludz et al., *DDR Handbuch*, 2d ed. [GDR Handbook] (Cologne: Wissenschaft und Politik, 1979), p. 286 [hereafter, *DDR Handbuch*].

2. "Das neue Programm der SED," *Deutschland Archiv 9*, no. 7 (1976), p. 747.

3. Edwina Moreton, *East Germany and the Warsaw Alliance: The Politics of Detente* (Boulder, Colo.: Westview Press, 1978).

4. The material for this section is drawn from ibid.; and from Gerhard Wettig, *Die Sowjetunion, die DDR, und die Deutschland-Frage, 1965–1976* [The Soviet Union, the GDR, and the German Question, 1965–1976] (Stuttgart: Bonn Aktuell, 1976).

5. *The Military Balance 1983–1984* (London: International Institute for Strategic Studies, 1983), p. 21.

6. Ibid., p. 16.

7. Jochen Bethkenhagen et al., *DDR und Osteuropa: Wirtschaftssystem, Wirtschaftspolitik, Lebensstandard* [GDR and East Europe: Economic System, Economic Policy, Standard of Living] (Opladen: Leske, 1981), pp. 167–178.

8. Doris Cornelsen et al., *Handbook of the Economy of the German Democratic Republic* (Westmead, England: Saxon House, 1979), pp. 244–245; Maria Haendcke-Hoppe, "DDR-Aussenwirtschaft unter neuen Vorzeichen [GDR Foreign Trade Under a New Design]," *Deutschland Archiv 16*, no. 4 (1983), pp. 378–385.

9. Cornelsen et al., *Handbook of the Economy of the German Democratic Republic*, pp. 245–248; Bethkenhagen et al., *DDR und Osteuropa*, pp. 173–178.

10. Zentralverwaltung für Statistik, *Statistisches Jahrbuch 1980 der Deutschen Demokratischen Republik* (Berlin: Staatsverlag, 1980), p. 329 [hereafter *Statistisches Jahrbuch 1980-DDR*].

11. *UNESCO Statistical Yearbook 1980* (New York: United Nations Statistical Office, 1981), p. 511–531.

12. *DDR Handbuch*, pp. 400–401.

13. Cornelsen et al., *Handbook of the Economy of the German Democratic Republic*, pp. 249–256; Bethkenhagen et al., *DDR und Osteuropa*, pp. 161–165.

14. Horst Lambrecht, "Entwicklung der Wirtschaftsbeziehungen zur Bundesrepublik Deutschland [Development of Economic Relations with the Federal Republic of Germany]," in Hans-Adolf Jacobsen et al., eds., *Drei Jahrzehnte Aussenpolitik der DDR* [Three Decades of Foreign Policy of the GDR] (Munich: Oldenbourg, 1979), pp. 453–472.

15. Bethkenhagen et al., *DDR und Osteuropa*, pp. 161–162.

16. Ilse Spittmann, "Die Milliardenkredit [The Billion Credit]," *Deutschland Archiv 16*, no. 8 (1983), pp. 785–788.

17. Peter Jochen Winters, "Das deutsch-deutsche Verhältnis 1981 [The German-German Relationship 1981]," *Deutschland Archiv 14*, no. 12 (1981), pp. 1233–1236.

18. Trade data calculated from *Statistisches Jahrbuch 1980-DDR*, p. 235.

19. Harald Kleinschmid, "Grosse Brücken und kleine Brücken: Zum Honecker-Besuch in Österreich [Large Bridges and Small Bridges: On the Honecker Visit in Austria]," *Deutschland Archiv* 13, no. 12 (1980), pp. 1236–1239.

20. Trade data calculated from *Statistisches Jahrbuch 1980-DDR,* p. 235.

21. Johannes Kuppe, "Honeckers Staatsbesuch in Japan [Honecker's State Visit in Japan]," *Deutschland Archiv* 14, no. 7 (1981), pp. 673–679.

22. Bethkenhagen et al., *DDR und Osteuropa,* p. 309.

23. Maria Haendcke-Hoppe, "Die Umgestaltung des Aussenhandelsapparats in der DDR [The Transformation of the Foreign Trade Apparatus in the GDR]," *Deutschland Archiv* 14, no. 4 (1981), pp. 378–384.

24. Trade data calculated from *Statistisches Jahrbuch 1980-DDR,* p. 235.

25. Maria Haendcke-Hoppe, "DDR-Aussenwirtschaft unter neuen Vorzeichen [GDR Foreign Trade Under a New Design]," *Deutschland Archiv* 16, no. 4 (1983), p. 380.

26. Trade data calculated from *Statistisches Jahrbuch 1980-DDR,* p. 235.

27. Johannes Kuppe, "Zum Staatsbesuch Honeckers in Mexiko [On Honecker's State Visit to Mexico]," *Deutschland Archiv* 14, no. 10 (1981), pp. 1022–1026.

28. Trade data calculated from *Statistisches Jahrbuch 1980-DDR,* p. 235.

29. Michael Sodaro, "The GDR and the Third World: Supplicant and Surrogate," in Michael Radu, ed., *Eastern Europe and the Third World* (New York: Praeger, 1981), pp. 106–140.

9
Conclusion

In some respects the German Democratic Republic offers itself as a test case for evaluating communist-style socialism. Whereas the Soviet Union, China, and most other communist regimes of East Europe and Asia undertook the ostentatiously un-Marxist task of conducting a "workers' revolution" in overwhelmingly traditional, peasant-dominated societies, East Germany possessed many of the economic and social preconditions consonant with a more authentic Marxist image of revolutionary change: chiefly, a strong urban-industrial base and a large, skilled, and organized working class. What was missing, of course, was a broad sense of national identity and a government endowed with elemental sovereignty. Neither of these considerations had figured prominently in Marx's optimistic prescience.

I began this overview of East Germany's culture, social structure, economic system, and political order by noting the confluence of four influences: (1) the impact of German history and the consequent legacy of values and social resources; (2) the extent of Soviet penetration, through which Moscow's security needs and ideological aims shape East German institutions and policies; (3) the adoption of Marxist socialism, providing both assets and liabilities for economic change; and (4) the emergence of new ecological problems, as urban-industrial concentrations give rise to novel modes of human, physical, and international interdependence.

In reviewing the list of East German achievements and deficiencies, it is very tempting to ascribe certain achievements to one or more of these influences and to blame deficiencies on other influences. Westerners, of course, especially those in the Anglo-Saxon capitalist nations, are inclined to attribute all "positive" aspects of East German life to its German heritage and its modern social processes. The "negative" features are attributed, naturally, to the Soviet presence and the restrictive consequences of socialism.

At this point, three critical methodological obstacles should be noted. First, any effort to classify change in the GDR into positive and negative features presumes a universality of evaluative criteria, which simply does not exist. Although the Western cultural tradition, including most varieties of the Marxist value system, ascribes high priority to such goals as personal freedom, equality, and material abundance, there remains great disagreement concerning the optimum distribution of these values among social segments, as well as the presumed extent of incompatibility—the necessary trade-offs—among social goals.

Second, the specific endeavor to assess the independent consequences of either Soviet penetration or socialist institutions must fail, because these two influences have not operated independently. Not only are East German socialism and Soviet influence inextricably intertwined, but their combined impact on East German politics and society has also been affected by numerous other changes in East Germany's environment. In other words, the specific consequences of neither socialism nor Soviet penetration were ever predetermined. At each stage of the GDR's history, these two sets of influences acquired concrete significance partly in response to exogenous forces. For example, Soviet-induced measures to transform the mechanisms of political control in East Germany should not be understood without reference to demonstrations of hostility emanating from the Western powers and to disruptive internal developments in Yugoslavia, Hungary, and Poland. Similarly, disappointments in East German efforts to modernize the socialist economy cannot be readily comprehended without acknowledging the discriminatory effects of Western trade policies.

Finally, an effort to determine whether the GDR represents a faithful continuation of its German heritage, or some sort of deviation from its past, fails for want of what experimental social scientists would term a "control." This simply means that the real effect of outside influences could be gauged only if the GDR could be compared to another case (the control) that had been allowed to develop in the absence of outside influences. This point may seem gratuitous to conscientious social scientists. But it requires emphasis here, in light of the fact that Western writers have often implicitly—and mistakenly—claimed that the Federal Republic of Germany should serve as such a standard of control, since it has followed a more "naturally German" path of change. My point is simply that both the GDR and the Federal Republic have reached their present respective stages of development as a result of processes in which external factors were heavily involved. Moreover, the differential impact of external factors, as was noted in Chapter 8, has decidedly favored the Federal Republic.

Social Progress and National Identity

Having made these methodological reservations, it is nevertheless appropriate to conclude by summarizing some of the ways in which each of the four sets of influences is reflected in the contemporary German Democratic Republic.

German Heritage

In addition to the substantial economic and demographic assets inherited from the past, the GDR exhibits a number of attitudinal characteristics that might be regarded as typically—if not exclusively—German. Above all, economic development and social progress have drawn heavily on a strong popular sense of individualism and a pervasive achievement orientation. As avenues of social mobility were restructured, especially in the possibilities for education and job skills improvement, a great many people responded, chiefly in the quest for greater material rewards. This process has led to real changes in life chances, as well as to marked improvement in the quality of human resources available for economic growth. At the same time, a customary accommodation toward the exterior trappings of the status hierarchy, such as official rank and educational credentials, has led the majority to channel their aspirations for upward mobility toward acquiring these formal attributes. In other words, people try to get ahead by following the rules for advancement; there has been no surge of populist egalitarianism.

An additional feature is a continuing appreciation for aesthetic culture, revealed in extensive participation in government-supported efforts to vitalize the performing, graphic, and literary arts. In addition, this particular attachment to culture is linked to an assertive nationalism and an occasionally expressed feeling of cultural superiority. This long-standing German trait is accentuated in the face of the encroachment of Soviet culture and the penetration of "Western" materialism. The considerable public attention to the nation's athletic prowess further expresses a desire to document this alleged superiority.

Finally, the German heritage has left East Germans with a thinly disguised contempt for Russians and other Slavic peoples, as well as a persistent tendency to judge domestic achievements by the standards of the industrialized West. The latter occurs, above all, by reference to the Federal Republic.

Soviet Penetration

The military and political presence of the Soviet Union is manifest in multiple ways. Most visibly, the architecture of East German political structures imitates that of the Soviet Union in detail. The SED is indeed faithful to the image of the Communist Party of the Soviet Union (CPSU). With minor exceptions in the makeup of nominal legislative bodies, the GDR government structure also bears an unmistakable Soviet imprint. By and large, the evolution of the structure of political power— from an extremely narrow concentration of authority toward a marginally looser constellation of expert elites under Politburo guidance—replicates a similar Soviet experience. To be sure, Walter Ulbricht's rule in the 1960s displayed elements of ideological innovation and economic reform not fully consonant with the Soviet pattern, but these modest deviations were subsequently remedied.

Ineluctable East German incorporation into the Soviet sphere of influence brought extensive economic interdependence, with limited benefits and palpable costs. In addition, diplomatic dependency has meant severe restrictions on the GDR's capacity to conduct normal foreign relations. In one sense, the presence of Soviet military units has served the GDR's security needs well, but only at great cost in financial support and in the loss of internal legitimacy. In recent years, the alliance with the Soviet Union has induced East Germany to devote considerable resources to support economically marginal and politically fragile regimes in Africa.

Finally, Soviet omnipresence has provided the East German people with a concrete focus for everyday disenchantment. Almost any abrasive problem, from consumer-goods shortages to the high cost of gasoline, from "wasted" foreign aid to the obtuse monotony of the SED's propaganda organs, can be blamed on Soviet interference.

Socialism

East German socialism, the virtual substitution of central planning and state ownership for the mechanism of market capitalism, has materially altered the conditions of life for most citizens. Most visibly, it has sharply reduced the income disparity between the highest and lowest economic classes. It has also gone far toward eliminating the role of property accumulation as a support for social inequality. Family background can still provide marginal cultural advantages and useful career contacts. Yet a concerted emphasis on achievement criteria, such as school performance and other employment credentials, has done much to extend equal opportunity to previously disadvantaged social segments.

Although income differentials remain as an incentive for occupational advancement, a comprehensive social wage insures that all citizens receive the vital necessities of life. Extensive subsidies for food and housing guarantee at least minimum comfort for the elderly and others with low incomes. Comprehensive funding for education, health care, and recreation, and progressive support programs for families compare favorably with most social policies in wealthier Western nations, despite the heavy financial burden on a limited work force.

At the same time, the large and often arbitrary administrative structures created to implement both economic and social policy are notoriously inefficient and unresponsive to popular needs. The housing stock remains gravely inadequate, industrial production cannot keep pace with technological change, a weak financial infrastructure impedes rational investment, and a cumbersome transportation network repeatedly results in supply bottlenecks and wasted labor. Economic growth continues, and the East German standard of living is still the highest in the Soviet alliance. But a full realization of the nation's economic potential awaits the introduction of new measures to permit more rational price calculations and more flexible responses to the fluctuating requirements of the global economy.

Urban-Industrial Ecology

To a large degree, East Germany's comprehensive social policies are designed to ameliorate the economic stresses of living in a modern, interdependent society. Yet East Germany, like so many Western "post-industrial" societies, is facing unanticipated consequences of contemporary urban life. Growing concentrations of population, combined with the aggressive development of industrial production, have produced threats to human health in the form of noise and air and water pollution. The pressures of material accumulation and the stresses of occupational advancement increasingly require that individuals and families have adequate "private space" and recreational opportunities, as a means of psychological and physical regeneration. This is difficult to achieve in a society that has so consistently neglected investment in housing and in any other facilities that did not directly contribute to the nation's productive capacities.

Moreover, urban-industrial life brings with it value changes, which increase popular pressures on government. Citizen preference for fewer children and nuclear families means a dwindling labor force, as well as a need to alter the distribution of housing and leisure facilities. Higher levels of education and greater attention to information media can lead citizens to evaluate government performance by more rigorous standards, to demand more material benefits, more channels of participation, and more vigorous adherence to principles of legal and social equity.

East Germany's Identity Today

Quite clearly, life in East Germany today is a peculiar amalgam of these four principal influences. The GDR is German, socialist, and modern, with a strong admixture of Soviet penetration. Each of these four influences collides with the others, sometimes in turbulent ways. Moreover, each stream of influence contains its own inherent contradictions. It is no wonder, then, that the real identity of the German Democratic Republic remains a mystery.

Western journalists and others who have lived in the GDR for extended periods report that most citizens are reflective and expressive on the subject of national identity. Most display considerable awareness of the virtues and defects of their own political system and a reasonably informed comprehension of the outside world. Some are implacable and cynical, and a few even undertake overt opposition to the current regime. Many pretend indifference to all political questions and simply focus their attention on the minimum requirements of work and the greater rewards of family and leisure pursuits. And there are others, generally younger adults, who persist in seeing some reasons for optimism, who believe that—since they are Germans, after all—there must be some way to make this system work.

Bibliography

General

Bottomore, T. B., and Maximilien Rubel. *Karl Marx: Selected Writings in Sociology and Social Philosophy*. London: C. A. Watts, 1963.

Buch, Günther. *Namen und Daten: Wichtiger Personen der DDR* [Names and Dates: Important Persons of the GDR]. Berlin: J.H.W. Dietz, 1979.

Erbe, Günter, et al. *Politik, Wirtschaft, und Gesellschaft in der DDR* [Politics, Economy, and Society in the GDR]. Cologne: Westdeutscher, 1979.

Legters, Lyman (ed.). *The German Democratic Republic: A Developed Socialist Society*. Boulder, Colo.: Westview Press, 1978.

Ludz, Peter C., et al. *DDR Handbuch*. 2d ed. Cologne: Wissenschaft und Politik, 1979.

Merritt, Anna J., and Richard L. Merritt. *Politics, Economics, and Society in the Two Germanies, 1945–1975: A Bibliography of English Language Works*. Urbana: University of Illinois, 1978.

Statistisches Bundesamt. *Statistisches Jahrbuch 1981 für die Bundesrepublik Deutschland*. Stuttgart: W. Kohlhammer, 1981.

————. *Statistisches Jahrbuch 1979 für die Bundesrepublik Deutschland*. Stuttgart: W. Kohlhammer, 1979.

Steele, Jonathan. *Socialism with a German Face*. London: Cape, 1977.

Zentralverwaltung für Statistik. *Statistisches Jahrbuch 1980 der Deutschen Demokratischen Republik*. Berlin: Staatsverlag, 1980.

Zimmermann, Hartmut. "The GDR in the 1970s." *Problems of Communism* 27, no. 2 (1978):1–40.

History

Badstübner, Rolf, et al. *DDR: Werden und Wachsen* [GDR: Becoming and Growing]. Frankfurt am Main: Marxistische Blätter, 1975.

Doernberg, Stefan. *Kurze Geschichte der DDR*. [Short History of the GDR]. Berlin: Dietz, 1964.

Leonhardt, Wolfgang. *Die Revolution entlässt ihre Kinder*. Cologne: Kiepenhauer and Witsch, 1955.

Lippmann, Heinz. *Honecker and the New Politics of Europe*. New York: Macmillan, 1972.

McCauley, Martin. *Marxism-Leninism in the German Democratic Republic*. New York: Harper and Row, 1979.

Schenck, Fritz. *Im Vorzimmer der Diktatur* [In the Anteroom of the Dictatorship]. Cologne: Kiepenheuer and Witsch, 1962.

Stern, Carola. *Porträt einer bolschewistischen Party* [Portrait of a Bolshevik Party]. Cologne: Politik und Wirtschaft, 1957.

State and Party

Baylis, Thomas A. *The Technical Intelligentsia and the East German Elite.* Berkeley: University of California, 1974.

Bender, Peter. "Episode oder Alarmzeichen für Honecker?: Anmerkungen zum 'Spiegel-Manifest' [Incident or Alarm for Honecker?: Observations on the 'Spiegel Manifesto']." *Deutschland Archiv* 11, no. 2 (1978):113–116.

Glaessner, Gert-Joachim, and Irmhild Rudolph. *Macht durch Wissen: Zum Zusammenhang von Bildungspolitik, Bildungssystem, und Kaderqualifizierung in der DDR* [Power Through Knowledge: On the Relationship of Education Policy, Education System, and Cadre Training in the GDR]. Opladen: Westdeutscher, 1978.

Kuppe, Johannes, and Siegfried Kupper. "Parteitag der Kontinuität [Party Conference of Continuity]." *Deutschland Archiv* 14, no. 7 (1981):714–737.

Ludz, Peter C. *Parteielite im Wandel* [Transformation of the Party Elite]. Cologne: Westdeutscher, 1968.

Mampel, Siegfried. "DDR-Verfassung fortgeschrieben [GDR Constitution Revised]." *Deutschland Archiv* 7, no. 11 (1974):1152–1157.

"Das neue Programm der SED." *Deutschland Archiv* 9, no. 7 (1976):744–779.

Neugebauer, Gero. *Partei und Staatsapparat in der DDR* [Party and State Apparatus in the GDR]. Opladen: Westdeutscher, 1978.

Protokoll des X. Parteitages der Sozialistischen Einheitspartei Deutschlands [Protocol of the Tenth Party Congress of the Socialist Unity Party of Germany]. Berlin: Dietz, 1981.

Rheinhold, Otto. "Gestaltung der entwickelten sozialistischen Gesellschaft im Lichte des Programmentwurfs [The Formation of Developed Socialist Society in Light of the Draft Program]." *Einheit*, no. 3 (1976):285–289.

Schmid, Karin. *Die Verfassungssysteme der Bundesrepublik Deutschland und der DDR* [The Constitutional Systems of the Federal Republic of Germany and the GDR]. Berlin: Berlin-Verlag, 1982.

Sieveking, Klaus. "Kommunalpolitik und Kommunalrecht in der DDR [Local Government Policies and Law in the GDR]." *Deutschland Archiv* 16, no. 11 (1983):1163–1174.

"Das Spiegel Manifest und die Reaktion der DDR [The Spiegel Manifesto and the Reaction of the GDR]." *Deutschland Archiv* 11, no. 2 (1978):199–219.

Statut der Sozialistischen Einheitspartei Deutschlands. Berlin: Dietz, 1976.

Economy

Alton, Thad, et al. *Economic Growth in Eastern Europe, 1965, 1970, and 1975–1980.* New York: L. W. Financial Research, 1981.

Bethkenhagen, Jochen, et al. *DDR und Osteuropa: Wirtschaftssystem, Wirtschaftspolitik, Lebensstandard* [GDR and East Europe: Economic System, Economic Policy, Standard of Living]. Opladen: Leske, 1981.

Bryson, Phillip J. *Scarcity and Control in Socialism.* Lexington, Mass.: Lexington, 1976.

Buck, Hannsjörg F., and Bernd Spindler. "Luftbelastung in der DDR durch Schadstoffemissionen [Air Pollution Through Toxic Emissions in the GDR]." *Deutschland Archiv* 15, no. 9 (1982):943–958.

Cornelsen, Doris, et al. *Handbook of the Economy of the German Democratic Republic.* Westmead, England: Saxon House, 1979.

Haase, Herwig E. "Wachsende Finanzielle Belastungen der DDR-Wirtschaft und ihr Ausweis im Staatshaushalt [The Growing Financial Burden of the GDR Economy and Its Impact on the State Budget]." *Deutschland Archiv* 12, no. 8 (1979):818–838.

Heibel, Dieter. "Zur Neuordnung des Lohnsystems in der DDR [On the New Arrangement of the Wage System in the GDR]." *Deutschland Archiv* 10, no. 11 (1977):1226–1228.

Holmes, Leslie. *The Policy Process in Communist States.* Beverly Hills, Calif.: Sage, 1981.

Kupper, Siegfried. "Geplante Stagnation: Zur zukunftigen Entwicklung der Wirtschafts-beziehungen DDR-Sowjetunion [Planned Stagnation: On the Future Development of Economic Relations GDR-Soviet Union]." *Deutschland Archiv* 13, no. 3 (1980):225–228.

Leptin, Gert, and Manfred Melzer. *Economic Reform in East German Industry.* New York: Oxford University Press, 1978.

Mellor, Roy E. H. *The Two Germanies: A Modern Geography.* New York: Harper and Row, 1978.

Pritzel, Konstantin. "Die Umweltpolitik in den intereuropäischen und innerdeutschen Beziehungen [Environmental Policy in Inter-European and Intra-German Relations]." *Deutschland Archiv* 13, no. 8 (1980):834–843.

Raestrup, Reiner, and Thomas Weymar. " 'Schuld ist allein der Kapitalismus': Umwelt-probleme und ihre Bewältigung in der DDR ['Only Capitalism Is Guilty': Environmental Problems and Their Solutions in the GDR]." *Deutschland Archiv* 15, no. 8 (1982):832–844.

Ruban, Maria Elisabeth, and Heinz Vortmann. "Subventionen kontra Investionen [Subsidies Versus Investments]." *Deutschland Archiv* 13, no. 12 (1980):1277–1281.

Schultz, Hans-Dieter. "Vor dem Einkauf schnell zur Bank [Quickly to the Bank Before Shopping]." *Deutschland Archiv* 12, no. 5 (1979):451–453.

Stinglwagner, Wolfgang. "Die Braunkohleindustrie in der DDR—ein tragfähiger Brücke ins Atomzeitalter? [The Brown Coal Industry in the GDR—A Durable Bridge to the Atomic Age?]." *Deutschland Archiv* 14, no. 12 (1981):1296–1299.

Strassburger, Jürgen. "Ein neues lohnpolitisches Experiment? [A New Wage Policy Experiment?]." *Deutschland Archiv* 9, no. 9 (1976):950–958.

Zimmermann, Hartmut. "In der DDR wird das Lohnsystem reformiert [The Wage System Is Reformed in the GDR]." *Die Quelle* 3, no. 3 (1977):114–117

Society

Amnesty International Report 1980. London: Amnesty International, 1980.

Bahro, Rudolf. *Die Alternative: Zur Kritik des real existierenden Sozialismus* [The Alternative: On a Critique of Real Existing Socialism]. Cologne: Europäische Verlagsanstalt, 1977.

Belwe, Katharina. *Mitwirkung im Industriebetrieb der DDR* [Collaboration in Industrial Enterprises in the GDR]. Opladen: Westdeutscher, 1979.

Erbe, Günter. *Arbeiterklasse und Intelligenz in der DDR* [The Working Class and the Intelligentsia in the GDR]. Opladen: Westdeutscher, 1982.

Fischer, Peter. *Kirche und Christen in der DDR* [Church and Christians in the GDR]. Berlin: Holzapfel, 1978.

Fricke, Karl Wilhelm. *Politik und Justiz in der DDR* [Politics and Justice in the GDR]. Cologne: Wissenschaft und Politik, 1979.

————. "Zwischen Resignation und Selbstbehauptung [Between Resignation and Self-Assertion]." *Deutschland Archiv* 9, no. 11 (1976):1135–1139.

Glaessner, Gert-Joachim. "Bildungsökonomie und Bildungsplanung [The Economics and Planning of Education]." *Deutschland Archiv* 11, no. 9 (1978):937–956.

Gransow, Volker. *Kulturpolitik in der DDR* [Cultural Policy in the GDR]. Berlin: Volker Spiess, 1975.

Grünert-Bronnen, Barbara. *Ich bin Bürger der DDR und lebe in der Bundesrepublik* [I Am a Citizen of the GDR and I Live in the Federal Republic]. Munich: Piper, 1970.

Havemann, Robert. *Ein deutscher Kommunist: Ruckblick und Perspektiven aus der Isolation* [A German Communist: Reflections and Perspectives from Isolation]. Hamburg: Rowolt, 1978.

———. "Über Sozialismus und Freiheit [About Socialism and Freedom]." *Deutschland Archiv* 9, no. 8 (1976):1104–1106.

Helwig, Gisela. *Frau und Familie in beiden deutschen Staaten* [Women and the Family in Both German States]. Cologne: Wissenschaft und Politik, 1981.

———. " 'Wir müssen und wollen Flagge zeigen': Zur derzeitigen Situation der evangelischen Kirchen in der DDR ['We Must and We Will Show the Flag': On the Current Situation of the Evangelical Church in the GDR]." *Deutschland Archiv* 14, no. 4 (1981):345–347.

———. "Standhafte Kämpfer heranbilden: Zum Hochschulbeschluss des SED-Politburos [Educate Steadfast Fighters: On the Higher Education Decree of the SED Politburo]." *Deutschland Archiv* 13, no. 5 (1980):462–463.

———. "Zum Stellenwert der Familienerziehung in der DDR [On the Priority of Family Upbringing in the GDR]." *Deutschland Archiv* 12, no. 12 (1979):1311–1315.

Holm, Hans-Axel. *The Other Germans: Report from an East German Town*. New York: Random House, 1970.

International Labour Office. *The Cost of Social Security, 1975–1977*. Geneva: International Labour Office, 1981.

Jäger, Manfred. *Kultur und Politik in der DDR* [Culture and Politics in the GDR]. Cologne: Edition Deutschland Archiv, 1982.

———. "Das Ende einer Kulturpolitik: Die Fälle Kunze und Biermann [The End of a Cultural Policy: The Cases of Kunze and Biermann]." *Deutschland Archiv* 9, no. 12 (1976):1233–1235.

Kleinschmid, Harald. " 'Fehler sind Natur': Zur Kulturpolitik der DDR im zweiten Halbjahr 1980 ['Mistakes Are Natural': On the Cultural Policy of the GDR in the Second Half of 1980]." *Deutschland Archiv* 14, no. 1 (1981):39–44.

———. "Die geistige Auseinandersetzung in der DDR findet im Westen statt [The GDR's Intellectual Confrontation Is Taking Place in the West]." *Deutschland Archiv* 10, no. 10 (1977):1011–1017.

Loewe, Lothar. *Abends kommt der Klassenfeind* [The Class Enemy Comes at Evening]. Frankfurt am Main: Ullstein, 1977.

Lolland, Jörg, and Frank S. Rodiger (eds.). *Gesicht zur Wand: Berichte und Protokolle politischer Häftlinge in der DDR* [Face to the Wall: Reports and Testimony of Political Prisoners in the GDR]. Stuttgart: Seewald, 1977.

Mallinkrodt, Anita. *Das kleine Massenmedien* [The Small Mass Media]. Cologne: Wissenschaft und Politik, 1982.

Manz, Günter, Gunnar Winkler, et al. *Theorie und Praxis der Sozialpolitik in der DDR* [Theory and Practice of Social Policy in the GDR]. Berlin: Akademie, 1979.

Pritzel, Konstantin. "Konvergenz und Divergenz im Gesundheitswesen der beiden deutschen Staaten [Convergence and Divergence in Health Care of the Two German States]." *Deutschland Archiv* 14, no. 12 (1981):1284–1296.

Rittershaus, Joachim, et al. *Jahrbuch für Soziologie und Sozialpolitik 1981* [Yearbook for Sociology and Social Policy 1981]. Berlin: Akademie, 1981.

Rueschemeyer, Marilyn. *Professional Work and Marriage: An East-West Comparison*. London: Macmillan, 1981.

Russ, Werner. "Altersrente in der DDR [Retirement Pensions in the GDR]." *Deutschland Archiv* 14, no. 1 (1981):53–55.

Schaffer, Harry G. *Women in the Two Germanies*. New York: Pergamon, 1981.

Scharf, C. Bradley. "Correlates of Social Security Policy, East and West Europe." *International Political Science Review* 2, no. 1 (1981):57–72.

———. "Labor Organizations in East German Society." Diss., Stanford, 1974.

Schweigler, Gebhard. *National Consciousness in Divided Germany.* Beverly Hills, Calif.: Sage, 1975.

Smith, Jean-Edward. *Germany Beyond the Wall.* Boston: Little, Brown, 1969.

Social Security Administration. *Social Security Programs Throughout the World 1981.* Washington, D.C.: U.S. Government Printing Office, 1982.

Spittmann, Ilse. "Der Fall Bahro [The Bahro Affair]." *Deutschland Archiv* 10, no. 10 (1977):1009–1011.

Foreign Affairs and Military Policy

Axen, Hermann. "Die DDR schreitet zuverzichtlich vorwärts [The GDR Strides Confidently Forward]." *Deutsche Aussenpolitik* 14, no. 12 (1969):1401–1406.

Doeker, Gunther, and Jens A. Brückner. *The Federal Republic of Germany and the German Democratic Republic in International Relations.* 3 vols. Dobbs Ferry, N.Y.: Oceana, 1979.

Forster, Thomas M. *The East German Army.* London: Allen and Unwin, 1980.

Fricke, Karl Wilhelm. "Okkupanten oder Waffenbrüder? Die Gruppe der Sowjetischen Streitkräfte in Deutschland [Occupiers or Brothers-in-Arms? The Soviet Armed Forces Group in Germany]." *Deutschland Archiv* 15, no. 3 (1982):269–272.

Haendcke-Hoppe, Maria. "DDR-Aussenwirtschaft unter neuen Vorzeichen [GDR Foreign Trade Under a New Design]." *Deutschland Archiv* 16, no. 4 (1983):378–385.

————. "Die Umgestaltung des Aussenhandelsapparats in der DDR [The Transformation of the Foreign Trade Apparatus in the GDR]." *Deutschland Archiv* 14, no. 4 (1981):378–384.

Herspring, Dale R. *East German Civil-Military Relations: The Impact of Technology, 1949–1972.* New York: Praeger, 1973.

Jacobsen, Hans-Adolf, Gert Leptin, Ulrich Scheuner, and Eberhard Schulz (eds.). *Drei Jahrzehnte Aussenpolitik der DDR* [Three Decades of Foreign Policy of the GDR]. Munich: Oldenbourg, 1979.

Kleinschmid, Harald. "Grosse Brücken und kleine Brücken: Zum Honecker-Besuch in Österreich [Large Bridges and Small Bridges: On the Honecker Visit in Austria]." *Deutschland Archiv* 13, no. 12 (1980):1236–1239.

Kuppe, Johannes. "Honeckers Staatsbesuch in Japan [Honecker's State Visit in Japan]." *Deutschland Archiv* 14, no. 7 (1981):673–679.

————. "Zum Staatsbesuch Honeckers in Mexiko [On Honecker's State Visit to Mexico]." *Deutschland Archiv* 14, no. 10 (1981):1022–1026.

The Military Balance 1983–1984. London: International Institute for Strategic Studies, 1983.

Moreton, Edwina. *East Germany and the Warsaw Alliance: The Politics of Detente.* Boulder, Colo.: Westview Press, 1978.

Sodaro, Michael, "The GDR and the Third World: Supplicant and Surrogate." In Michael Radu (ed.), *Eastern Europe and the Third World.* New York: Praeger, 1981.

Spittmann, Ilse. "Die Milliardenkredit [The Billion Credit]." *Deutschland Archiv* 16, no. 8 (1983):785–788.

UNESCO Statistical Yearbook 1980. New York: United Nations Statistical Office, 1981.

Vali, Ferenc. *The Quest for a United Germany.* Baltimore: Johns Hopkins, 1967.

Wettig, Gerhard. *Die Sowjetunion, die DDR, und die Deutschland-Frage, 1965–1976* [The Soviet Union, the GDR, and the German Question, 1965–1976]. Stuttgart: Bonn Aktuell, 1976.

Winters, Peter Jochen. "Das deutsch-deutsche Verhältnis 1981 [The German-German Relationship 1981]." *Deutschland Archiv* 14, no. 12 (1981):1233–1236.

Abbreviations

Benelux	intergovernmental union of Belgium, Netherlands, and Luxembourg
BPL	Bezirksparteileitung
bpo	basic party organization
CDU	Christian Democratic Union
CMEA	Council for Mutual Economic Assistance
CPSU	Communist Party of the Soviet Union
DBD	Democratic Farmers' party
DFD	Democratic Women's Federation
DSF	Society for German-Soviet Friendship
DTSB	German Gymnastics and Sports League
EOS	Expanded Secondary School
FDGB	Free German Labor Union Federation
FDJ	Free German Youth
FRG	Federal Republic of Germany
GDR	German Democratic Republic
GNP	gross national product
KB	Culture Federation
KdT	Chamber of Technology
KPD	Communist Party of Germany
KPL	Kreisparteileitung—district party leadership
LDPD	Liberal Democratic Party of Germany

NATO	North Atlantic Treaty Organization
NDPD	National Democratic Party of Germany
OPEC	Organization of Petroleum Exporting Countries
SED	Socialist Unity party
SPK	State Plan Commission
Stasi	State Security Service
WTO	Warsaw Treaty Organization

Index

About the Book and Author

Politics and Change in East Germany:
An Evaluation of Socialist Democracy
C. Bradley Scharf

This text avoids preoccupation with "the German question" and East-West German comparisons, looking at the German Democratic Republic (GDR) in its own right while recognizing that a legacy of German history and political precedent persists in the GDR as much as in the Federal Republic. Dr. Scharf shows how the GDR is subject to the same developmental forces that appear in any urban-industrial society. He also looks at the influence of socialism, which he describes as an authentic impulse in the GDR, though its applications—borrowed from Soviet practice—often seem alien.

Dr. Scharf's analysis of the GDR acknowledges the overwhelming presence of the USSR and West Germany, both as models of sociopolitical change and as actors in the immediate external environment, and illustrates why that dual presence effectively precludes for the GDR policy options open to other nations. The legitimacy of the governing party is undermined by its inability to reconcile the competing claims of East and West at the crossroads of Europe.

Integral to the text is an emphasis on public policy; policy effects are measured and illustrated with reference to European and U.S. comparisons. Employing accepted political science concepts without forcing unique phenomena into contrived categories, Dr. Scharf has succeeded in his effort to make the policies and problems of the GDR comprehensible in familiar terms.

C. Bradley Scharf is an associate professor of political science at Seattle University, where his particular interests are Eastern European politics and comparative social policy. From 1978 to 1983 Dr. Scharf was *East-Central Europe*'s managing editor for GDR material.